The Language of Love

Other Books of Interest from St. Augustine's Press

Stanley Rosen (Martin Black, editor), *Essays in Philosophy: Ancient*

Stanley Rosen (Martin Black, editor), *Essays in Philosophy: Modern*

Stanley Rosen, *Metaphysics in Ordinary Language*

Stanley Rosen, *Nihilism: A Philosophical Essay*

Stanley Rosen, *Plato's Statesman: The Web of Politics*

Stanley Rosen, *Platonic Productions: Theme and Variations*

Stanley Rosen, *The Question of Being: A Reversal of Heidegger*

Stanley Rosen, *G. W. F. Hegel: An Introduction to the Science of Wisdom*

Stanley Rosen, *Plato's Symposium*

Stanley Rosen, *Plato's Sophist: The Drama of Original and Image*

Stanley Rosen, *The Ancients and the Moderns: Rethinking Modernity*

Stanley Rosen, *The Limits of Analysis*

Nalin Ranasinghe (Editor),
Logos and Eros: Essays Honoring Stanley Rosen

Rémi Brague, *Eccentric Culture: A Theory of Western Civilization*

Ronna Burger and Patrick Goodin (editors),
The Eccentric Core: The Thought of Seth Benardete

Peter Kreeft, *Socrates' Children: The 100 Greatest Philosophers*

Peter Kreeft, *Ethics for Beginners: 52 "Big Ideas" from 32 Great Minds*

John von Heyking, *Comprehensive Judgment and Absolute Selflessness:
Winston Churchill on Politics as Friendship*

Joseph Bottum, *The Decline of the Novel*

Barry Cooper, *Consciousness and Politics:
From Analysis to Meditation in the Late Work of Eric Voegelin*

D. Q. McInerny, *Being Ethical*

Roger Scruton, *The Politics of Culture and Other Essays*

Roger Scruton, *The Meaning of Conservatism*

Roger Scruton, *An Intelligent Person's Guide to Modern Culture*

The Language of Love:
An Interpretation of Plato's *Phaedrus*
STANLEY ROSEN

Edited with an Introduction by Martin Black

ST. AUGUSTINE'S PRESS
South Bend, Indiana

Manufactured in the United States of America.

1 2 3 4 5 6 26 25 24 23 22 21

Library of Congress Cataloging-in-Publication Data
Names: Rosen, Stanley, 1929-2014, author.
Black, Martin (Philosophy teacher), editor.
Title: The language of love : an interpretation of Plato's Phaedrus /
Stanley Rosen ; edited with an introduction by Martin Black.
Description: South Bend, Indiana : St. Augustine's Press, [2016]
Includes index.
Identifiers: LCCN 2016012553
ISBN 9781587314544 (clothbound : alk. paper)
Subjects: LCSH: Plato. Phaedrus.
Classification: LCC B380 .R67 2016
DDC 184--dc23 LC record available at
https://lccn.loc.gov/2016012553

St. Augustine's Press
www.staugustine.net

"…mais *tange montes et fumigabant*. Aussi tost qu'on s'écarte tant soit peu du sentiment de quelques Docteurs, ils éclatent en foudres et en tonneres."

Leibniz, Letter to Landgraf E. von Hessen-Reinfels

CONTENTS

EDITOR'S ACKNOWLEDGEMENTS   ix

INTRODUCTION   xi

ABBREVIATIONS   xxii

CHAPTER ONE: The Non-Lover   1

CHAPTER TWO: The Concealed Lover   25

CHAPTER THREE: The Lover   68

CHAPTER FOUR: The Language of Love   169

CHAPTER FIVE: Conclusion   253

EDITOR'S ACKNOWLEDGEMENTS

The editor would like to recognise with gratitude Bruce Finger-hut's appreciation of Stanley Rosen's works and his dedication to publishing them. Benjamin Fingerhut generously took over this task with the same capability and their qualities, including remarkable patience with dilatory editors, have made a genuine contribution to the common good.

The editor's chief debt is to Stanley Rosen: βουλαὶ δὲ πρεσβύτεραι/ἀκίνδυνον ἐμοὶ ἔπος σὲ ποτὶ πάντα λόγον/ἐπαινεῖν παρέχοντι (Pindar, *Pythian* II, 65–67).

Earlier versions of portions of Chapters One and Two were previously published:

Part of Chapter One was delivered as "The Nonlover in Plato's *Phaedrus*" at the Society for Ancient Greek Philosophy in Washington, D.C., in December, 1968; published as "The Role of the Non-Lover in Plato's *Phaedrus*", *Man and World* 2 (1969): 423–37; and as "The Nonlover in Plato's *Phaedrus*," as Chapter Four of *The Quarrel Between Philosophy and Poetry* (Routledge: New York, 1988), pp. 78–90.

A portion of Chapter Two was published as "Socrates as Concealed Lover" in *Classics and the Classical Tradition* (Penn State University Press, University Park: 1973), pp. 163–78, and as Chapter Five of *The Quarrel Between Philosophy and Poetry* (Routledge: New York, 1988), pp. 91–101.

INTRODUCTION
Martin Black

A Platonic dialogue is a vivid reminder that if human beings love wisdom it must be that we do not understand what we normally mean by "love." Similarly, a commentary on a Platonic dialogue by Stanley Rosen is not restricted to textual, linguistic, literary, and conceptual analysis, but provides an expression or reminder of the dialogue's animating impulse: to live the philosophical life by thinking through the fundamental questions of human existence. Rosen's considerable learning is always employed to the end of understanding, rather than philological—let alone historical—purposes.

Rosen first published as a poet of noted ability and promise, attracted to the view that "philosophy and poetry are two different languages about the same world."[1] Since the perspectives illuminated by language are dependent upon pre-discursive intuition, then either poetry or philosophy must see more truly, if there is indeed a world or cosmos at all. Rosen came to the view that discursive thought and philosophy are ultimately better able to aspire to an understanding of the whole that was reflexive or that included the perspective of the thinker within it and thus realise the classical aim of self-knowledge.

Rosen reconstituted the argument for the priority of theory or of the goodness of the philosophical life against the grain of twentieth- and twenty-first-century thought, which generally if

---

1   Cf. Stanley Rosen, "Chicago Days" in *Essays in Philosophy: Ancient* (St. Augustine's Press, 2013), p. 1. Rosen's first work was a collection of poems, *Death in Egypt* (Golden Goose Press, 1952.)

unreflexively promulgated the impossibility of theory in the classical sense, of which the contemporary use of the word "theory" to mean a discursive hypothesis is one commonplace sign.[2] The modern formulations of the priority of practice to theory have been so deeply absorbed by institutions ostensibly devoted to learning that they regularly justify their existence and increasingly absurd fees by reference to various goods that have nothing to do with learning. Our scholars and intellectuals routinely reduce life and thought to linguistic and historical constructions, that is, to ephemera, and ultimately to the function of rationalisations of power structures, or what have you, thus deprecating their own way of life: has there been a time when so many people wrote, read, and talked as if all discourse was ideology, i.e., devoid of genuine significance?

Plato's writings in part responded to contemporary formulations of the same sophistry, because the priority of theory must always appear paradoxical. It seems to detach us from the ordinary concerns of life; it is, in the famous metaphor, "learning to die and being dead" (*Phaedo* 64a4-6, 64b7-9). As Rosen shows, the *Phaedrus* is a prime example of Plato's demonstration that a teaching that makes intelligence instrumental to other desires not only debases the intelligence but also the passions. On the other hand, if philosophy is possible and the principles of action and thought are intelligible, then intelligibility itself is good, or the "idea of the good" and the "cause of knowledge and truth."[3] That may mean that *theoria* in the classical sense is possible, but theory can be only understood as being for its own sake if it embodies human excellence or is the natural object of the human desire for happiness or

2　Rosen exercised considerable care in criticising the key reflexive attempts to deny the possibility of *theoria* which animate the analytical and continental philosophical streams of academic philosophy in *Nihilism* (New Haven: Yale University Press; 1969; 2nd edition: South Bend, Indiana; St Augustine's Press, 2000, which contains the Preface to the Portuguese Translation).

3　Cf. Plato's *Republic* 508e2-4 with Chapter Five of Rosen's *Nihilism*, *op. cit.*

perfection. The preservation of the meaning of human action is possible only if theory is prior to practice. Plato has Socrates show that philosophy is possible and good in part through a myth of the soul's end that itself shows the necessity for human beings to use myth. This philosophical poem, which Socrates attributes to Stesichorus, depicts the human soul in its tragi-comic journey through the cosmos in search of a glimpse of the truth of the beings to which we wish to ascend, culminating in a silent glimpse of silent beings that occurs "through time" amid the conflicts of human existence. *The Language of Love* contains Rosen's most de-tailed discussion of the dependence of human self-understanding in general, and of philosophical discourse in particular, on the *cos-mos noetos* or the intelligible principles of things that lend art, myth and discourse in general their significance and which Plato's in-terlocutors call the ideas or forms.

Nothing ought to delay the reader's making direct acquain-tance with Rosen's text. What follows may be justified as an ex-planation of the happenstance of the work's publication and an explanation of one of the book's suggestions that some readers may find of interest.

The *Language of Love*

In 2009 Stanley Rosen was compelled to resign from formal teaching because of ill health. A number of overly hot or overly drafty rooms decorated with beige, vaguely child-safe looking plastic furniture and unmemorable carpet on the campus of Boston University immedi-ately resumed the aspect of absolutely commonplace classrooms; when until that time, for several hours every week, they had been the light-filled and enticing antechambers to visions conjured by the pos-ing and analysis of the questions most urgent and most important to human life. Rosen's difficulties, and the eccentricity of his parking angles, had visibly increased over recent semesters. I cannot help re-calling his saying in a class in 2008, "BU has just asked me to sign a ten year contract…the fools!" with an expression of mock cunning, followed by gentle laughter. Rosen and his beautiful and gracious wife Francoise, who had been a teacher of Greek, Latin and French, removed to Philadelphia, or, as he once put it, "to the city of brotherly love—just don't be out after 6pm." Cleaning out Rosen's office turned up, in addition to the expected flotsam of a lifetime of teaching, several unexpected and wonderful things; e.g., notes on the mathematics of the theory of relativity; the draft of a letter to Seth Benardete proposing "one more dance"; and a dense set of notes on the 1958 seminar—now notorious in some quarters—by Leo Strauss on Plato's *Statesman*. However, the least expected and most wonderful find was a manuscript of some 350 typed buff pages, with the title that the reader now sees on the cover of this volume.

A rapid examination showed the manuscript to be a complete work on the *Phaedrus*. The First Chapter discusses the relation between the *Phaedrus* and the *Symposium*, the dramatic setting of the dialogue, and the speech of Lysias read by Phaedrus that advocates that a beautiful young beloved should surrender his favours to a non-lover rather than a lover. The Second Chapter, which treats Socrates' rendition of the same conceit, Rosen entitles "The Concealed Lover," to bring out Socrates' implication that such a speech is not just shameful but self-cancelling. The Third Chapter interprets Socrates' "palinode" (or song of recantation), in which he praises *eros* as the fourth kind of divine madness which, in contrast with the varieties of all too human madness, are responsible for the greatest goods in which human beings share. The Fourth Chapter analyses the subsequent discussion of rhetoric and the Fifth Chapter concludes with synoptic reflections on the themes of the whole work.

When I called him, Rosen's explanation was that he had written and intended *The Language of the Love* as his second publication, to follow his ground-breaking interpretation of *Plato's Symposium* (1968; the Second Edition was duly published with a new Preface in 1988). Instead, he followed the recommendation of his editor at Yale, Jane Isay, whose views he respected, to publish "a more general work." *Nihilism: An Essay in Philosophy*, one of the more significant works of philosophy written after the Second World War, was published in 1969. Since the manuscript's first two chapters included corrected excerpts from two essays that were published in 1969 and 1973, work on *The Language of Love* had presumably continued into the 70s.[4]

Confronted with the continued existence of this work and the demand that the world be allowed to know of it, Rosen made the off-hand remark that "students of philosophers should have such things," and then kindly assisted when this ambiguous statement was interpreted as an imperative to bring the book before the public. Since the type-written manuscript was complete, together with Rosen's handwritten corrections, the major editorial difficulty concerned the transfer from 1950s to twenty-first-century "information processing technology." Changing a perispomenon to a paroxytone accent was practically the peak editorial intervention. I have supplied translations of Greek, where no translation or explanation was given in immediate context.

The Way Up and the Way Down

Rosen opens *The Language of Love* with the claim that "The first task which confronts the student of the *Phaedrus* is to account for its relation to the *Symposium*." Lest the reader suspect that this is the first task only for those students of the *Phaedrus* who have just published their comprehensive and ground-breaking interpretation of the *Symposium*, some explanation may be justified.

4   Rosen remarks in the notes to "Socrates as Concealed Lover" that it and "The Nonlover in Plato's *Phaedrus*" form a sequence that "constitute parts of a longer interpretation which is in progress" (*The Quarrel Between Philosophy and Poetry*, Routledge: New York, 1988; 205, n. 2). In *Metaphysics in Ordinary Language*, Rosen introduces "Erotic Ascent" with the remark that it is "an extract from what was originally intended to be a reconsideration of the Platonic doctrine of eros," which he had decided not to complete (39). While "Erotic Ascent" is not continuous with *The Language of Love*, it builds on this work and provides a helpful synopsis of Rosen's view of eros in the *Phaedrus*, *Symposium* and *Republic*. There is also a discussion of the *Phaedrus* in Rosen's critique of Derrida's reading of the dialogue in Chapter Two of *Hermeneutics as Politics* (Oxford, 1987; 2nd ed., New Haven, 2003).

The *Symposium* gives us a dramatic exhibition of what Socrates terms in the *Republic* the "ancient quarrel" or "primeval variance between poetry and philosophy" (607b6-7). It is Rosen's contention that all of the speeches in the *Symposium*, with the apparent exception of that of Socrates, attempt to justify a view of human existence from within the horizon of genesis. Their various viewpoints cannot account for the stable and knowable structure of the view they propound. The primary example would be reflected in the inability of Aristophanes' lovers, who are halves of a whole split apart by Zeus, to say what it is they actually want or what their *eros* is for: "the soul of each wants something else [than sexual union], something that it is unable to put into words; instead, it divines it and expresses itself in riddles" (*Symposium* 192c7-d2). Aristophanes has Hephaestus articulate their desire to become one out of two, "which no *one* [*heis*] would deny"; that last "one" brings out the implication of the whole speech, that the end of desire is not only unknowable but its satisfaction would lead to the extinction of the desiring individual. Making the origin of human desire temporal—deriving from "our ancient nature" (192e9-10)—means Aristophanes is unable to account for the self-knowledge expressed in his speech either as a lover or as a poet who makes the gods necessary to civil life.

Diotima's teaching of Socrates is only an apparent exception. While apparently concluding that theory transcends *praxis* or *poiesis*, Diotima seems to define eros' end not as the good but as one's own and then as "production in the beautiful," thereby conceding something to both poets, Aristophanes and Agathon, respectively. Her description of *eros* ascends from the desire to reproduce and raise children to the desire for fame, whose peak is the poets' production of their own beautiful children, the gods. Her ultimate "mysteries" describe the ascent to the vision of the beautiful itself. However, this apparent culmination in theoretical vision seems to be undercut by its taking place in the element of production and without showing how a transcendence of the particulars is possible, which is why it requires a guide whose knowledge of the right way is not explained.

Rosen summarises the meaning of the dialectic of the *Phaedrus* when he states that the "key to the difference between the

Symposium and the *Phaedrus* is the recognition that the way up is not the same as, and in fact is posterior to, the way down." This formulation, which appears at telling points in several of Rosen's other works, is only here explained. It clearly refers to Heraclitus, fragment 60: "[the] way up [and the way] down: one and the same," an apothegm that itself stands in need of clarification. Rosen's reading appears to be that it reflects Heraclitus' teaching that there are no stable principles that differentiate the high and the low, since "all things become in accordance with strife and necessity" (fr. 80) with the implication that Heraclitus cannot account for the awakening of the philosopher to the divine truth from the dreams of *nomos*.[5] Diotima promulgates an ascent to being from genesis while indicating that this ascent depends upon the prior ascent of a guide, but the latter's ascent can only be possible if there is another guide, and so on *ad infinitum*. In other words, there must be a descent, or a revelation of what transcends genesis, before there can be an ascent.

By contrast, in the *Phaedrus*, our "comprehension of genesis is rooted in [our] transcendence of genesis." This transcendence is depicted in the myth of our souls seeing the beings in their discarnate journey to the roof of the cosmos, and the difference between the two dialogues is symbolised by Eros' promotion from a *daimon* in the Symposium to a god in the *Phaedrus*. Rosen's non-mythological

---

5   Cf. frr. 1, 88, 103, 104. Note the implications of the alteration that Plato's Socrates makes to the image of the philosopher as awake and the the person of praxis as asleep (*Republic* 476c1-d3; references to Plato will be to the Oxford text edited by Burnet, except for the new editions of the *Republic*, ed. S. R. Slings, 2003 and of Vol. 1, ed. E. A. Duke et al., 1995). Wakefulness is redefined as being able to see the difference between original and image, whereas being asleep is taking an image for the original. That human beings have access to the original, that is, to the form, in the image or the particular is what, I believe, Rosen means by the descent that must precede the ascent. Cf. the guide mentioned in 479d10-e4 and the role of the guide in Rosen's discussion of Diotima's ascent to the beautiful itself in Chapter One below.

understanding of the descent that precedes the ascent of the potential philosopher is variously expressed through his arguments for
the necessary hypothesis of the forms or, as he here terms them, the
"ontological subjects" of thought, speech and experience. These con-
tentions share the same purpose as Rosen's argument for the recognition of "ordinary experience" as the non-reductive matrix of deed
and word within which the distinction between the ordinary and
extraordinary experiences becomes visible.

In the *Phaedo*, Plato has Socrates remark on the fact that the
forms which he introduced, i.e., the pre-discursive grounds of discourse, are "much discoursed about."[6] Rosen's title for the work
contains another version of this jest, by pointing to the silence of
the soul's apprehension of the objects of its longing as distinct
from the discourse to which that longing, in civilized persons,
gives rise. That silence also characterizes the forms themselves,
which are necessarily pre- and so non-discursive if speech is to
be intelligible, that is, if there is a cosmos of meaning independent
of the peculiarities of anything put into speech or language
(whether thought silently or spoken aloud).

Rosen's response to this characterisation was not to make the
pietist or nihilistic gestures towards silence of a Wittgenstein or
Heidegger, nor to contribute to the contradictory garrulity of their
epigones, but to demonstrate that reflexive speech must accom-
modate the poetic nature of humanity's self-understanding in its
aspiration for the comprehension of what lies beyond speech. The

6   *Phaedo* 100b5 (in the new Vol. 1 of the Oxford edition; b4-5 if the
    reader has sacrificed the new MS and papyrus readings for the rel-
    atively sane approach to textual intervention of Burnet's established
    edition). By referring to the beings themselves as "those much bab-
    bled about things (ἐκεῖνα πολυθρύλητα)," Socrates simultaneously
    expresses not only the fact that the grounds of discourse are neces-
    sarily non-discursive but also recognises the fact that discourse
    about them is apparently without limit. It is impossible not to be
    amused by the proportion of scholarship that has failed to grasp this
    point and so has devoted volumes of discourse to the conceptuali-
    sation of the pre-conceptual.

denial of ontological subjects or of ideas in the Platonic sense necessarily leads one to find irrational or low ends for reason, a denial that underlies Lysias' speech and the speech of the concealed lover. The denial of the forms implies the denial that the soul has specific ends, which means that reason and the other specifically human faculties serve the body's satisfaction. If there is no desire for a comprehensive understanding of our desire, all understanding reduces to misunderstanding, fantasy, or deception. The poetic mind too is no longer mimetic or imaginative but productive of simulacra that reflect the most ordinary of realities, and, to cite the unconscious self-condemnation of reductive thinking by one of its most influential wholesalers, "Nothing is more tediously arid than commonplace fantasies."[7]

Rosen appeared to differ most from his great teacher, Leo Strauss, in addressing more directly the question of the forms and in addressing less directly the question of esotericism. Rosen agreed with Strauss' remark, made in the context of a reading of the *Phaedrus*, that "[t]he study of the literary question is...an important part of the study of what philosophy is."[8] He differed regarding the correct rhetoric for our time and regarding the necessity for arguing directly for the possibility or philosophy. This is not a denial of the value or necessity of poetry. Since discursive thought as a whole and philosophy in particular depend upon the pre-discursive intelligibility of the world, there is a whole only when it is completed by "poetry" giving conceptual form to our intuitions of pre-conceptual form and providing paradigms that illuminate the hierarchy of the states of the human *psyche*.[9] *The*

7   Karl Marx, "Introduction" to the *Grundrisse in Later Political Writings* (Cambridge: Cambridge University Press, 1996), p. 130.
8   Leo Strauss, *The City and Man* (Chicago, 1964), pp. 52.
9   Cf. Plato, *Parmenides* 135b5-c6 and Rosen's Preface to the Second Edition of *Plato's Symposium* (New Haven, 1987; First Edition, 1968), pp. xxviii-xxxv, and his early article "Ideas," *The Review of Metaphysics*, 16 (1963). This essay, on the condition of philosophy, belongs with the essays on its beginning and end, "Thales," and "Wisdom," published in the same journal.

Language of Love contains the clearest exposition we have of these two senses of form in Plato, as the "ontological subject" of intellectual intuition and as the object of *diaeresis*, respectively.

The difference in Strauss and Rosen's approach might be expressed by suggesting that they reflect different notions of the silence towards which speech is meant to direct us. It might also be characterized by way of Strauss' articulation, in the final paragraph of *The City and Man*, of the procedure governing that work. He argues that Aristotle's dictum that one must begin with what is first for us in order to comprehend what is first in itself or by nature has the following implication in our time: we must first move from "what is *'first* for us'" to what is *"primary* 'for us'"; that is, we must move from Aristotle's political science, in which the phenomena of political life has been realised in concepts, to the pre-philosophical representation of the political community in Thucydides.[10] Only by undertaking this additional step of moving back to the beginning in the city's self-understanding as subject to the divine, "in the ordinary understanding of the divine," can we then come to see philosophy as it was originally understood. Only with this addition will we "be open to the full impact of the all-important question which is coeval with philosophy although the philosophers do not frequently pronounce it—the question *quid sit deus*."[11]

Rosen endorsed Strauss' partial agreement with Husserl that our concepts need to be "desedimented," in his own interpretation of what is first for us as "ordinary experience," which necessarily eludes definition because it is context for discourse altogether. He suggested, however, that there is a danger that the image of our descent to a second "unnatural" cave from which one must ascend to the "natural" cave might involve itself in historicism in the very attempt to overcome it.[12] Without denying,

10 Leo Strauss, *The City and Man, op. cit.*, pp. 240–41. Emphasis added.
11 *Ibid.*, p. 241.
12 See, e.g., Rosen, *Hermeneutics as Politics*, Chapter 3, esp. pp. 137–38; See Leo Strauss, *Philosophy and Law*, tr. Eve Adler (New York, 1995),

indeed while insisting on the need to see that philosophy has political and literary conditions and that the history of philosophy consists in the systematic covering over of original insights with conceptual apparatus, there is a danger of conflating a return to the temporal origins of philosophy in its Greek exemplars with a return to the origins in the sense of the ahistorical principles themselves.

In the course of making his comparison of the *Phaedrus* with the *Symposium*, Rosen remarks that "The root of the difference between friendship and desire is therefore the difference between time and timelessness. If the latter difference does not obtain, neither does the former." This is the ground for his argument that "[f]riendship is higher than desire because it has attained its end. The object of friendly love is present to the lover in a way that cannot be dissolved into the past. Our friendship with a man does not properly cease with his death, and it is perfectly intelligible to speak of friendships in which both persons are dead."[13] In the *Phaedrus*, Plato has Socrates provide the philosophical answer to the question *quid sit deus* (249c6, cf. 246c6-d3). The reader now has the opportunity to share in a friendship of the intellect with Rosen in reading his interpretation of the question which is coeval with philosophy because it is coeval with the question of the perfection of human life.

pp. 136, n. 2: "To that end and only to that end is the 'historicizing' of philosophy justified and necessary: only the history of philosophy makes possible the ascent from the second, 'unnatural' cave." See also, Leo Strauss, *Persecution and the Art of Writing* (Chicago, 1988), pp. 155–56. Cf. Stanley Rosen, *Hermeneutics as Politics*, op. cit., especially pp. 137–38.

13 Rosen, *Symposium*, pp. 216–17.

ABBREVIATIONS

This list contains only those titles of scholarly works which have been abbreviated in the footnotes. It is not a complete bibliography of works consulted or mentioned in the present study.

Allen, R. E. *Studies in Plato's Metaphysics* (London: Routledge, Kegan Paul, 1967)

Bigger, Charles P. *Participation* (Baton Rouge, Louisiana State University Press, 1968)

Diels, Hermann. *Die Fragmente der Vorsokratiker* (Berlin: Weidmannsche Verlagsbuchhandlung, 1956)

Diesendruck, Z. *Struktur und Charakter des platonischen Phaidros* (Vienna and Leipzig: Wilhelm Braumüller, 1927).

Friedländer, Paul. *Platon*, Bd. III (Berlin: Walter de Gruyter, 1960)

Gadamer, H.-G. *Platos dialektische Ethik* (Leipzig: Felix Meiner Verlag, 1931)

Gaiser, Konrad. *Platons ungeschriebene Lehre* (Stuttgart: Ernst Klett Verlag, 1963)

Hackforth, R. *Plato's Phaedrus* (Cambridge: Cambridge University Press, 1952; Bobbs Merrill Reprint, n.d.)

Helmbold, W. C. and Holther, W. B. "The Unity of the *Phaedrus.*" *Classical Philology*, Vol. XIV, 1950-52

Merlan, Philip. *From Platonism to Neo-Platonism* (2nd ed., Hague: Martinus Nijhoff, 1960)

Pieper, Josef. *Enthusiasm and Divine Madness* (New York: Harcourt, Brace & World, 1964)

Robin, Léon. *La Théorie platonicienne de l'amour* (Paris: Alcan, 1933)

——————. (ed.). *Phèdre*, in *Ouevres complètes*, Tome IV, 3e Partie (Paris: Budé, 1947)

——————. (*La Théorie platonicienne des Idées et des Nombres d'aprés Aristote* (Hildesheim: G. Olms Verlag, 1963)

Rosen, Stanley. "The Role of Eros in Plato's *Republic*" in *Review of Metaphysics*, 18, March, 1965; Now reprinted in *The Quarrel Between Poetry and Philosophy* (New York: Routledge, 1988)

——————. *Plato's Symposium* (New Haven: Yale University Press, 1968; Reprint: South Bend, Ind.: St. Augustine's Press, 1999)

——————. *Nihilism* (New Haven, Yale University Press, 1969; Reprinted with the "Preface to the Portuguese Translation," South Bend, Ind.: St. Augustine's Press 2000).

——————. "I See What You Mean," (unpublished lecture)

Sinaiko, Herman L. *Love, Knowledge, and Discourse in Plato* (Chicago, University of Chicago Press, 1965)

Skemp, J. B. *The Theory of Motion in Plato's Later Dialogues* (Cambridge: Cambridge University Press, 1942)

Stefanini, Luigi. *Platone*, II (Padua: Cedam-Casa Editrice Dott. Antonio Milani, 1949)

Stenzel, Julius. *Kleine Schriften* (Darmstadt, Wissenschaftliche Buchgesellschaft, 1957)

Thompson, W. H. *The Phaedrus of Plato* (London: Whittaker and Co., 1868)

von Arnim, Hans. *Platos Jugenddialoge und die Entstehungszeit des Phaidros* (Leipzig-Berlin: Teubner Verlag, 1914)

CHAPTER ONE:
The Non-Lover

I.

The first task which confronts the student of the *Phaedrus* is to account for its relation to the *Symposium*. Although the famous banquet of Agathon is never explicitly mentioned in the *Phaedrus*, its ghost is perpetually present, like a half-formed memory that haunts the reader's imagination. This relation between the two dialogues is reflected in the fact that recollection is not discussed at all in the *Symposium*, whereas it constitutes an essential if obliquely developed theme in the *Phaedrus*. It would be no exaggeration to say that one purpose of the *Phaedrus* is to stimulate us into a recollection of the *Symposium* which is at the same time a transformation or *Aufhebung* of the earlier treatment of Eros. The ascent of the erotic psyche, so briefly described by Diotima, becomes now the central theme of a long and beautiful Socratic myth. The key to the difference between these two accounts is the elevation of Eros from the status of *daimon* to that of god. The ascent as it is alluded to by Diotima must be accomplished by the mortal *psyche* as a resident of the incarnate or terrestrial dimension of genesis, driven by an ambiguous force which is continuously ceasing to be what it is, and coming to be what it is not. The teaching of the *Symposium* is a discontinuous account of a discontinuous world, which must be literally re-collected from the higher, more comprehensive viewpoint of the *Phaedrus*.[1] Diotima

---

1   Robin has seen something of the relation between the two dialogues; cf. *Phèdre*, p. cxxxvi: "Le discours de Lysias et le premier discours

provides us with the promise or prophecy of a subsequent unification of human existence which is not fulfilled in the *Symposium*. As I shall argue, it cannot be fulfilled because there is no divine madness in the *Symposium*, but only a human madness, which consequently depreciates the quality of human sobriety.

The importance of the doctrine of recollection in the *Phaedrus*, as well as the oblique manner in which it is presented there, is already evident in the title of the dialogue. The name and opening scene of the *Phaedrus* constitute jointly an invitation to return to the beginning of the *Symposium*. Phaedrus, we remember, is the "father of the logos"; the dialectical ascent in the *Symposium* begins dramatically from the fact that he is the beloved of the physician Eryximachus. Eryximachus, himself a moderate drinker, turns the banquet from drinking to a praise of Eros, in response to Phaedrus' complaint that the god has been neglected by poets and encomiasts. Despite the atmosphere of celebration, excitement, and hybristic self-exaltation, the *Symposium* begins in a sober mixture of medicine and utilitarianism. This note of sobriety is never absent from the banquet, even during the presence of the drunken Alcibiades, who reveals to us the sober interior of Socrates' erotic hubris. In fact, one may say that the human sobriety of the *Symposium*, with the single exception of Socrates, turns all too easily into human madness. The continuous self-transformations of the non-Socratic discourses mirror the nature of Eros itself as described by Diotima. As for Socrates, his nocturnal behavior toward the young Alcibiades would seem to suggest something more than sobriety, or something less than divine madness. As is evident in his exchanges with Diotima, the young Socrates must have been defective in Eros, and apparently this

de Socrate sont l'equivalent des points de vue incomplets des cinq premiers discours du *Banquet*." He also makes the interesting observation that Stesichorus replaces, and so corresponds to, Diotima. But he does not see, or at least he does not explain, the dialectical development of these relationships. Cf. Robin (*Amour*), p. 52; Stefanini, pp. 45–50 *passim*.

condition continued to mark his relations with beautiful young men. Or perhaps the peculiar Eros of Socrates cannot be made intelligible, does not present itself as itself, under the conditions of the *Symposium*. However this may be, the sobriety of Socrates would seem to be the "erotic" peak or fulfillment of the manifestly base sobriety of Phaedrus.

This inner connection between Socrates and Phaedrus is reinforced by the dramatically later dialogue bearing Phaedrus' name. This time, however, instead of being obscured by the darkness of night, the presence of other speakers, and the peculiar indirectness of a recollection of a recollection, Socrates and Phaedrus are isolated in the light of high noon, and presented directly to the reader without any dramatic mediation. In terms of dramatic time, the *Phaedrus* is the present, the *Symposium* is the past. Put somewhat differently, the *Phaedrus* manifests the timelessness of recollection, whereas the *Symposium* is circumscribed by the origin and decay of human time. For the moment, however, let us restrict ourselves to an exact observation of the dramatic setting in the two dialogues. In the *Phaedrus*, we are not in the home of the elegant tragedian Agathon, but in the countryside just outside the city wall. In the *Symposium*, Socrates takes the unusual step of wearing shoes; in the *Phaedrus* he is unshod, but is portrayed for the only time in the Platonic corpus as walking in the country. The sunlight, the dramatic immediacy, the isolation of Socrates and Phaedrus, the simplicity of their surroundings, all suggest initially a much more sober setting for a dialogue on love than is apparent in the *Symposium*. At the same time, the dramatic details of the *Phaedrus* take us away from human things, whether mad or sober, and place us in the mixture of the divine and the natural, as mediated by myth. Both madness and sobriety take on a new appearance in these surroundings. The setting of the *Phaedrus* is thus in a way the inverse of the setting of the *Symposium*, but there are certain features common to both. The first is the emphasis on something unusual concerning Socrates. The second is Socrates' interest, for whatever reason, in speeches, especially those delivered by sophists or students of sophists. This

interest in speeches, of course, provides us with the initial explanation of the link between Socrates and Phaedrus. Both are more
interested in talking than in doing; both prefer the sobriety of
speeches about Eros to the madness of erotic possession. The central role of Phaedrus in the present dialogue therefore suggests at
once that sobriety will continue to be an essential element in the
new teaching about Eros. But the changes in setting and dramatic
detail suggest further that this element will receive a new context.

In the *Symposium*, Socrates insulates himself from the dangerous erotic currents of the banquet by wearing shoes; here, he
counters the excessive sobriety of Phaedrus by meeting him in a
beautiful country location with a specially erotic mythological
significance: the rape of Oreithuia. However, let us note that, even
in responding to the erotic defectiveness of Phaedrus, Socrates
has recourse to speech—rather than to deed. One might almost
say that in the *Symposium*, Socrates employs corporeal protection
(a bath and special clothing), whereas in the *Phaedrus* he employs
psychic protection (myth and the praise of madness). In more accessible terms, the sobriety of the *Symposium* is human or incarnate; and because of its connection with the body, turns all too
easily into human madness (as is evident in the case of Alcibiades,
who alone among the speakers in the *Symposium* links philosophy
to μανία [madness – ed]). The sobriety of the *Phaedrus*, on the
other hand, once the base or "demythologizing" sobriety of Phaedrus has been countered, turns upon a radical abstraction or ascent from the human or "lived" body. The *Phaedrus* deals with the
psyche and what we may call here the vision of the Ideas in a
purer form than does the *Symposium*.[2] The purity of this form is
not contradicted by the praise of madness.

2   Cf. Robin (*Phèdre*), p. cxxxix ff. It should be noted from the outset
    that the abstraction from the body is not the same as an abstraction
    from the cosmos. Also, the expression "vision of the Ideas" does not
    appear in the *Phaedrus*; Socrates speaks regularly of the "hyper-
    Uranian beings."

The previous reflections lead to a general comment on the relative perspectives of the *Symposium* and the *Phaedrus*. Whatever the ultimate deficiencies of Plato's teaching may be, each dialogue is marked by an intentional limitation, which is necessary in order to bring into sharp focus that aspect of human existence to which each is specifically dedicated. In the *Symposium*, Plato shows us how far one may go in the effort to provide a thoroughly human account of human existence. In the last analysis, that effort, which is characterized by the radical exclusion of eternity, or a world "beyond" the world of genesis, collapses because of the internal contradictions of genesis itself. Plato represents these contradictions in the previously mentioned nature of Eros, or the continuous manifestation of birth and death. The internal collapse of what I shall call an "immanent" account of genesis (in which, incidentally, one finds the ancestors of the various forms of modern dualism) is not eluded in the *Symposium*, not even by the prophecy of Diotima. One may quarrel with my view, expressed elsewhere, that the beautiful in itself, as cryptically described by Diotima, is not a "separate" Idea. But even if it were, I believe there can be no doubt that it is held out to us as a hope for escape from the incoherences of genesis, rather than presented as a goal already accomplished. The journey upward toward the achievement of this hope, even in the brief sketch with which Diotima provides us, is shown to be itself a resident of genesis, a human production and in that sense a poem. As the daimonic manifestation of a daimonic force, Eros provides us with no secure basis for the appropriation of the divine. The almost complete silence about madness in the *Symposium* is a token of its silence about the divine (except, of course, in the sense of the Olympian gods, who are themselves "poems" or residents of genesis).

The absence, or compromised presence, of the divine in the *Symposium* is evident from the fact that Eros is identified as a daimon rather than as a god. Eros is given a problematic relationship even to the Olympian gods. But entirely apart from this, as a force whose roots are planted on Mount Olympus, Eros shares in, or exemplifies, the qualities of Olympus. The best that can be said for Olympus is that, as a mountain peak, and so connected to the earth, it nevertheless reaches up toward, and in that sense approaches, hopes for, or promises, heaven in the sense of the truly divine: of what is beyond genesis. To state the point as briefly as possible, the philosophical criticism of poetry is at the same time a criticism of the "divine" status of Olympus. This criticism is decisively informed by the characteristic of the daimonic. Eros is *polymorphous perverse*. Even its promotion to the status of a god (*Phaedrus* 242d9 ff.) is in itself not sufficient to bridge the gap between genesis and a coherent account of genesis. We need philosophy in the sense of a divine madness or portion, that is, as a vision of the hyper-Uranian beings. This step is taken in the *Phaedrus*. At the same time, however, the *Phaedrus* is marked by the complete silence of the psyche in Socrates' account of its exercise of divine madness.[3] I shall argue in some detail that this silence is "reflexive" in the sense that it indicates the inadequacies of the account of the divine in the *Phaedrus*. In other words, I am speaking here only of Plato's intentions, or his own understanding of limitations intrinsic to the human enterprise of philosophy. One cannot sensibly criticize those intentions until they have been accurately understood. Let us simply summarize here what will be spelled out at greater length throughout the present study. In the first place, any account of the divine must necessarily be poetic, whether altogether or in part. Every attempt to purge such an account of its poetic nature results in the creation of a "mathematical ontology," which suffers from the double defect that it is itself a poem or human product, and one which renders human existence unintelligible. In the second place, no account of the divine can be given for purely technical or "logical" reasons, if by "account" we mean a logical analysis of the formal structure of the cosmos.

3 The silence of the psyche in Socrates' second speech has not, so far as I am aware, been noted by previous commentators. Perhaps Diesendruck comes closest; cf. pp. 25, 45 ff., and 51 ff., for some related comments on vision, beauty, and silence concerning mathematics.

Despite its more comprehensive or higher perspective than that of the *Symposium*, the *Phaedrus* is also compromised by the silence of poetry. According to Plato's teaching, this "compromise" is an essential characteristic of human nature. It cannot be overcome by restricting oneself to technical or "analytical" devices of pure logic, such as diaeresis, or the division and collection in accordance with kinds. For if poetry is silent about the logical structure of human existence, logic itself is silent about the poetic horizon within which, like all human activities, it lives and moves and has its being. Man needs both poetry and logic (or mathematics); his need for both is illustrated in the *Phaedrus*, as it is not in the *Symposium*. But the *Phaedrus* also illustrates that the joint need can itself be expressed only through the use of poetic language. With respect to the first or last things, poetic language (even when it employs logic and mathematics) is necessarily silent, just as the psyche is silent about how he "knows" the nature of this psychic ascent, just as the hyper-Uranian beings are themselves altogether silent in the face of man's effort to see them, and to capture this vision forever in speech. In sum, the *Phaedrus*, despite its philosophical superiority to the *Symposium*, does not present us with an answer to the question of the complete philosophical speech, or even to the question as to the possibility of speaking at all about eternity. One may say that it does not answer the question as to the connection between reason and the good. But it takes us several steps closer to that answer than does the *Symposium*. There will be enough time, after we have ourselves taken those steps, to ask whether still more progress is possible.

II.

By writing the *Phaedrus*, Plato tells us that the *Symposium* is a necessary but insufficient step in understanding the nature of Eros. We have to start again, and we start once more with Phaedrus. The name "Phaedrus" designates a human being rather than something inanimate. It means literally both "bright" and "beaming," like the light, and also "cheerful" or "joyous": as one might say, "beaming with joy"—a meaning which, as we shall see, tells us something about the dialogue itself, and why it takes place at high noon, in the brightest sunlight. "Phaedrus," to continue, does not name an abstraction, like "The Republic," an event, like "The Symposium," or a human type, like "The Sophist." Furthermore, "Phaedrus" is the name of a historical person, not a mythical one like "Minos." The person is an approximate contemporary of Socrates, unlike "Parmenides," and someone to whom Socrates is clearly superior, as is not apparent in the case of "Timaeus." This superiority does not preclude regular association; Socrates may not be a friend of Phaedrus in the strict sense of the term, but he is a companion of Phaedrus, as he is not of "Protagoras." This companionship is a kind of imitation of friendship, as is not true of Socrates' relations with "Gorgias," "Meno," or "Hippias." Phaedrus is not a young boy whom Socrates meets for the first time and whose nature he tests, like "Charmides" or "Theaetetus." He is not silent like "Philebus," not a fanatic like "Euthyphro," not an old and sober friend like "Crito," not a disciple like "Phaedo." So far we seem to be proceeding entirely by negation. Even if this were so, the results would be instructive, since a negative description, as we know from theology, is perhaps the only way to define a unique entity. But we can now be rather more positive. The connection between Socrates and Phaedrus turns upon Eros. However, Socrates does not claim to be in love with Phaedrus,[4] as he does with Alcibiades, nor is it ever suggested that Phaedrus loves Socrates. The point is that Socrates and Phaedrus share a love for speeches. The love of speeches is more sober than the love of bodies; differently stated, its daimonic nature is higher than that of the corporeal Eros because it permits a detachment from, and ascent beyond, the body.[5] Socrates and

4 The context of 228d8-e1 shows that Socrates is ironical here in saying "much as I love you . . ." The sense is: I love Lysias' speech more than your necessarily defective memory of it.
5 This is true even when corporeal Eros plays a contributory role in the love of speeches. At the same time, the problematic character of

Phaedrus are united by the sobriety of their Eros, if not by the divine principle of that Eros. For Phaedrus' sobriety is base, or excessively human, because directed primarily toward the care of his body; whereas Socrates' sobriety is noble, or divine, because directed primarily toward the care of his psyche. Phaedrus and Socrates represent the two poles of erotic sobriety. And the peak of sobriety is at once the peak of madness: the distinguishing mark, I may add, of Plato's conception of philosophy.

The *Phaedrus* is not simply about Eros, as one might perhaps say of the *Symposium*. It is also about speeches or rhetoric, and it culminates in a discussion of writing. In the *Symposium*, speeches are delivered as a consequence of Eros; in the *Phaedrus*, we are given a discussion about the writing of speeches to Eros. Similarly, the *Symposium* culminates in cryptic reference to a conversation between the sober Socrates and the drunken poets Aristophanes and Agathon about writing.[6] In the *Phaedrus*, the discussion culminates in a technical conversation between the sober and non-poetic Socrates and Phaedrus about writing. The greater sobriety of this dimension of the *Phaedrus*, despite or because of its introduction of divine madness, in comparison to the *Symposium*, is shown by its movement from Eros to the *technē* of writing, and thus to the mention of dialectic. The link between Eros and writing is the psyche. More specifically, it is the myth of the varieties of psychic madness, and primarily, of the divine or philosophical madness. But the structure of the *Phaedrus*, and so the relationship between Eros and writing or discourse, is extremely complex.[7] Let us observe from the beginning that Socrates never explicitly says

---

    speech is shown by the fact that the silent ascent of the psyche is motivated by the love of beautiful bodies. There is a difference between erotic ascent and speech about erotic ascent.

6   *Symposium* 223c2 ff. The fact that Aristophanes falls asleep before Agathon gives perhaps slight support to the thesis that the *Symposium* is a tragedy.

7   Scholars have debated since antiquity whether or not the *Phaedrus* possesses a structural unity. For a summary of this debate, cf. Diesendruck, pp. 1 ff.

that one must be mad in order to discourse well. He refers to himself as "a lover of divisions and collections" (266b3-4), and not of beautiful bodies. Good discourse depends upon knowledge of the psyche, but Socrates does not say that knowledge of the psyche depends upon erotic madness. This means ultimately that Socrates does not associate knowledge of the psyche with the noetic apprehension of a hyper-Uranian being (cf. 246c6 ff.). Instead, he exhibits the erotic nature of the psyche in an "inspired" myth. *He does not tell us how he knows the content of this myth*, which is in fact attributed to the poet Stesichorus. As I previously indicated, the transcendence of Mount Olympus is accomplished by means of powers associated with Mount Olympus. There is no discursive account, or as we would now say, no epistemological analysis, of inspired or manic knowledge. If Socrates' knowledge of the psyche is "mad," it would seem to be in a sense different from the madness which raises the psyche to the roof of the cosmos. Nothing is said in the myth to support the inference that noetic apprehension leads to self-consciousness; as we shall see below, the reverse is rather the case. The knowledge of madness, in the sense of self-consciousness or knowledge of the nature of the human psyche, is apparently discontinuous from both the exercise of madness and the sobriety of discursive or diaeretic dialectic. In another sense, of course, it is continuous with both, in that we can speak about ourselves as well as the hyper-Uranian beings, once we have seen them. This is perhaps the simplest explanation of the sense in which discourse, whether poetic or logical, is recollection.[8] For example, as the phrase "self-consciousness" suggests,

8   In one sense or another, speech would seem to depend upon the erotic pathos; it is either a mark of Eros, or about Eros, or both. For a sober account of the dependence of true discourse on pathos, cf. *Sophist* 234d2-e6. The function of diaeresis is pedagogic; namely, it is designed to bring the student as close as possible to the objects of discourse, given that, because of his youth, the student is ἄνευ τῶν παθημάτων ["without those experiences" – ed.]. If the student possessed those *pathēmata*, presumably diaeresis would be unnecessary. I shall return to the status of diaeresis below.

we must first have been conscious as a self, in order to identify reflexively that consciousness as "self-consciousness."

Thus we see again and again the reciprocal relationship between madness and sobriety, and the difference between that relationship as it is expressed in the *Symposium* or in the *Phaedrus*. To this extent, at least, the *Phaedrus* would seem to be appropriately named: Socrates describes the perfect writing as a living being, and Phaedrus is a living being who loves speeches, or a sober man with a tincture of madness. In less playful, or more sober, terms, the ascent to the divine madness, as a necessary completion of the teaching of the *Symposium*, requires first a criticism of the teaching of the *Symposium*. And this requires another look at the principle or progenitor of the earlier discussion: Phaedrus. We require another look at sobriety in its human form before we are ready to move on to madness in its divine form. And this is an excellent recipe for philosophy: two parts of sobriety to one part of madness.

Although the sober Phaedrus and Socrates both claim to be erotic about speeches, neither is a writer. Poetry and sexual generation are both associated with madness; the sobriety of the Eros of Phaedrus and (so far as we know it here) Socrates gives it in both cases an explicitly passive inflection. Neither Phaedrus nor Socrates generates speeches of his own. Of course, both "speak," but in the crucial instances, they either speak the speeches of others, like actors (hypocrites); or else, as in the case of Socrates at least, they repeat and test the speeches generated by others. However, both may be regarded as indirect generators of speeches. According to Socrates, Phaedrus has inspired more speeches than anyone except Simmias. According to the Platonic dialogues, Socrates goads or stimulates men into making speeches, thanks to a process which he calls "midwifery," but which is perhaps more frankly portrayed in the *Apology* as a kind of disagreeableness or ungentlemanliness. Phaedrus is a "father" of speeches because of his beauty, whereas Socrates seems to cause others to generate speeches because of his ugliness. Phaedrus' physical beauty seems to prevent his lovers from ascending to the love of his not so beautiful psyche. Socrates' "ugly" behavior, together with the manifest ugliness of his body, seems to pose no insurmountable obstacle to the love of his unusually beautiful psyche; no obstacle, that is, for those with eyes to see. In terms of the erotic ascent described by Diotima, the transition from corporeal to psychic Eros requires a "guide." Diotima does not explain how this "guide" leads the lover to prefer the extremely beautiful psyche of an ugly body to the not so beautiful psyche of a beautiful body.[9] A genuine understanding of the difference between love for Phaedrus and love for Socrates is not visible in the *Symposium*. Thus Alcibiades is laughable to the other guests because of his obvious if incoherent erotic attraction toward Socrates. Love of Socrates ceases to be laughable when we understand the divine portion or fate by which madness is transformed into sobriety, and sobriety into madness, or by which the beautiful becomes ugly and the ugly beautiful.

Let me approach this point in a slightly different way. Phaedrus espouses the cause of the non-lover, both here and in the *Symposium*. Socrates, although he defends the lover in the *Phaedrus*, does so by developing a myth of the psyche, attributed to the poet Stesichorus, the highest function of which consists in guiding us to the essentially passive enterprise of looking at the hyper-Uranian Beings. In the *Symposium*, Socrates presents himself as a student of the prophetess Diotima, that is, as a young man who is defective in his erotic understanding, and who is taught that the peak of erotic activity is, again, a kind of passive looking. Prophetess and poet agree that the highest erotic man is, if not non-erotic, a divine voyeur. What does this mean so far as the three main themes of the Phaedrus are concerned? Eros is first criticized and then praised by two passive or "sterile" erotics, who nevertheless paradoxically stimulate others to generate. This praise, having been prepared by criticism, culminates in a speech about the psyche, according to which human perfection, paradoxically called a species of divine madness, is identified as the passive-erotic vision of the non-erotic hyper-Uranian beings. And

9   Cf. Rosen (*Symposium*), pp. 265 ff. and *Symposium* 210a4 ff.

discussion of the themes introduced in the first two parts of the dialogue leads to the technical discussion of the technē of writing, a technical discussion between two amateurs or non-practitioners of the art in question.

One might well be tempted to conclude that the *Phaedrus* is a comedy, on the basis of the observations just made.[10] If so, however, we must append that it is a divine comedy, and hence not lacking in tragic overtones. The praise of passivity is inseparable from the Platonic conception of human perfection as a transcendence of the corporeal Eros. The sobriety of the non-lover has therefore something essential in common with the madness of the philosopher. The sterility of the passive erotic is similar to the anti-poetic vision of the eternal beings beyond heaven. Even further, the attenuation or cessation of the corporeal Eros, although accompanied by a flowering of the psychic Eros, leads, precisely if the latter is successful, to the suppression of one's human individuality. Wisdom as the fulfillment of philosophy, at least if wisdom is perfect vision of perfection, amounts to the transformation of man into a god—or rather, into a noetic formal monad. The silent ascent to perfection would seem to terminate in perfect silence, rather than in speech, whether perfect or imperfect. Only in this case, one may suggest, would the meaning of the otherwise mysterious saying of Parmenides become perspicuous: τὸ γὰρ αὐτὸ νοεῖν ἐστίν τε καὶ εἶναι.[11]

10 "In this dialogue it ought to be evident by now that very little is flatly stated, though much is of high seriousness in spite of the irony"; Helmbold and Holther, p. 408. Cf. Pieper, p. 3: "The Socrates of this dialogue embodies seemingly irreconcilable features: wit, pleasure in mockery, and an inclination toward parody, such as we scarcely encounter in the other dialogues."

11 Diels, Fr. 3. ["For to think and to be are the same." For a more elaborate translation and an interpretation of this ambiguous and much disputed fragment, see Rosen's "Parmenides B3: Commentary on A. A. Long's 'Parmenides on Thinking Being'" in *Essays in Philosophy: Ancient*, ed. M. Black (St. Augustine's Press, 2013), pp. 92–101 – ed.]

III.

Socrates encounters Phaedrus on the way from Lysias, son of Cephalus, who was Socrates' host in the *Republic*. Phaedrus is walking in the country for reasons of health, in accord with the advice of Acumenus, the physician and father of Eryximachus. He no doubt needs the exercise in order to recuperate from what Socrates calls the "banquet" of speeches offered by Lysias (227a1-b7).[12] Phaedrus allows medicine to tend his body and rhetoric to tend his psyche. The defect of rhetoric as psychic medicine is suggested by the fact that it lacks moderation; as a consequence, the lover of rhetoric seems actually to be ruled by the corporeal physician. In any case, Phaedrus has no trouble in interesting Socrates in the topic discussed at this new banquet, although not quite for the reason he supposes. Lysias has written that a beautiful youth "ought to gratify the non-lover rather than the lover" (227b8-c8).[13] Phaedrus refers to Lysias' speech as "refined"; Socrates points out that, with some expansion, its elegance would properly be called "useful to the demos," with whom he ironically associates himself by reason of his poverty, age and lack of distinction. However, even as it stands, the speech is of sufficient interest to Socrates that he himself is willing to engage in a long therapeutic walk in order to hear it.[14] Let us bear in mind the "medical" conjunction of the non-lover, the demos, and utility. Meanwhile, we observe

12 Epicrates was a rhetor and demagogue, Morychus a wealthy and "eminent bon vivant" (Thompson, *loc. cit.*). Note also that Socrates confirms Acumenus' advice as though he, too, were a physician (227b3).

13 Socrates quotes Pindar, *Isthmian* I, lines 1–2, in such a way as to compare Phaedrus to "my mother Thebes." Pindar places the glory of his polis beyond everything else. For Socrates, the love of speeches transcends the polis; this is related to the location of the dialogue outside the city wall.

14 227c7-d5: Socrates says that he would be willing to obey the advice of Herodicus, another physician who is mentioned in the *Protagoras*.

that Phaedrus regards Lysias as the most talented writer of the day, and would rather be able to memorize his speeches than come into a fortune (228a1-4). Phaedrus imitates the philosopher in valuing speeches and memory beyond money. Unlike the philosopher, he admires "democratic" rather than aristocratic speeches.[15] Presumably he believes that rhetoric is more useful than money, although in view of his tastes, this may be an error on his part. The most charitable, as well as the most cautious, interpretation is probably that Phaedrus loves speeches or rhetoric for selfish reasons, but transcends his selfishness by virtue of his love for speeches. And this love is passive or imitates the non-lover whose praise he admires: Phaedrus wishes that he could memorize Lysias' speeches, but not that he could write his own.

Now Socrates introduces the distinction between corporeal and psychic medicine by the confession that he has a "disease for listening to speeches" (228b6), which, he implies, can be ameliorated by Phaedrus.[16] Phaedrus' "medicine" will be shared by doctor and patient alike; the repetition of Lysias' speech will induce a mutual corybantic enthusiasm that replaces the atmosphere of intoxication (to the extent that it is genuine) in the *Symposium*.[17] To anticipate Socrates' remark upon the conclusion of the speech, Phaedrus is transformed by rhetoric into a Dionysian reveler, an appropriately feminine condition in which Socrates claims to share

15   We should also note that Phaedrus explicitly accuses himself of having a bad memory, a defect which will have considerable importance in the dialogue, and especially in the final third, where we find the technical discussion of rhetoric. Socrates, on the contrary, indicates that his memory of Phaedrus' and his own nature, at least, is excellent (228b5-6).

16   The passage 228a5-c5 exhibits Socrates' prophetic powers, as he unveils both past and future. There is another interesting subtlety that should not be overlooked here. At 228c3, Socrates indicates that Phaedrus would use force to detain him, whereas at 228c9, he agrees that he will use force to detain him. The significance of the force is of course verbal rather than physical: it refers to the constrained or accommodated nature of the conversation.

17   The corybants were priestesses of Cybele.

(234dl-6).[18] How different this is from Phaedrus' characteristic passivity, we may easily infer from his conversation with Socrates about the myth of Boreas and Oreithuia. Phaedrus is vague on the geographical details, and obviously does not believe in the truth of the story.[19] As Socrates implies, Phaedrus interprets myths in terms of physics, like Anaxagoras and Metrodorus. Socrates finds this kind of de-mythologizing "charming"—that is, it indeed charms men away from the more important task of understanding themselves, and hence amounts to a "kind of boorish wisdom" (229c6-230a6).[20] Socrates must devote his time to investigating his own puzzling nature, which he compares to mythical beasts. It is not clear to him whether he is more complex and puffed up than Typhon, or whether he has a more divine and less vain nature; as we might say, Socrates has not yet understood the nature of his own hybris. He does not therefore deny the possibility of giving physical interpretations to myths, but rather its utility. A proper study of the prodigious nature of man requires a kind of acquiescence in conventional religious views (230al ff.). Stated somewhat differently, religious acquiescence is a necessary condition, and perhaps even a mask, for the non-political or "selfish" concern with one's own nature or psyche. This speech of Socrates thus sets the tone for (at least) the next two-thirds of the dialogue.

18 As further evidence of the curiously "feminine" dimension to Socrates' nature, note that at 230b2, he swears "by Hera!" a woman's oath.

19 229c4: I take his oath to show exasperation with those who believe such tales; this is certainly how Socrates responds to Phaedrus' question.

20 Cf. *Theaetetus* 146a5 ff.: οὐ τι που . . . ἐγὼ ὑπὸ φιλολογίας ἀγροικίζομαι ["surely I'm not acting boorishly out of a love of speeches" – ed.] The love of logos or "argument" (=de-mythologizing) can make one boorish with respect to human civility. Socrates will call himself a φιλόλογος ["love of speeches" – ed.] at *Phaedrus* 236e5. Sinaiko, p. 13, mistakenly attributes to Socrates here a dismissal of "both the makers and the rational interpreters of myths." In fact, only the latter are rebuked.

Despite his Bacchic susceptibilities, Phaedrus does not share this respect for *nomos*. His enthusiasm for rhetoric is selfish rather than political; Socrates indicates that this selfishness leads to self-neglect and ignorance. There is a sobriety in Socrates' madness, but a "madness" in Phaedrus' sobriety. Although Phaedrus is accustomed to walk in the countryside, whereas Socrates is not, he is ignorant of the topography and associated myths, which Socrates knows. The countryside and trees do not wish to teach Socrates, but he has learned their human significance from men (230d3).[21] This love of learning, interestingly enough, permits Socrates to appreciate the natural beauty of the locale in a "most unusual" manner—as though he were a stranger seeing it for the first time. Socrates suggests that this is indeed the case, and that he has been lured into the country by his hunger for speeches (230d5 ff.). Whether this is true or not, Socrates is not "drugged" (230d6) by the prospect of a feast, so as to be unable to make an intense and articulate response to the environment. Phaedrus, on the contrary, is aware of almost nothing but Lysias' speech and his desire—quickly divined by the mantic Socrates (228d7)—to recite it to Socrates.

We are now approaching high noon, the hottest part of the day and in the hottest season of the year. The two companions have "turned aside" from their walk to sit down beneath a plane tree, with bare feet—normal for Socrates, unusual for Phaedrus—for wading in the stream. The location is marked by grace, purity, and clarity: as Socrates says, it is a good place for maidens to play (but not perhaps for Bacchic maidens). Light and shade, heat and coolness, reclining humans and a flowing stream, feminine nature and masculine logos: the setting takes on the character of a harmony of opposites (229a1-c3). This is especially appropriate for the demonstration of the identity between the divine forms of

---

21 Cf. Robin's note at 230d for Socrates' excursions beyond the city walls. They are taken for political reasons, or to visit the Lyceum and Academy. Thompson, in his note on καταγωγή ["resting place" – ed.], gives a brief description of what he takes to be the locale of the dialogue as it appeared in May, 1856.

sobriety and madness. Phaedrus, mad with love for Lysias' apparently non-erotic speech, has been prevented by Socrates' prophetic sobriety from testing his memory, and will read to Socrates from the copy he had concealed beneath his cloak.

IV.

Lysias, author of the demotic and utilitarian praise of the non-lover, is a rhetorician and *logographos*, especially famous for his courtroom speeches. He appears at the beginning of the *Republic*, in the home of his father, Cephalus. The members of this family are there portrayed as conceiving of justice in terms of utility. The ascent in the *Phaedrus* from the non-lover to the lover is parallel to the ascent in the *Republic* from a utilitarian interpretation of justice to the virtual identification of justice with moderation and its subordination to philosophy. In the *Symposium*, which emphasizes the hybristic nature of Eros, justice is not mentioned as one of his attributes. The one man who seems seriously concerned with justice is Alcibiades, whose intoxicated appearance at the banquet transforms it into a trial of Socrates for hybris, with himself as the plaintiff. Alcibiades' speech soon reveals, however, that even though he may be correct in his perception of Socrates' nature, his own complaint against Socrates is unjust and rooted in immoderateness. I suggest that the *Phaedrus* begins with Lysias' speech in order to indicate something about the defective or incomplete nature of the *Symposium*. Eros and justice, as the *Republic* makes explicit, are, if not simply incompatible, opposites which need a "third" element to bind them into harmony. The sobriety of the non-lover is more like moderation than is the madness of the lover. An immoderate criticism of the passive Eros is no more just than a praise of Eros that is silent about justice. In the *Phaedrus*, the ascent from sobriety to madness is not an "abstraction" but rather a sublation, just as, in the *Republic*, the notion of utility is not discarded but sublated into the final interpretation of justice.

In the *Symposium*, Phaedrus is the father of the logos; in the *Phaedrus*, it is Lysias who serves this purpose. The speech of

Lysias both criticizes the end of the *Symposium* and returns us to the theme of the beginning. Our new start is an improvement on the beginning of the *Symposium* in two ways. First, it is the speech of a professional rhetorician or generator of discourses, and not simply of a lover of discourses. Second, the professionalism of the author renders his speech free from contradictory or obscuring effects that might arise from the enthusiasm of the speaker. Lysias' mastery of the rhetorical technē permits him to give a "disinterested" or just presentation of the merits of the non-lover. His speech imitates philosophy to this extent: it combines technical skill with praise for the utility of sobriety; Lysias is a sober, rather than a mad or inspired, poet. On the other hand, this latter fact represents the defective nature of Lysias' speech; it inspires Phaedrus, but for the wrong reasons, because it is not itself inspired.

Let us now turn to the main points of Lysias' speech. As is befitting its sober message, the speech begins (and indeed continues throughout; see Hackforth's outraged commentary[22]) with no rhetorical flourish; its rhetoric, one might almost say, is anti-rhetorical. The boy knows the situation, and the non-lover has already spoken of their "joint interest" (230e7): there is to be an exchange of goods, or a wholesale rather than a retail business contract. Lovers confer benefits freely only while their desire lasts; the cessation of the erotic desire thereby endangers, perhaps terminates, the advantages enjoyed by the beloved. The non-lover, on the contrary, because he acts from freedom rather than necessity, in a sober and business-like manner, which does not interfere with an efficient and technically accurate calculation of profits and losses, nor lead him to quarrel with relatives over the distribution of property, may devote his energies to the benefit of the beloved (231a1-b7). The non-lover's case rests upon a distinction between "what I need" ($\dot{\omega}v$ δέομαι) and the desire (ἐπιθυμία) of Eros. Is this defensible? At least in this sense: according to the non-lover, he desires gratification, as an "objectified" commodity, independent of the personality of the

---

22   R. Hackforth, *Plato's Phaedrus* (Cambridge: 1952; LLA reprint).

boy, who is to him not a beloved but a reified unit in the free-market economy, whose wares are subject to the laws of supply and demand. The non-lover agrees in part with Marx's analysis of capitalism, but approves of the results. Objectivity grounded in a technically competent selfishness is preferable for buyer and seller to the authentic, human esteem praised by Marxists and existentialists.

Like the modern exemplar of the Protestant ethic, the non-lover prides himself upon his autonomy and industrious efficiency; like the philosopher, he is a sober master of the technē of division and collection (i.e., of profits and losses). He acts in accordance with his own capacity, both toward himself and his family as well as toward reified youths; whereas the lover is carried beyond his capacity, with consequent injustice to all concerned, by the transcendence of madness. In sum, he combines the qualities of hedonism, utilitarianism, and technicism in such a way as to abstract from such human qualities as the beautiful and ugly or the noble and the base. Like the philosopher, he disregards human individuality in his pursuit of the general or steadfast. But the manner in which he does so leads to a transformation in the meaning of the true and the false; by beginning from the lowest or common denominator of animal passion, the non-lover terminates in the advanced sciences of cost-accounting, game theory, and, in an anticipatory sense, of computer-based psychology. The origin of this line of development is in the distinction between erotic and non-erotic desire; the former turns upon the personality or humaneness of the beloved, and the latter upon the common physiological structure of buyer and seller. The lover is presented as faithful, not to the beloved, but to his desire for the beloved as beloved; whereas the non-lover is uninterested in the loveableness of the boy, but is faithful exclusively to the possibilities for gratification, considered physiologically or in terms of the body in virtual disregard for the psyche—probably even for certain bodily qualities, although nothing is said on this point. The non-lover minimizes the connection between his position and desire; however, reflection shows that his more serious claim is not to eliminate desire but to make it autonomous. His own autonomy is not from desire but from the ἀνάγκη ["compulsion" or "necessity" – ed.] of Eros, or the trans-human, i.e., what we call the *divine*. The non-lover is a "humanist" as well as a hedonist, utilitarian, and technicist. But his humanism is inseparable from, or rather identical with, a debasement of the human to the physiological. In slightly different terms, the successful application of the quasi-mathematical version of division and collection to human affairs depends upon the debasement of Eros by physiology.[23]

Eros is an illness leading to immoderateness or the inability to master oneself (231d2 ff.); the combination of rhetoric and medicine represented by Lysias and Phaedrus cures the illness, or makes self-mastery possible thanks to a new and lower interpretation of the self. There are very few lovers, or at least few excellent lovers, whereas there are many candidates for the title of "extremely useful"; as Socrates initially observed, the non-lover is a democrat in addition to being a humanist, hedonist, utilitarian, and technicist (231d6-e2). Since "desire" means "physiological gratification," the non-lover brings us egalitarianism or freedom from the subjectivity of value judgments. Strictly speaking, it should even be irrelevant whether non-lovers and non-beloveds are physically beautiful, young, or in any other corporeally-oriented sense (even perhaps their sex) pre-eminent. But now the defect in Lysias' exoteric or obvious teaching becomes manifest. In a democratic business society of the kind sketched by the non-lover, there is a contradiction between physiological egalitarianism and the difference between the rich and the poor. This is related to an implied physiological difference between the non-lover and the object of his "non-erotic" desire. The non-lover takes it for granted throughout his speech that the boy is not himself motivated by erotic but by financial considerations, or at least by concern for his reputation: for "keeping up appearances" (231e3-232e2). Thus he regularly refers to his relationship

23 Cf. *Sophist*, 227a7 ff.

with the boy as one of φιλία rather than ἔρως, of "gratification" rather than of "desire."[24] The pederastic relationship is regularly contrasted to the relation of friendship (cf. 231cl, 233c6 *et passim*) or said to interfere with it. But "friendship," as we know, means "advantage," and since "advantage" is essentially economic, while certainly not erotic, it would seem to be most advantageous for the youth to gratify only the wealthiest non-lovers. Even further, his best interests may lie in the sober plundering of wealthy lovers whose technical vision is blinded by the madness of erotic passion. This continues to hold true even if the youth is also motivated by the non-erotic or physiological need for gratification. Where all other factors are irrelevant, a rich "friend" must be preferable to a poor one.

It is not clear that the non-lover sees this defect in his position. For example, he observes that lovers must fear rivals possessing greater wealth or intelligence (232c4-8). Apparently the non-lover does not share these fears because he has achieved what he needs δι' ἀρετήν ["through virtue" – ed.] (232d4-5); i.e., through his own efficient management of the joint advantage of himself and the boy in question—through his intelligence or technē. We have to realize, furthermore, that only a man of a certain degree of wealth or business acumen could profitably avail himself of the argument of the non-lover. The non-lover clearly assumes that, although others may be richer than he, he is rich enough; if others are more intelligent, he is intelligent enough. Indeed, if he loses one boy to a superior rival, there are surely many others, just as there are many non-lovers. His teaching, like many another technē, is a substitute for personal excellence, and its very persuasiveness is a better protection for his own interests than the advantages traditionally predicated of a lover. Nevertheless, in the last analysis, the teaching of the non-lover turns upon the difference between rich and poor; it is oligarchical rather than democratic.

24 E.g., 231e1-2, 232b4 (where φιλία is equated with ἡδονή ["pleasure" – ed.]), 232d4, 232el, 232e6. [φιλία is usually translated "friendship" in contrast with ἔρως, "love" or "passionate desire" – ed.]

What of the tacit assumption that the boy is either non-erotic or prefers money to the higher considerations? According to the non-lover, friendship comes from intelligence rather than from Eros, again, incidentally, an imitation of the philosophical teaching. That is: in the erotic relation, physical desire for a specific individual precedes, and is the condition for, friendship. In the case of the non-lover, who is disinterestedly interested in physical gratification, and objective toward, or disinterested in, the personal or lovable attributes of the person, friendship—i.e., a rational relationship based upon mutual advantage—precedes physical gratification (232e3-233a5). This means that the non-lover, thanks to the impersonal, and hence sober or less compelling, nature of his physical desire, can guarantee the financial advantage of the boy prior to gratification. It is the vulgarity or bestiality of the non-lover's position, and not his freedom from desire, that makes his suit more advantageous. In fact, the non-lover is moved by Eros, but by a very low form of Eros. The success of his argument then turns upon the possession of wealth, and the capacity to corrupt the young by employing the technē of rhetoric to excite greed rather than lust. The non-lover is in fact a concealed lover, however base a lover.

Before we rebel against the baseness of the non-lover, let us remember the results of the earlier stage of our investigation. It is perfectly reasonable to claim that passion interferes with friendship, as well as with the pursuit of the useful, the just, and the true. Furthermore, the non-lover praises moderation, intelligence, and a prudent concern for the future (233b6 ff.). He is eager to improve the condition of his friend, to free his perception of pleasure from the pain accompanying Eros, to teach him self-mastery, and to balance justice with mercy. I have pointed out that this whole argument is, among other things, a legitimate criticism of the general teaching of the *Symposium*. This is made clear in an amusing way. The erotic man (as the *Symposium* asserts) is the most needy man. If one must gratify the most needy, then one must gratify the worst rather than the best. In philosophical language, if we love what we do not have, must not the lover of goodness be bad?

Those men who strive most assiduously for perfection must themselves be worthless (233d5 ff.). In other words, the erotic mania, if it is not regulated by a divine fate, or a prophetic synopsis, is extraordinarily dangerous, and more likely even in the rarest cases to produce an Alcibiades than a Socrates. We must first have what we desire, thanks to divine madness, precisely in order to desire it soberly. Thus the non-lover warns us that, to follow Diotima's advice, would mean inviting beggars rather than friends to our "private banquets" (233e1). He suggests, in effect, that this is the mistake made by Agathon; and, appropriately enough, at this point his speech sounds more like that of Pausanias (Agathon's lover) than like that of Phaedrus, or like a mixture of the speeches of Pausanias and Phaedrus. One should gratify those moderate, sober, stable, clever lovers (who for prudential reasons call themselves "non-lovers") who are best able to show their gratitude. In exoteric terms, one should gratify those on whose pensions (οὐσία)[25] one can rely; in esoteric terms, one should gratify those who already possess the good or οὐσία in the ontological sense (233e6-234c5). In sum: the baseness of Lysias' speech contains a serious teaching, or rather two serious teachings, in however ironical a form. As always in Plato, the low prefigures the high; the philosopher must learn to understand dirt and other low things if he is to understand the psyche and, finally, the cosmos. The difference between the philosopher and the gentleman leads the latter to recoil from vulgarity, whereas the philosopher has inured himself to practice his ἀκριβολογία even upon a "tedious piece of rhetoric" which, in Hackforth's words, "deserves little comment."[26] The non-lover, then, teaches us something about human baseness, but he also has something to say about the nature of philosophy.

25 [οὐσία originally refers to what one owns or one's "property" or "substance" and becomes a central word for "being" among the philosophers. It is translated by Rosen as "essential being" on p. 99 – ed.]
26 Hackforth, *op. cit.*, p. 31.

CHAPTER TWO:
The Concealed Lover

I.

According to the speech of Lysias, there is an opposition between friendship and erotic desire. The hypocritical nature of the non-lover's argument should not prevent us from perceiving the truth in such a contention. Even in terms of Eros, it is not simply false to distinguish between an ecstatic desire that immediately transports us "out of our senses," and a physiological need that employs calculation in order to guarantee a stable mode of gratification. It is not simply false to suggest that friendship is more compatible with a rational calculation of common advantage than with an overpowering, maddening passion. Consider, for example, the situation of Phaedrus and Socrates. To the extent that either is subject to madness, it is in the form of a "sickness" or desire for speeches (cf. 228b6 and 231d2). In different senses, each may function as physician to the other, or provide for mutual gratification, and precisely because neither is erotically attracted by the other as an individual person. The "Dionysian revelry" in which Socrates and Phaedrus are united (234d1-6) is entirely impersonal, a daimonic, even divine perception of beauty, powerful enough to raise Phaedrus from the selfishness which first led him to admire Lysias' speech. Even though Socrates is ironical in his own expression of enthusiasm, he undoubtedly does share in the beauty perceived by Phaedrus, which is purified from its base origins by the transformation it undergoes in Phaedrus' "shining" joy. Phaedrus is an icon of the Idea of beauty, upon which Socrates gazes in self-transcending delight.

Having done so, however, Socrates shows his sobriety by returning to earth and, like the non-lover, attending to the process of improving or educating the person who has just gratified him. As is so frequently the case in the dialogues, he begins by assuring his companion of the need for them to reach agreement (234e8-9, 235a3-4).[1] In the *Symposium*, Socrates first establishes agreement with Agathon before beginning his own speech. To this extent, Socrates' first speech in the *Phaedrus* is analogous to his second dialogue with Agathon in the *Symposium*. But whereas, in an occasion devoted to speeches, Socrates employs dialogue to establish agreement, in a dialogue about speeches, he delivers a speech. Phaedrus, in other words, is more amenable to speeches than to conversations.[2] In the same context, there is another inverted reference to the *Symposium* and Agathon. Socrates there tells Agathon that one cannot be filled up with another's wisdom by touching him, as water is drawn by a thread from one vessel to another.[3] Here, Socrates assumes that he has himself been filled up like a vessel from the springs of other people's knowledge; only he refers now to hearing, whereas previously he spoke of touch (235c8 ff.). Wisdom may not be transferred by erotic contact, but knowledge may be transferred by the more sober sense of hearing: again a point in favor of the non-lover. Agathon is far more erotic, and infinitely more clever, than Phaedrus. But because Phaedrus loves to listen, Socrates may be able to pour some knowledge into him, knowledge that was previously obtained from Sappho, Anacreon, or some other writer.

Phaedrus was inspired by the sober speech of a sober professor of rhetoric. Socrates indicates that he is being inspired by a speech which was probably written by a poet, that is, by an inspired or

1   Cf. *Gorgias* 486e5 ff., esp. 487d7-e7, for the rhetorical importance of agreement.
2   Cf. *Symposium* 194d1 ff., where Phaedrus interrupts the first dialogue between Socrates and Agathon, in order to ensure that the speeches continue.
3   *Symposium* 175d3 ff.

mad rather than sober author. And as we are about to see, this speech is about a lover disguised as a non-lover, just as was the case in Lysias' speech, only here explicitly admitted. The shift from the first to the second speech is one of increased daimonic power, an essential step in the education of Phaedrus, whom Socrates here calls ὦ δαιμόνιε (235c5).[4] In accordance with Socratic practice, pedagogic disagreement may be rooted in, even disguised as, agreement. The agreement here consists in the fact that the case of the non-lover is not altogether abandoned. Instead, Socrates makes partially clear that the non-lover is a particular form of Eros. His vagueness about the name of the author supports the general impression of the "inspired" character of the speech; the author may be a poet, or even some more daimonic force which has "infused" the speech directly into Socrates' breast. And Socrates' modesty or apparent unwillingness to deliver this speech, by which he ironically reverses roles with Phaedrus (236c1 ff.), is here intended to excite the appetite of his too-sober student.[5]

Phaedrus rises to the bait, and offers Socrates a bribe if the latter will recite his speech. The nine Athenian archons must dedicate a statue of themselves to Delphi if they break their oath and take bribes. Phaedrus will dedicate a statue of himself *and* Socrates in exchange for the speech: Phaedrus is a corrupt "archon." Or perhaps one may suggest that there is a Platonic joke here, and that "nine" refers to the Muses, invoked by Socrates just as he begins to recite his first speech, which is later identified as a myth (237a7, 241e8). As the location of the dialogue beyond the city walls also implies, there is something contrary to political "music" about the praise of divine madness. But the reference to an icon of Socrates, repeated at 236b3-4, has another and ultimately related meaning. We are at once reminded of Alcibiades' speech in the *Symposium*, which its

---

4   [Literally "daimonic one," a vocative usually expressing surprise or wonder. – ed.]

5   At the same time, of course, Socrates is preparing the way for his eventual disowning of the speech; cf. 242b8 ff. But this point has not yet been made.

author calls an icon, and which contains the famous icon of Socrates as a Silenus-figure.[6] Alcibiades reveals that Socrates' external ugliness conceals inner "statues of gods." Phaedrus now imitates Alcibiades' hybris by offering (ironically) to erect Socrates' icon at the two divine sanctuaries of Delphi and Olympus. Phaedrus, of course, lacks Alcibiades' genius. Whereas Alcibiades speaks for himself, Phaedrus demands that Socrates reveal the beautiful speech secreted within his breast. Whereas Alcibiades speaks in drunken and erotic madness, Phaedrus tries to conclude a business contract with Socrates for an exchange of goods. Finally, in the *Symposium*, the banquet occurs at the home of a tragedian and, as the speeches of Aristophanes and Alcibiades indicate, there is a strong element of tragedy throughout the dialogue. It would be no exaggeration to say that everyone at the banquet but Socrates teaches, or unconsciously contributes to the teaching, that life is a tragedy. Phaedrus, on the other hand, here indicates that he and Socrates are both behaving like vulgar comedians; and Socrates emphasizes the laughable character of the role he is about to play.[7] In the *Phaedrus*, which despite or because of its praise of divine madness is more sober than the *Symposium*, the lot of the non-philosopher and philosopher alike is more comic than tragic. And this preponderance of comedy over tragedy has to do with the setting outside the city.

Led on by Socrates, Phaedrus threatens to use force if need be to obtain the second speech; his Dionysian revelry is now heightened by desire into a comic imitation of the mythical Boreas, in whom he does not believe.[8] Or rather, Socrates forces Phaedrus to force him to deliver the speech (cf. 241e4, 242a4). Phaedrus at last delivers the coup de grace: he swears by the plane tree that, if

6 Cf. Rosen (*Symposium*), pp. 294 ff.
7 236c2, 236d4; cf. *Symposium* 198c5-6.
8 As Thompson points out, ξύνες ὅ σοι λέγω ["comprehend what I'm telling you" – ed.] echoes a "well-known fragment of Pindar, Boeckh, No. 71," in which Pindar says "do not strive to be a god." Phaedrus may well be giving similar advice to Socrates; i.e., "you are a devotee of a god, not a god; hence you must yield to my will and provide me with another speech."

Socrates does not recite the praise of the non-lover, he will never again repeat any speeches to him. Socrates is constrained by his φιλολογία ["love of speeches" – ed.] to acquiesce. In terms of the previous chapter, he is a friend rather than a lover, and of speeches rather than of bodies (236e4-5; cf. 230d3). Phaedrus, in other words, gives a sober interpretation to his threat of force, as is symbolized by his "demythological" replacement of a tree for a god in his oath. Instead of threatening Socrates' body, he threatens his psyche. Socrates then covers his head, i.e., his body; whereas, by speaking, he seems to reveal his psyche. Of course, as will later be made explicit, his words are also veiled by irony, and he later indicates that, in the course of his first speech, his head is veiled in shame (243b6). Without denying this interpretation, we may nevertheless suggest that the veiling of the head indicates here the ambiguous erotic status of the body. And this is Socrates' major correction of Lysias' version of the argument of the non-lover.

II.

Socrates begins by invoking the Muses to assist him in attacking another god: Eros. Even though Socrates' non-lover is a lover in disguise, the speech is in fact, as Socrates later insists, an attack upon Eros. Hence Socrates' invocation implies a dispute in heaven between music (in the generic sense) and Eros. The praise of the non-lover begins appropriately with the suggestion that not all music is erotic. This is a corollary of the fact that the "necessity" (237a9) which constrains Socrates to speak is derived from φιλία rather than from ἔρως. On the other hand, the difficulty in such a distinction is shown by the fact that the non-lover is actually a lover in disguise. If friendship arises from Eros by a "veiling over" of, or abstraction from, the body, there is still a subterranean connection between the two. For example, if the difference between "friendship" (φιλία) and Eros turns upon the difference between possession and desire, must not the psyche be "individuated" or stamped as a separate, private person in order to "possess" in a genuine sense? How can X possess Y unless Y is identifiable as belonging to X rather than to non-X? Is it not the body that renders the psyche "private," and so the identifiable possessor of private property? In the case of φιλολογία, of course, two or more individuals may befriend the same speech without necessarily infringing upon each other's property rights. But the notion of friendship is unintelligible apart from the privacy of an individual psyche. The problem of the relation between lover and non-lover is thus closely related to the problem of the difference between friendship and Eros. Both of these problems are rooted in the difference between the body and the psyche, or the nature of the individual psyche. Thus the opening of Socrates' first speech is a "prophecy" of the main theme of his second speech.

Socrates is constrained to speak, not simply from philological motives, but in order to educate or improve Phaedrus.[9] Since Phaedrus is susceptible to speeches rather than to conversation, or in effect identifies rhetorical skill with wisdom, Socrates must present himself to Phaedrus as a "wise" orator, and on a topic which is dear to Phaedrus' heart. Let us note in passing the striking fact that Phaedrus does not seem to remember having once before heard Socrates discourse on Eros. I believe that this extraordinary silence, so far as Phaedrus is concerned, is another indication of his defective memory, or poor powers of recollection, which we have had occasion to observe before, and which we will see again. In any case, the obvious (but not the only) function of Socrates' first speech is to establish his credentials as a wise teacher for Phaedrus (237a10-b1). Socrates is a friend of Phaedrus' psyche, it would seem, as well as of speeches. He does not speak to all men, nor does he pronounce all speeches, but rather he speaks particular speeches to particular men at particular times. Socrates is a friend of particular speeches and psyches; even more

9   It is not yet clear *why* Socrates wishes to educate Phaedrus. I will return to this point in the discussion of rhetoric; to anticipate, Phaedrus is an "intellectual," or himself a teacher of men or former of taste. Socrates may have an effect on Phaedrus which he could not accomplish with the many.

specifically, his friendship consists in choosing the right speeches for the right psyche. Socrates is in this sense like a match-maker rather than a midwife, for the latter assists indiscriminately in those births for which she is paid, or is a kind of sophist.[10] Socrates' rhetoric turns, not upon the priority of utility, but rather of knowledge, and knowledge of the particular. Socrates is more practical than the sophistic rhetorician, who is an expert in the general principles of oratory, and so in the general desires of men, but who does not tailor his speech to the needs of the individual. The rhetorician speaks to the crowd: he says the same thing to everyone. The nature of his technē forces him to substitute the desires of the crowd for those of the individual; his utilitarianism is necessarily demagogic rather than pedagogic. He therefore agrees with the sophist that the art of rhetoric in general is the greatest good for men generally, i.e., anonymously. The good of the technē is independent of the individuality of the person. By accepting this technical notion of "good," the person thereby transforms himself into a unit of the crowd. From this point of view, sophistic rhetoric is like mathematics. It reduces men to homogeneous monads, or to the lowest common denominator.

According to Lysias' non-lover, there are few lovers (231d6). Socrates quietly corrects this assertion by assigning many lovers to the handsome youth of his story (237b1-2). This is related to the most obvious difference between the speeches of Lysias and Socrates: the Socratic protagonist is a lover in disguise. As I suggested earlier, the teaching of the non-lover will not be rejected, but revised or assimilated into a more comprehensive interpretation of Eros. It is immediately visible that desire is of two kinds, corporeal and psychic. The most immediately visible link, and so bridge, between the two is the desire for beauty. The corporeal desire for the beautiful is dominated by an implicit interpretation of the good (i.e., the object of desire) as the useful, and of the useful as the pleasant. The psychic desire for the beautiful is by

10 Cf. Xenophon, *Symposium* III. 10, 13, where Socrates describes himself as a pander.

nature more akin to an interpretation of the good as the visible; that is, as the true, or as what is not reducible to the corporeally useful. The body, or the "principle of individuation," delimits the psyche and thus makes it self-conscious, or capable of transcending the body. Thus the immediate visibility of the difference between corporeal and psychic desire is itself a result of the transcendence of the body. Reflection upon desire is the consequence of man's most characteristic and powerful desire: the desire for truth. We were prepared for the discussion of this desire by Socrates' comment on Phaedrus' love of speeches, which raised him above his love of corporeal utility. The love of base speeches in a way transcends the love of the baseness of what is said. This is the paradigm for grasping the ascent from corporeal to psychic Eros. Perception of rhetorical beauty, even in the form of speeches catering to self-interest, is *disinterested*. But we must never forget that this disinterestedness, however divine, is not altogether dissimilar to the sobriety of the non-lover. The element of transition, of course, entails a transition from the body to the psyche.

Socrates' non-lover is in fact a disguised lover. His speech is fundamentally an attempt at corporeal seduction; it begins, but does not complete, the shift in priority from the body to the psyche. The speech also serves the dramatic function of an attempt at the psychic seduction of Phaedrus; that is, it prepares him for the speech on the myth of the psyche. This dual function gives the speech a peculiar complexity; it imitates the ambiguous situation of the actual erotic experience, which draws us simultaneously toward and away from the body. As we shall see later, the same characteristic is true of Socrates' second speech, which describes the ascent of the psyche to the roof of the cosmos in obviously sexual language. In fact, the language of the second speech is far more erotic than the language of the seduction speech. The turn from the body to the psyche would seem to entail an increase in erotic strength. The concealed lover begins his seduction of the body with a criticism of the many. In all matters, and not simply with respect to love, "they forget that they do not know the nature of each thing." The concealed lover introduces his case with a discussion of the "one principle" of deliberation. The question of erotic gratification is thus presented as an instance of prudential calculation, of sobriety rather than madness (237b7-c3). Whereas this was also the thesis of Lysias' speech, the defect of the non-lover's case was one of intelligence. The concealed lover is "wily" (237b4), like the wily Odysseus who also found it useful to conceal his identity on more than one occasion.

Whatever we may desire, it is necessary to deliberate on the best means for obtaining satisfaction. And this in turn depends upon knowledge of the nature (οὐσία) of what we desire: one must know the object of deliberation (237cl). There is a necessary link between desire and knowledge which demands a mitigation of erotic madness by disinterested sobriety. In the present case, we need to know the nature of Eros itself. But the possession of knowledge about Eros would seem to be incompatible with being possessed by Eros. And yet, the *Symposium* (not to mention the subsequent myth in the *Phaedrus*) suggests that, unless one is possessed by Eros, one cannot possess knowledge of Eros. The difficulty may be rephrased in a more illuminating way when we notice the relationship between the appetitive and deliberative components of Eros. Appetite is prior to deliberation in the sense that the latter is not necessary for the former. We are "given" or "possessed by" our appetites, whereas deliberation depends upon our regaining possession of ourselves. But we would not deliberate if we had not first desired. Desire "excites" not merely our appetite but also our intelligence. The contradiction between appetite and intelligence (or deliberation) has its roots in a more fundamental harmony. But "more fundamental" does not mean "more profound" in the sense of providing greater intelligibility. The difficulty arises from the invisible, or at least obscure, nature of the foundation. *To speak about the fundamental nature of Eros is already to rise above the foundation.* This is the approximate motive for Aristophanes' speech in the *Symposium*: speech "alienates" man from his original nature. But Aristophanes was also aware of the fact that silence destroys man's original nature. Hence his tragic interpretation of man; the destructive character of both speech and silence makes man's origins altogether inaccessible.

For reasons of this kind, it is both true and false to say that man's nature is fundamentally desire. It is false because man's most characteristic desire is to speak about, i.e., to know, his nature, and knowledge is not simply or "naturally" given by Eros. We must acquire knowledge, and in order to do this we must regain possession of ourselves from desire, without losing the initial impetus that only desire provides. This is precisely the conduct of the concealed lover. In order to satisfy his appetite, he must deliberate, presumably because the youth does not share his desire, or because of some other external obstacle. In order to deliberate, however, he must first "conceal" his desire *from himself*: concealment from the youth is a secondary (if necessary) consequence of the lover's self-possession. Most people forget their ignorance of the things they desire because they mistake desire for knowledge; the concealed lover "forgets" his desire in order to obtain this knowledge. We see here a still more sober restatement of the sobering dimension of Diotima's teaching in the *Symposium*. The concealed lover emphasizes the deliberative and cognitive elements of the erotic pursuit, in order to determine its most useful conclusion for ordinary human life. Diotima emphasizes the visual enjoyment of superhuman, immortal or divine beauty, toward which goal the pursuit of knowledge is itself directed.[11] One could scarcely deny that, in this sense, the teaching of the concealed lover is far more useful to the majority of mankind than is the teaching of Diotima. In the same sense, Phaedrus is more useful than Agathon as a basis for agreement about the nature of Eros.

The concealed lover, then, is a more intelligent utilitarian than the non-lover. According to him, knowledge is necessary, not as an end in itself, nor even to facilitate individual gratification, but, as he emphasizes, for the sake of agreement (237c3, c5, d1). In addition, whereas the non-lover began almost at once with the issue

11 *Symposium* 210e2 ff.

of need and desire (231a1, a3), the concealed lover begins with the issue of deliberation. One receives the initial impression from his opening remarks that the useful is not corporeal gratification but deliberative agreement. The concealed lover "politicizes" the situation, in a way not unlike that of Socrates, who regularly emphasizes, as I have already noted, the essential need for agreement with his interlocutor.[12] This is reinforced by the formulation of the alternative to Eros, which is that "one should rather proceed into [the condition of] friendship" (237c7-8). Our second impression of the opening lines is then that deliberation about erotic desire is useful if (1) it proceeds on the basis of knowledge about the nature of Eros (237c8) and (2) terminates in friendship. By emphasizing deliberation, knowledge, agreement, and friendship (which is a kind of agreement), the concealed lover "covers over" the body, just as Socrates did symbolically when beginning to speak.

The importance of agreement is made clear by the fact that the concealed lover "defines" Eros in accordance with common opinion: "that Eros is a kind of desire, is clear to all" (237d3-4). We may remember that precisely this was not clear to the young

12   Cf. Sinaiko, pp. 32–33. He does not seem to observe the "existential" significance of the shift to agreement, namely, that a seduction is taking place, and at two different levels. Thus his very good remarks on generalization and division (34 ff.: "In a dialectical discourse, then, the concrete difference between generalization and division is largely a matter of one's point of view...") are compromised by the apparent conclusion that the need for agreement is part of the philosophical determination of the truth. That this is not Sinaiko's view is evident from pp. 43–45; more accurately, Sinaiko's own distinction between persuasion and inquiry contradicts his "existential" thesis concerning dialectic. Thus he says of the abstract concept of love: "the mere statement of this generalization, however, is dialectically useless if it is not fully understood and accepted by those to whom it is addressed" (45). Part of the confusion between truth and persuasion is due to Sinaiko's failure to distinguish between kinds of addressees, and so levels of teaching. Sinaiko, so to speak, "democratizes" Socrates' rhetoric.

Socrates, who for that reason was led to consult Diotima.[13] The young Socrates had noticed the widespread manifestations of erotic desire, but not the kind of desire, its power or work. The concealed lover begins with the commonsensical assumption that Socratic ignorance on this point is impossible. We are instructed silently by our bodies as to the work of Eros. Of course, such instruction, because it is silent, does not provide us with knowledge, but with a kind of opinion (δόξα). It almost seems as though Socrates, in reporting his conversation with Diotima, claims that one may proceed from ignorance to knowledge about Eros, whereas the concealed lover claims that we all begin from something like opinion, and so that knowledge of love is a form of *recollection*. Nevertheless, however clear the erotic desire may be, there is a difficulty: "we know also that even non-lovers desire beautiful things. In what way can we distinguish the lover and the non-lover?" (237d4-5). This assertion that the non-lover desires the beautiful is in conflict with the definition of Eros as the love of beauty, agreed upon by Socrates and Agathon in the *Symposium* (201a8-10). If there is a non-erotic desire for the beautiful, philosophy may have a non-erotic as well as an erotic origin. Or the function of the non-lover may be to indicate that there is a non-erotic as well us an erotic component in the nature of philosophy. This is not contradicted by the fact that the "non-lover" who calls our attention to this suggestion is actually a concealed lover. The issue of concealment does, however, leave open the likelihood that the final interpretation of Eros will include the component of what is here called non-erotic desire. To repeat an earlier comment: it was not clear from the *Symposium* how one could love Socrates. The non-lover, in however complex a form, stands for the possibility of such love, which is, or is close to, friendship.

If Eros is a kind of desire, it does not follow from this alone that Eros is a desire for the beautiful. For example, just as

13 Cf. *Symposium* 206b1-6 for his ignorance concerning the ἔργον ["work," deed" or "action" – ed.] of Eros, 207a5-c4 for his ignorance concerning its αἰτία ["cause, blame" – ed.]

(according to the concealed lover) the non-lover also desires the beautiful, so the lover might also desire the non-beautiful, either altogether or in part. The concealed lover is therefore correct in his assertion that Eros cannot be defined solely in terms of the beautiful. He goes on to introduce a new distinction in order to facilitate deliberation: "one must perceive (νοῆσαι) that in each of us there are two kinds of ruling and leading form (ἰδέα) which we follow as we are led; one is a natural desire (ἔμφυτος . . . ἐπιθυμία) for pleasure, and the other an acquired opinion (ἐπίκτητος δόξα) that aims at the best (ἐφιεμένη τοῦ ἀρίστου)" (237d6-9). The distinction between the lover and the non-lover thus turns upon a distinction between "desiring" and "aiming at," or between two forms of desire (since ἐφιεμένη can also mean "longing after"). These two forms remind us of our previous division of Eros into the appetitive and deliberative components. The natural desire for pleasure resembles very closely the appetitive component of Eros, which is immediately furnished by our corporeal nature. The acquired opinion that leads us to aim at the best is similar to deliberation, or the self-possession, i.e., the re-acquiring of the self from desire (the *recollecting* of oneself), in order to determine the best course of action for obtaining the object desired. In fact, deliberation is actually about the object as well as the means of acquisition (and the object is here distinguished from the end, whether in a Platonic or Aristotelian sense). We inquire whether the object is really desirable, or what we really desire. The concealed lover thus makes the very reasonable observation that the natural desire for pleasure is not the same as a desire for the best. Nature does not furnish us with opinions about the best, i.e., about the order of excellence of the desires, or the objects desired; these must be acquired. In an easily intelligible sense, opinion, the fruit of deliberation, is not natural. Let us, however, notice one more point. The concealed lover begins by emphasizing the need for knowledge; he now traces this need back to an acquired opinion. At least in the case of deliberation, which is approximately co-extensive with human action, or practice, the judgments we make, even though relative to natural desires, are grounded in opinion. We are not yet told exactly how this "opinion" is acquired; in Socratic terms, the distinctions of the concealed lover could be preserved by attributing the acquisition of such an opinion to a "divine portion" or a kind of madness that leads us to rise above the natural instructions of the body (cf. 244c3).

These two "forms" (ἰδέα is here used), which conflict within each of us for mastery, are now defined in such a way as to underline the concealed lover's criticism of the *Symposium*. "When opinion leads us by logos (λόγῳ) toward the best, and rules, the name of the ruler is temperance (σωφροσύνη). But when desire drags us irrationally [ἀλόγως might almost be translated as "silently"] toward pleasures and rules in us, hybris is the name given to the ruler" (237e2-238a2). Eros is also identified with hybris by Socrates in the *Republic*, a dialogue in which justice and temperance are highly praised. In the *Symposium*, on the other hand, Eros is tacitly identified with hybris by Diotima. But she does not attribute justice and temperance to Eros, whereas Socrates is regularly presented as hybristic.[14] I have shown elsewhere that the criticism of Eros in the *Republic* is not equivalent to a denial of the erotic dimension of philosophy. It would be much more difficult, or rather, impossible, to argue that the praise of hybristic Eros in the *Symposium* is not equivalent to a denial of the restriction of philosophy by (political) justice. In the *Phaedrus*, we have a praise of erotic madness, which one might call a more polite (and in that sense "political") name for hybristic Eros, and which is preceded by an ambiguous but still recognizable restatement of the explicit teaching of the *Republic*. The *Phaedrus* somehow harmonizes the *Symposium* and the *Republic*, with respect to the interpretation of Eros. But let us not forget that the dramatic

---

14 Cf. Rosen (*Symposium*), pp. 234 ff.; Rosen (*Republic*), and *Republic*, Bk. IX, *passim*. At *Symposium* 188a1 ff., Eryximachus identifies the base or pandemic Eros as hybristic and the noble or Uranian Eros as orderly. This distinction in a way corresponds to the one made by the concealed lover. The same may be said of Pausanias' distinction between noble and base Eros.

setting and the praise of madness both place the principle of the harmony outside the city. We should expect that, if justice is to be ascribed, either explicitly or implicitly, to Eros in the *Phaedrus*, it will not be the demotic justice of the *Republic*.

The concealed lover began his diaeresis with the monad of desire, which was divided into erotic and non-erotic kinds. These were in turn defined as temperate and hybristic; we now learn that hybris itself has many forms (ἰδεῶν: 238a3). It seems from the development of this point that Eros is a species of, rather than co-incident with or a synonym of, hybris. Whichever form of hybris becomes pre-eminent in a man, it lends him its name, "the possession of which is neither something noble (καλήν) nor honorable" (238a3-6). The examples given by the concealed lover are gluttony and drunkenness; adding Eros to these, we find that hybris is illustrated by means of three corporeal functions which are necessary for life: food, drink, and reproduction. The other forms which he has not named are, he says, "all as clear" as the clear examples given (238b5-7). The concealed lover thus argues that the difference between the body and the psyche is proportional to the difference between nature and opinion. Nature drags us toward pleasure, and these desires are (or easily become) hybristic. Since there are many opinions, we must say that the acquisition of the right opinion, by means not here explained, will direct us, contrary to the desires of nature, toward a longing for the best, and therefore to temperance with respect to the body. Presumably an appetite for the best is not an appetite for the pleasant; we might support this inference by citing the well-known maxim χαλεπὰ τὰ καλά. ["The noble things are hard" – ed.] On the other hand, it is not stated whether corporeal temperance is accompanied by a kind of psychic moderation; in view of the difficulty, both of restraining the body and acquiring the best, one would assume not. If not, then, is there a form of hybris corresponding to the psychic excess which is implicit in the concealed lover's teaching? Could the non-corporeal, non-erotic hybris correspond to philosophy?

Since Eros is a species of hybris, the concealed lover should have begun his diaeresis by dividing desire into its hybristic and non-hybristic forms. His failure to do so, together with the previous distinction between desire (ἐπιθυμία) and longing for (ἐφιεμένη), supports the inference that there are no non-hybristic desires. It leaves intact the questions just raised, namely, whether the concealed lover has committed, perhaps intentionally, the logical error of separating "longing for" and hybris. Perhaps a superior dialectician would have conducted the diaeresis as follows:

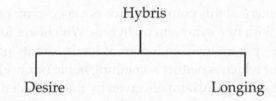

In any event, as it stands thus far, the teaching of the concealed lover asserts a dualism of nature and opinion or convention; were philosophy to be mentioned in his schematism, it could only fall under opinion, and so be understood as the attempt to master nature. The difference between the concealed lover and Descartes, however, is this. According to Descartes, the attempt to master nature is itself a natural consequence of human passions (=desires). According to the concealed lover, this cannot be true. And therefore, precisely because he distinguishes the "acquired opinion" from the (essentially corporeal) desires, the concealed lover is closer than Descartes to the Socratic teaching, attributed to Stesichorus, that in effect, the longing for the best is a divine gift or portion.

Despite the deeper ambiguity concerning the nature of non-erotic longing, there is a superficial clarity in the diaeresis employed by the concealed lover, corresponding to the obvious difference between body and psyche. The concealed lover soberly repudiates the mysterious nature widely attributed to Eros by giving it a physiological interpretation. As his language indicates, Eros is as "clear" or manifest as the body itself[15]; the concealed lover "demythologizes" the corporeal desire for beauty. Eros is

15 237d3-4, 238b5, 238b6-7; cf. Robin's note to 237a: "Ligurian" = clear.

desire without speech that overcomes the opinion directing us toward the correct.[16] The silence and manifest visibility of Eros are intimately related; for ambiguity is a property of speech, or of opinions about phenomena, and not of phenomena themselves. What "appears" is, prior to speech, simply what shows itself. Prior to speech, the phenomenon has the status, in certain respects, of the so-called Platonic Idea. But the inadequacy of phenomenal clarity is evident from the fact of the concealed lover's speech itself. To say that X "shows" itself is to refer implicitly to an audience. The attribution of silent visibility to the corporeal Eros is part of the "motion" by which the concealed lover's opinion leads him toward the best (or correct). It is a speech, or itself an acquired opinion, an interpretation of the phenomena, and therefore itself subject to interpretation.

The difference between the silent manifestation of a phenomenon that "is what it is" and the variety of discursive accounts of that phenomenon, contains *in nuce* the problem of the difference between our noetic apprehension of the hyper-Uranian beings and the discursive accounts we give of the "logical forms" of those beings. I mention this here to indicate how the most difficult theme in the *Phaedrus* is implicit in the discussion of the non- and concealed lovers. We shall analyze this problem in considerable detail when we come to the myth of the psyche. Meanwhile, let us notice that the concealed lover argues implicitly that the evidence of the nature of Eros goes beyond that of opinion. There can be no question of the body's pursuit of pleasure derived from corporeal beauty, a pursuit in which Eros leads, but with the assistance of the related desires (238c1-2). However, it is precisely the concealed lover's point that the corporeal evidence of desire is amenable, despite its clarity and certitude, to alternative interpretations. He does not deny the force of desire, but he denies

16 238b7ff. I note that the substitution of τὸ ὀρθόν for τὸ ἄριστον (237d9) is a weakening of the power of δόξα ["the correct", "the best", "opinion" – ed.]. We may long for the best, but "right opinion" is the "best" we can obtain.

that we ought to submit to this force. The force of desire is such as to give rise to an opinion which identifies the enjoyment of beautiful bodies with the best or the correct. The concealed lover does not exclude the enjoyment of corporeal beauty from participation in temperate behavior, but rather one way in which this enjoyment is experienced. In this respect, he resembles Pausanias, who in the *Symposium* distinguished between noble and base pederasty. His opinion about the best or correct is more intricate than the opinion based upon the immediate teaching of the body. As a result, we are led to see that the locus of complexity, and so of significance, is not in Eros, but in speech or opinion about Eros. We might silently submit to the natural force of the erotic hybris. But the absence of speech would be equivalent to the invisibility of the best or correct. It is self-contradictory for a human being to offer a verbal opinion that silence is *better* than speech, since the visibility of that superiority depends upon speech. The body desires, but it does not compare the merits of its desires, and certainly not the merits of the *ways* in which these desires may be satisfied.

III.

Having defined Eros through the persona of the concealed lover, Socrates interrupts his speech for a brief exchange with Phaedrus. This intermission is a kind of diaeresis, separating the definition from examples of the disadvantages of Eros. Within the first section, there is a division between Eros and longing; in the second section, longing is not mentioned; and Socrates explicitly refuses, in response to an objection by Phaedrus, to elaborate upon the advantages of the non-erotic suitor. It would therefore seem that the first section of the concealed lover's speech is more "scientific" or technical than the second. Of course, Socrates breaks off his speech for the ostensible purpose of calling to Phaedrus' attention its inspired, almost dithyrambic character. But the very fact of his doing so is a mark of Socrates' sobriety. Whereas poets invoke the Muses as they sing, they do not interrupt their song to remind the audience of their inspired condition.[17] Socrates engages in a brief dialogue, his normal procedure, in the midst of his speech, in order to reinforce the sobriety of the concealed lover with evidence of his own sobriety. The intermission is more like an Aristophanean parabasis than a tragic chorus. The "divine pathos" which Socrates claims to have undergone (238c5-6) is thus compatible with the previously discussed theoretical passivity symbolized by the non-lover. Just as previously Socrates claimed to share in a Dionysian or characteristically feminine frenzy, so here he warns Phaedrus not to wonder, should the local divinity render him "nymph-possessed" (νυμφόληπτος) in the balance of his speech (238c9-d2). The receptivity of the female, like the sobriety of the non-lover, resembles the passive openness of the philosopher before the Ideas, whereas the divine possession corresponds to the madness which is a gift of the gods. Receptivity, sobriety, and divine madness: we see here a representation of the philosophical nature.

According to Phaedrus, Socrates has been speaking "beyond the customary fluency" (238c7). As the context shows, this refers to the poetic nature of the concealed lover's rhetoric. It may perhaps also be Plato's way of suggesting that Socrates is presenting us with an unusual criticism of Eros, and in a sense that goes beyond what Phaedrus himself understands. In any event, there can be no doubt that this is what is actually happening. Like the stream by which he sits, Socrates' speech "flows" in such a way that, although the depth is visible through the surface, it appears initially in a distorted form. The problem of bringing the surface into focus with the depth is indicated by the fact that Socrates attributes his rhetorical flow first to divine inspiration, but second to the human causality of Phaedrus (238d5: τούτων μέντοι σὺ αἴτιος). One could say that there is no contradiction here; Socrates was led by Phaedrus to speak, and his speech was elevated by

17 Except perhaps in the parabasis of a comedy; but the effect remains that the poet is detached from the mood or source of inspiration. We see here another indication of the "comic" nature of the *Phaedrus*.

the local divinity. But apart from the fact that the intermission it-self casts doubt on Socrates' "enthusiasm," the reconciliation of the two causes shows that the divine is subordinate to the human. Phaedrus is the cause of Socrates' divine inspiration, and this im-mediately raises the complex question of how the low can cause the high. In order to be inspired by the local nymphs, Socrates had first to be inspired by Phaedrus. Here again is an anticipation of a later theme, namely, that recollection of the hyper-Uranian beauty is stimulated by the perception of an erotically attractive body. This holds good even if we transfer our attention from Phaedrus personally to the speech of Lysias, which, looked at commonsensically, is an instance of low or base rhetoric. It would be no exaggeration to say that the proper entrance into the *Phae-drus* lies in reflection upon why Socrates is interested in Phaedrus, or (what amounts to the same thing) why he responds in so "en-thusiastic" a manner to the speech of Lysias. And this is the re-flection that we are now making.

Thus far, according to Socrates, he has spoken by a divine pathos in a manner approaching the dithyrambic. Even in assert-ing his divine inspiration, however, Socrates qualifies it, or casts a doubt on the merits of Dionysian possession. Thus, he says: "perhaps the attack may be turned aside; but let us leave this to god, and let us return once more in the speech to the boy" (238d6-7). The onslaught of dithyrambic possession is thus treated by Socrates as an enemy, as is easily understood from the fact that the concealed lover represents the merits of sobriety. Socrates sug-gests that, in singing the praises of sobriety, he is being carried away by a divine force that corresponds to the love men feel for rhetoric or song. The implication is that one cannot speak well, even about sobriety, without transcending sobriety; as we say col-loquially, excellent speech is "inspired." But further, there comes a point when this inspiration interferes with the sobriety or ra-tional effectiveness of one's speech. Whereas previously Socrates seemed to be favorably disposed toward Dionysian enthusiasm, he here identifies it as the dangerous or bad kind of inspiration. And he appeals, not to the "local divinity," who is ostensibly responsible for his rising enthusiasm, but to "god" (θέῳ) for sober assistance. We noticed at the beginning of this speech an implied dispute between the Muses and Eros; now this implication is reinforced by the hint of a dispute between the god of enthusiasm and the god of sobriety. The god of enthusiasm has been identified first as Dionysus, then as a local nymph; the god of sobriety, although evidently associated with the Muses, has not been named. By the principle of parity, since the Muses, as feminine, correspond to the nymph, perhaps the unnamed god will be, like Dionysus, a male with special affinities for the feminine.

IV.

The first part of the concealed lover's speech, which contains the diaeresis of Eros and longing, and so the definition of erotic desire, begins with the salutation "o boy" (237b7: ὦ παῖ). The second part, which describes the bad consequences of Eros, but not the good consequences of longing, begins with the salutation "o best" or "bravest" (238d8: ὦ φέριστε). The "boy" has been endowed with bravery, i.e., the ability to "bear" (φέρω) or withstand the onslaughts of the lover, by learning the "scientific" definition of Eros as hybristic desire. Knowledge, in accordance with the Socratic definition of courage, teaches us what to fear. The definition answers the question "what is (τί ἐστι) Eros?" and so exhibits the form or shape of Eros. It shows us "Eros itself," or tries to, as though it were a Platonic Idea, at which we can look, because of its steadfast nature, as at a paradigm, and which thereby illuminates the appearances and disappearances of erotic desire within the unstable domain of genesis (238d8 ff., esp. βλέποντες δὲ δὴ πρὸς αὐτό ["looking towards it" – ed.]). In the *Symposium* (203d8 ff.), Diotima "defines" Eros, not by diaeresis, but mythically or poetically, as *constantly changing its shape*, or as always lacking what it desires; in short, as radically unstable, or a characteristic of the flux of genesis, and so as lacking a technical form. Instead, she speaks of beauty in itself (αὐτὸ καθ᾽ αὑτό: 211b1 ff.), albeit in almost entirely negative terms. According to the *Symposium*, one cannot look at Eros itself, but only at what it desires. According to the concealed lover, one can look at Eros itself, and interestingly enough, by lowering one's desire from psychic or noetic to corporeal beauty.

In the *Symposium*, we are shown the difficulties implicit in the attempt to ascend from the body (and from within the perspective of the body) to a vision of trans-corporeal beauty. These difficulties may be traced finally to the instability of genesis, or of the generating Eros. In the *Phaedrus*, we are shown a similar ascent to vision of hyper-Uranian beings, but this time from the perspective of the psyche. It is essential to note (as I shall explain in the appropriate place) that the psyche does not transcend (in the sense of "go altogether beyond") the body in the *Phaedrus*, either. But the vision of the body from the perspective of the psyche is quite different from the vision of the psyche viewed within the perspective of the body. The teaching of the concealed lover is directed downward toward the body, but necessarily from a perspective higher than the body, namely, from knowledge of Eros together with a kind of moderation or sobriety. We may say that the erotic deficiencies of the concealed lover, which in one way make him ugly or base, in another prefigure the beautiful or noble. The human sobriety of the concealed lover prefigures the divine madness of philosophy. This was already partially visible in the speech of Lysias, which is "corrected" or clarified by Socrates' first speech. The difference between these two speeches is this: the first is a parody of the utilitarian calculus in the service of corporeal hedonism, whereas the second is a parody of philosophy in the service of a defective corporeal hedonism. Lysias' non-lover is more sensual than Socrates' concealed lover; as we saw, he reifies physiological gratification, which alone, independently of the human medium, is the object of his rhetoric. The rhetoric of the concealed lover, as is shown by its criticism of Eros, is more likely to become its own object; put more cautiously, it prepares us for the purification of rhetoric in the service of love by a love of rhetoric, or for the emergence of philosophy. In sum: in the speech of the concealed lover, we see rhetoric being transformed into philosophy, through the complex medium of a criticism of corporeal Eros, a criticism stimulated by that Eros itself, even if only through its own deficiencies. Let us, however, remember that the body is veiled; it has not altogether disappeared.

The concealed lover's first diaeresis terminated in a definition of Eros; no formal definition was provided for longing, or the acquired opinion which directs us toward the best. He now makes a second diaeresis, looking toward the results of the first: "let us next say what benefit or harm will probably come to one who gratifies a lover and a non-lover" (238e1-2). Once again, however, the "non-lover," and so his benefits, will be ignored. Or more accurately, the concealed lover makes his case indirectly, leaving it to the youth to fill in the unstated definitions of longing and its advantages. We have here a simple instance of an important methodological principle in the dialogues. Conversation differs from formal logic in that the assertion or negation of a proposition immediately implies, to the interlocutor, its contradictory. Needless to say, by "implies" I do not mean "logically entails." The intelligent participant in a deliberative conversation, when he hears his advisor assert "non-P," immediately asks himself, "Yes, but suppose that P." If he fails to do this, he is irresponsible to his own interests, theoretical and practical. This simple observation, drawn from ordinary experience, must always be kept in mind while reading a Platonic dialogue. In logic, we cannot validly infer P from non-P. In conversation, we can frequently do so.[18]

In the speech of Lysias, the non-lover associated his own need for physiological gratification with friendship, economic advantage, and the prospects for future pleasure free of pain (e.g., 232b4-5, 233a5-b6). The reification of physiological pleasure, he in effect argued, by freeing sexual need from the influence of specifically human (as opposed to merely physiological) considerations, is in a way reminiscent of the procedure by which logicians abstract the logical form of an argument from its context in human speech. The non-lover "rationalizes" the erotic component; that is, he

18 Cf. Gadamer, pp. 45 ff.

applies a purely technical form of reason, a kind of logistics, to the problem of how to gratify sexual need without contradiction or concomitant impediments, undesirable side-effects, etc. Unlike the logician in his technical capacity, of course, he is motivated by an existential need, together with a confidence (normal among technicists) that his logistics will guarantee a contradiction-free future. As a human being rather than a mere technician, the logician, too, we may assume, plies his technē in service of the human desire to suppress contradiction. If the logician, however, equates reason with his technē, then he is obviously unable to give a rational justification for the desire for consistency. Instead, he must "point" to his desire as self-justifying: "consistency is desirable because I desire it." He may provide utilitarian justifications for this desire, exactly as does the non-lover for his "need." But in the last analysis, what he regards as "useful" must again be justified; the advantages provided by consistency for achieving X do not certify the utility of X (which, incidentally, may also be derived inconsistently from a contradiction). A technicist conception of reason necessarily leads to the justification of the utility of X in terms of desire or pleasure. But the lover of inconsistency is here on an equal footing with the lover of consistency. The need (or desire) for consistency (whether in physiological gratification or in logic), when justified in terms of pleasure (i.e., what I want), is subject to an internal transformation into inconsistency, because of the instability of pleasure. As our by now vast experience with the pathological or perverse should have instructed us, one man's pleasure is another man's pain, and vice versa. To state only the crucial case: given the very inconsistency of human nature against which logicians struggle, is it not easily conceivable that men may prefer the consistent pursuit of inconsistency to the consistent pursuit of consistency?

These reflections arise naturally from our attempt to understand the difference between the speech of Lysias and that of the concealed lover. Lysias inconsistently links the desire for consistency to hedonism; the concealed lover, who is at least more consistent than Lysias, identifies Eros as the desire for pleasure, and therefore criticizes the inconsistencies of hedonism: "now of necessity, he who is led by desire (ἐπιθυμίας) and enslaved by pleasure, must render the beloved as pleasant as possible to himself; to a sick man, what does not resist him is altogether pleasant, but what is stronger or equal to him, is his enemy" (238e2-5). The non-lover distinguished between the slavery of desire and the free pursuit of pleasure, but the concealed lover unmasks that freedom as bondage to desire. The reification of physiological gratification, if it frees us from the human, enslaves us to the sub-human. Thus, what the non-lover euphemistically referred to as his need (231a1: δέομαι), the concealed lover calls "necessity" (238e3: ἀνάγκη). In other words, by reifying the object of our desire, we reify ourselves as well. But the reification of desire leads to a division within the individual between his humaneness and that desire; man is thus "alienated" from his desire, and his humaneness or intelligence is enslaved by his sub-human and self-created master. Man makes, not himself, but his own enemy; thus divided and enslaved, he may legitimately be described as "sick." This sickness of division and enslavement generates contradictions within desire itself, so as to infect the desired pleasure with pain, and perhaps even to negate it entirely.

The concealed lover describes the dialectic of reified desire in terms of the disadvantages which accrue to the youth from the attentions of a lover. But it is easy enough to see that he is also criticizing the non-lover of Lysias' speech. The desire for pure physiological pleasure leads to enmity toward every element which might conceivably interfere with gratification or cause pain. The desire of pleasure's slave is therefore the desire for mastery, or the hybris of the tyrant. But there is a double contradiction implicit in the exercise of this tyranny, corresponding to the duality within the nature of the tyrant himself. If the "will to power" which transformed the non-lover into a tyrant originated in his need or desire, it was his intelligence which supplied the "will" with "power." The initially moderate desire, because of its moderation, was persuaded by intelligence to disregard all factors but that of physiological gratification. Conversely, intelligence, because of the moderation of desire, lacked the initial power to aim higher than at efficient gratification. But this emancipation of the moderate desire for efficient gratification is the origin of the self-contradictory tyranny of hedonism. Intelligence places itself at the service of gratification or pleasure, thereby accepting the role of slave, or utensil for the maintenance of efficiency in the pursuit of pleasure. If "intelligence" means "efficiency," however, and "efficiency" is in turn defined by gratification, then the difference between intelligence and desire disappears.

To the extent that no human being, however corrupt, is a mere desiring body, the deeper consequences of the identification between intelligence and desire is a division within intelligence, or the conscious enslavement of consciousness. As corporealized intelligence, the non-lover must pursue pure pleasure, hence brook no opposition, and therefore weaken or destroy those elements in the object of desire which might impede gratification in the terms desired. But the non-lover, as the concealed lover reveals, and as we already knew, is in fact a lover; that is, the moderate erotic of Lysias' speech is now exhibited as having been transformed into a hybristic tyrant. The tyrannical erotic (as he is described by the concealed lover, let us not forget) then necessarily destroys those qualities in the beloved which are lovable, thanks to the fact that, as lover, he is himself tyrannized by the emancipated desire for efficient pleasure. We may therefore certainly infer that, qua lover, or consciousness consciously enslaved, he suffers the pain of knowing that he must debase what he loves because he loves it; he must for that reason render it non-lovable. And qua "non-lover," or hedonist, by debasing the nature of the desired object, by objectifying it, he depreciates the hedonic capacities of the object itself.

Let us examine the latter point once more, and more closely. According to the concealed lover, the lover can be pleased only by what is weaker than himself, "and the ignorant is weaker than the wise, the coward than the manly, the one who is unable to speak than the rhetorician, the slow-witted than the shrewd" (239a2-4). We may recall that, in our analysis of Lysias' speech, the reification of physiological gratification was shown to abstract from human or personal qualities such as intelligence, character, and the like. On the other hand, as Phaedrus tells us at the beginning of the dialogue, Lysias' non-lover is attempting to seduce "some one of the beautiful youths" (227c6). His taste is initially the same as that of the lover; in other words, moderate erotic desire is aroused by the erotically desirable. The difference between the lover and the non-lover is not in what they "need," but in the way in which they attempt to satisfy this need; and this in turn depends upon the strength of their appetite, the degree of their intelligence, the nobility of their character, and so on. Put still more fundamentally, it is Plato's contention that all men desire the same thing, but fall short of achieving it in degrees varying as do their natural capacities (cf. 249e4 ff.). In the immediate context, the concealed lover argues that the utilitarian hedonism of the non-lover is a base form of moderate Eros, which, because of internal contradictions, is transformed into the hybristic or tyrannical Eros. An initially moderate love for the lowest aspect of lovable qualities is transformed into an immoderate desire for the lowest aspect of unlovable qualities. In still different terms, hedonism is an intellectual interpretation of corporeal appetite which fails to do justice to the intellectual or psychic dimensions of corporeal appetite. It is therefore a false, and even a contradictory, interpretation.

An ignorant, unmanly, inarticulate and dull-witted youth can scarcely be described as καλός, which means "noble" as well as "beautiful." Lest this be regarded as conjectural, however, let me add that the lover, as here distinguished, is a tyrant without tyrannical power. He may be able to impose his will on an unattractive fool, but, granted a corporeal beauty linked to a defective psyche, the lover will certainly have rivals. And in this case, the defective psyche of the beloved, necessary in view of the lover's tyrannical desire for pleasure free from pain, is a liability to the lover's capacity to ensure obedience. A beautiful fool is easy prey to others, and this must guarantee pain to the lover. The concealed lover goes on to develop the obviously painful exertions to which the lover must go, in order to safeguard his pleasure. The necessity of enslavement to pleasure (238e3) entails a necessary pleasure in natural defects of intelligence (239a4-6: note the repetition of ἀνάγκη in the two passages). If these defects are not innate in the youth, the lover must "prepare" them, or be deprived of his present pleasure (239a6-7; cf. 238e4). And this leads to the third necessity (239a7): jealousy, which is obviously painful,[19] and which would obviously be present even (or even more) in the case of a beautiful fool. The jealous lover must take pains to prevent the dianoetic (239a5) development of his beloved in two ways. First, he must prevent those associations and benefits by which the youth "would become a true man" (239b2). By associating the condition of "manliness" (which is closely related to the conception of the "gentleman" or καλὸς κἀγαθός) and the faculty of intelligence, the concealed lover indicates the impossibility of finding genuine pleasure in a beautiful fool. The relatively subtle argument of the non-lover would be unintelligible to such a youth, whereas a lover, i.e., one who desires the lovable, would not be in a position consistently to advance such an argument.

The case of the non-lover, then, depends upon the intelligence of the youth; but at the same time, it entails the suppression of his intelligence. The contradiction is visible in the attempt to link moderation with corporeal pleasures and benefits. The body is neither intelligent nor moderate; stated more fully, a body governed by a defective psyche, or a psyche that defines its advantage in terms of the body, is neither intelligent nor moderate. But it is not clear that the concealed lover's implied position is substantially more coherent. Courage and Eros are undoubtedly compatible, but the question arises whether the dianoetic moderation indirectly endorsed by the concealed lover is equivalent to the virtue of "a real man" (ἀνήρ). By sundering Eros from manliness, and linking the latter to intelligence, or by opposing intelligent

19 The dialectic of the jealous lover (φθονερός) is reminiscent of the analysis of malice (φθόνος) as a mixture of pleasure and pain, given in the *Philebus*, 47c1 ff.

moderation to the pursuit of pleasure, the concealed lover would seem to have delivered the youth to philosophy, or to have contradicted his concealed intentions. And indeed, the second way in which he accuses the tyrannical lover (=dialectically developed non-lover) is just this: his jealousy prevents the youth from consorting with those from whom he would become "most wise" (φρονιμώτιστος) or from whom he would acquire "divine philosophy, from which the lover must necessarily keep the boy as far as possible, from fear that he will become contemptible" (239b4-6); i.e., that philosophy will reveal the non-lover to be in fact a concealed lover, and so, as contemptible, it would seem, as the concealed lover himself. This is the first mention of "philosophy" in the dialogue, and in a crucial context.

The concealed lover has separated the erotic desire for (corporeal) pleasure from the (moderate) longing for the best, which has its source in an "acquired opinion." That is, the erotic desire for pleasure is attributed to nature (237d7), whereas the longing for the best is attributed to opinion or convention. The "good" opinion which restricts or tames "bad" nature is in effect equivalent to the teaching of the concealed lover himself. The concealed lover tacitly identifies himself as one of those whose company makes young men wise or prudent; he is, in short, an adept in "divine philosophy." Presumably, then, either he is himself (like every philosopher) a god, or he acquired his philosophical opinion from some other god than Eros. In either case we see again that this speech turns upon a conflict among the gods, or between two forms of divine music, the erotic and the non-erotic. But the immediate difficulty for the concealed lover is now evident. The very distinction between the erotic and the non-erotic, which he introduced in order to correct the teaching of the non-lover, leads finally to a confirmation or rehabilitation of the non-lover's teaching, and at a much higher level, one which seems to escape from the contradictions of the lower level. The concealed lover would seem to have been trapped by his own wiliness (237b4). In short, although Socrates subsequently refuses to sing the praises of the non-lover, he would seem to have done so already, in his criticism (through the Muses and the concealed lover) of the lover. We may also note in passing that, since Eros is a god, the speech praising (by implication) the non-lover does not deny divine madness, but rather its excellence. And the critique of divine madness is also a critique of nature.

The concealed lover, by taking the side of convention in its quarrel with nature, would seem to be a sophist rather than a philosopher. But this may be simply because he does not provide us with an adequate analysis of the divine, and so, of the source of his acquired opinion. If the divine is part of nature, and itself divided into mad and sober elements, then nature possesses a complex structure which must be dialectically exhibited. The internal complexity of nature is immediately suggested by the difference between body and psyche. This difference is manifested in the fact that, whereas the body functions according to innate desires, the psyche is able to transcend nature through the medium of acquired opinions (which in turn affect the body). In the simplified account of the concealed lover, nature is apparently the source of madness, whereas convention is the source of sobriety; he does not discuss the possibility of acquiring mad opinions, and this is, of course, a sign of the defective character of his initial diaeresis. But the defect has the result of directing the youth to philosophy rather than to corporeal hedonism. One of the interesting questions raised by the speech of the concealed lover is whether the recommendation of the philosophical life depends for its initial attractiveness upon noble or salutary lies. The philosopher, in his sober or dianoetic capacity, proceeds as if the world (nature) were rational, or accessible to discursive interpretation. If this is a mere opinion, or even if it is a form of divine madness, why should we believe it, or ground reason in revelation? Thus far in the *Phaedrus*, the implied answer to this question turns upon the notion of utility. The first two speeches, if we consider them carefully or soberly, teach us that the efficient satisfaction of corporeal desire depends upon the utility of intelligence and moderation, and that the necessary appeal to intelligence and moderation, if efficiently transacted, leads necessarily to the transformation from corporeal to psychic hedonism, or more radically, from hedonism to philosophy. The defect of the first two speeches (or more generally, of utilitarianism, whether base or noble) is that they present an inadequate because one-sided analysis of Eros, namely, as corporeal alone rather than as also psychic. The first two speeches denigrate madness, and this must be rectified by the third speech. In this way the *Phaedrus* will exhibit the previously noted recipe of philosophy as two parts of sobriety and one part of madness.

V.

The concealed lover divides the disadvantages of Eros into three kinds, corresponding to the mind, the body, and external possessions. Apart from a single reference to courage (239a3), and two references to temperance, one at the beginning and one at the end,[20] he represents the psyche exclusively by dianoetic or discursive intelligence. And this interesting fact illuminates a more general characteristic of the two "anti-erotic" speeches. In Lysias' speech, the word "psyche" does not appear at all; in the speech of the concealed lover, it is mentioned only once, toward the end, in a very strong sentence identifying the education of the psyche as most honored by mortals and gods alike (241c4-6: the word ἀλήθεια also makes its first appearance here).[21] In Lysias' speech, courage is not mentioned; temperance appears once, in an oblique way, through the verb σωφρονεῖν and in opposition to νοσεῖν as to mean "to be healthy" (231d3). The idea of temperance or moderation is implicit throughout the speech, in the sense of utilitarian calculus, or the employment of intelligence for the painless

20 The first is 237e3; I count 241a3 (νοῦν καὶ σωφροσύνην) and b1 (νοῦν ἤδη ἐσχηκὼς καὶ σεσωφρονηκώς) ["intellect and moderation" and "in possession of intellect and become moderate" – ed.] as a single, connected reference. The opposition between Eros and courage is also implicit in 239d4 ff., which spells out the corporeal consequences of 239a3.
21 In the *Republic* (376e2 ff.) the psyche is introduced as an explicit philosophical theme in conjunction with education (and there is an anticipatory discussion in connection with spiritedness at 375a11 ff.).

procurement of pleasure. In the concealed lover's speech, the link between moderation and intelligence is suggested at the beginning by its association with "opinion" (237d8 ff.), and made explicit at the end, in the phrase "mind and temperance instead of Eros and madness" (241a3-4; cf. b1). And finally, justice, the fourth of the cardinal virtues, is conspicuous by its absence from both speeches. These observations lead to the following general inference. The anti-erotic speeches, although they must necessarily suggest, and are indeed based upon, the distinction between body and psyche, tend to restrict the psyche to intelligence, or to a moderate use of the body through the employment of intelligence. In other words, they tend to abstract from the non-intellectual parts of the psyche, with the interesting result that justice is replaced by temperance or moderation. Although Eros is called hybristic here, and not characterized by justice in the *Symposium*, the anti-erotic speeches in the *Phaedrus* do not claim justice as a virtue of the union between intelligence and moderation. Sobriety is linked throughout the two speeches with what may he called base and noble forms of selfishness.

In the *Republic*, the effort is made to derive justice and patriotism from spiritedness (θυμός) rather than from Eros, which is criticized as hybristic or tyrannical. The defect of this effort is suggested by the portrait of the selfish character of sobriety in the *Phaedrus*. In the *Republic*, the self-interest of the philosopher leads him to seek political authority, with consequent restrictions upon his philosophical leisure. In the *Phaedrus*, the self-interest of both the sober and the mad aspects of the philosopher's nature lead him to transcend the city. This transcendence of the political is shown in two different ways. The anti-erotic speeches present the issue in terms of the body, and the speech praising divine madness presents it in terms of the psyche. The link between the two presentations is the intelligence: in the anti-erotic speeches, dianoia is primary; in the speech about madness, noēsis is primary.

The concealed lover directs the youth to look at the definition of Eros; the lover contrives to make the youth look at him (i.e., his body: 238d9, 239b6-7). Whereas the non-lover of Lysias' speech is frank to say that he is primarily concerned with the body, in Socrates' first speech, the primacy of the body is concealed by praise for intelligence and moderation. The situation is in a way reminiscent of Socrates' remarks in the *Phaedo* about his own turn from things to speeches. The concealed lover criticizes the lover for turning directly to the body; instead, he argues, if one wishes genuinely to acquire the benefits of the body, one must turn away from it toward the dianoetic account of Eros. The fulfillment of desire depends upon rational speech about, and to that extent a diminution of, desire. The lover who seeks, because of his own passionate thoughtlessness, for the maximum of pleasure, must inflict maximum damage on the discursive intelligence of the beloved (239b5-c2). As a consequence, the youth's body also suffers serious deterioration. The erotically controlled body is forced to run after pleasure rather than goodness (239c4-5). If intelligence is the virtue of the mind, its corporeal counterpart is courage or manliness: the strength needed to stand steadfast against the corruptions of pleasure. Still, one may object, the absence of intelligence, as experience shows, is not in itself incompatible with strong, brave, and beautiful bodies.

This objection is related to a previous difficulty in the concealed lover's teaching. By exaggerating his concern for the intelligence of the youth, he was forced to allude to "divine philosophy," or to become transformed momentarily from a concealed lover of the body to a genuine lover of the psyche. A complementary exaggeration is taking place in the present paragraph. The concealed lover wishes to praise a moderate Eros by showing how the non-lover of Lysias' speech is transformed by his lack of intelligence into a tyrannical lover. Since the tyrant brooks no opposition, or since he is himself the slave of his own hybristic desire, he must inevitably destroy the very qualities he desires in the body of the (reified) youth. That is, he seeks to transform the body of the youth into a slave's body, or more accurately, into that of an effeminate court-slave (since some slaves are warriors). He will therefore seek a body with the pallor of an upbringing protected from the sunlight and with the softness of a life free from exercise and other manly activities. Such a body, the concealed lover claims, because it has not been prepared for war, cannot be truly beautiful, but must disguise its blemishes with cosmetics and other artifices (239c5-d5). In short: the lover turns the youth into a girl, or even worse, into the opposite of what he desires. The concealed lover implies that his own attention to intelligence and moderation will produce a beautiful and manly warrior, or a truly lovable body. But if the psyche which animates such a body is as intelligent as the concealed lover desires, will he not understand that his manliness is a consequence of philosophy and moderation rather than of corporeal hedonism and madness? Will he not himself be transformed from a "lover" into a "non-lover?"

Let me restate the defect of the concealed lover's teaching, taken at its face value. The same dialectic by which the non-lover is transformed into a hybristic lover also transforms the concealed or moderate lover into a non-lover. Put differently: either the concealed lover becomes a philosopher, in which case he is no longer a pederast, or he will himself be caught up in the dialectical process that leads the non-lover to destroy the object of his desire. Without repeating everything that has gone before, I will merely mention that the concealed lover, as he is described, is actually a lover, i.e., a more intelligent lover of the body than the non-lover in Lysias' speech. His advocacy of a turn away from the body to rational speech is on behalf of a concealed allegiance to the body. His entire teaching rests upon the concealment of a disagreement between the desires of the body and psyche by an appearance of harmony between the two. If the harmony is genuinely established, the result is philosophy, or the rule of the body by the mind. If the established harmony is sophistic or a cleverly concealed enslavement of the psyche by the body, then the concealed lover becomes subject to all the contradictory pressures we found to characterize the non-lover. The problems faced by the concealed lover arise from his cleverness or attempt to be more consistent than the non-lover. But a genuinely consistent articulation of desire leads inevitably to philosophy, just as a genuinely consistent subordination of articulateness to desire leads to bestiality.

Since the majority of human beings are not consistent, they fall somewhere between the two extremes.

The damage inflicted by love upon mind and body makes the beloved a source of confidence to his enemies and of fear to his friends (239d4-7). The concealed lover refers to these consequences as "obvious" (239d8), which is something of an overstatement, as we have just seen. They could have been avoided by an inconsistent moderation which balances the influences of desire and intelligence so as to avoid the two extremes of bestiality and philosophy. But the general concern of the *Phaedrus* is not with ordinary existence in its own terms. Instead, it is concerned with the instability of the ordinary, or with the dialectical relationship between sobriety and madness. In order to prevent the comic aspects of human instability from deteriorating into tragedy, man requires divine assistance; the madness of sobriety must be transmuted into the sobriety of madness. The function of the concealed lover is to prepare us for this transmutation by allowing us to understand the inconsistent or unstable nature of the obvious. He turns next to the disadvantages of Eros with respect to possessions. These disadvantages are less obvious than those inflicted upon mind and body, because we see the latter directly exhibited in the speech and deeds of the beloved. Possessions may be divided into two kinds: human and material. Human possessions are described by the concealed lover to include parents, relatives, friends, wives, and children. The first three are called "most divine" (239e4) and separated from the last two by mention of money or material substance (240a2). The order of enumeration is chronological: the youth first acquires, or rather is acquired by, his progenitors; next, after inheriting his own property he may marry and generate children. But if we consider the situation more generally, the wife and children of one beloved are the mother and relatives (and friends) of another. Why are not both aspects of the family called "divine?"

This apparently minute difference in the concealed lover's speech has considerable significance for the logic of Eros. As the term "possession" (κτῆσις, κτῆμα) suggests, the concealed lover distinguishes between familial, political or heterosexual, and what we may call romantic or pederastic love. The romantic Eros is characterized by desire rather than by possession. Desire, as we know from the *Symposium*, is incapable of satisfaction or completion; there is a general difference between ἔρως and φιλία which played a role in the speech of Lysias' non-lover. The concealed lover alludes to the difference by linking friends with parents and relatives; the familial Eros is completed in the generation of children or citizens and the establishment of political friendship. The familial Eros is a divine possession that generates divine possessions. But the familial Eros may be divided into two kinds, depending upon whether the youth is considered as a son and relative, or a husband and father. Looked at from the second perspective, the familial or political Eros is a rival to the private, desiring, or pederastic Eros. The private Eros, as a citizen of the polis, and as a lover of youths, depends upon the political and generating functions of the familial Eros; but it also contradicts and transcends these functions. As is clear from its non-generating nature, the private Eros cannot be satisfied by the public or familial Eros. In speaking to the youth, the concealed lover pretends to associate himself with the public, but is actually a moderate representative of the private Eros. He therefore pretends (like Lysias' non-lover) that private Eros, if transformed into a doxic longing for the best, can be publicly legitimated and privately fulfilled. That is, he pretends that private Eros can be transformed into friendship, while still being directed by the body, or retaining its private nature. But this is impossible. Friendship is either political or philosophical; even though the political Eros is concerned with the welfare of the body, it interprets corporeal welfare in a psychic manner, as is obvious from the paramount importance of patriotism. To mention only the decisive case, the city regulates private or corporeal Eros in terms of public and religious laws or opinions. And as the concealed lover must himself argue, the effort to replace or moderate carnal desire by friendship in the private sphere is itself a transcendence of the body.

The acquired opinion which directs us to long for the best is opposed to the innate erotic hybris. The necessity (240a4) by which the lover destroys the possessions of the beloved is, then, one from which the concealed lover cannot escape. The words ἀνάγκη or ἀναγκάζω appear fourteen times in his speech, always with reference to the lover.[22] The opposition between the necessity of pleasure and the freedom of intelligence was introduced by Lysias' non-lover, but even he was forced to allude to the necessity of speech, or the dialectical link between desire and intelligence.[23] Conversation, whether with others or with oneself, the characteristic of dianoetic intelligence, is also a pleasure, and consequently a rival of corporeal pleasure. The non-lover, however, did not emphasize the pejorative function of necessity to the degree that the concealed lover does. And this, we may suggest, is because the concealed lover, as in fact a lover, or as moved by a stronger Eros than the non-lover, is radically aware in his own person of the necessity imposed by the desire for pleasure. The concealed lover is attempting to moderate his own desire, rather than merely to liberate it by the instrument of calculative intelligence. If he fails, he will himself become a non-lover, and so ultimately a slave of hybristic Eros. But if he succeeds, he will become either a virtuous citizen or a philosopher.

We turn now to the way of life imposed by the hybristic Eros on lover and beloved alike. In this section, the concealed lover makes entirely explicit the contradiction between the tyranny of desire and the pursuit of pleasure. The silent or irrational inclination of desire toward corporeal pleasure (238a1), precisely because it has not been guided by logos, misses its target almost

---

22 237c1, 238e3, 239a5, a7, b5, c5, 240a4, c4, dl, el, 241b4, b5, b7, c2.

23 ἀνάγκη appears in a pejorative sense at 231a4 (the initial opposition between necessary and voluntary action), 232a7, and 233b4. But at 232b3-4 the non-lover says that people will not blame the youth for associating with him, εἰδότες ὅτι ἀναγκαῖόν ἐστιν ἢ διὰ φιλίαν τῷ διαλέγεσθαι ἢ δι' ἄλλην τινὰ ἡδονήν. ["knowing that conversation is a necessity on account of friendship or some other pleasure" – ed.]

completely. The concealed lover indicates a diaeresis of evils: those in which a daimon has mixed some pleasure, and love, which is least pleasant of all (240a9 ff., b5-7). Since love is in the province of the gods, we have here a further reference to the previously noted conflict among the Olympian forces. More precisely, there is here a distinction between daimonic or partly pleasant evils, and almost completely painful evils of which the divine Eros is the only example. In the first example of a mixed evil, the concealed lover replaces the indefinite "some daimon" with the definite "nature" (240b2: ἡ φύσις). Since he initially referred to the hybristic Eros as "innate" (237d7), it would seem to follow that there is a division within nature herself between the daimonic and the divine. The two examples of the daimonic or mixed evils are the flatterer and the courtesan. The flatterer contains a certain "not uncouth pleasure" (240b2); the courtesan, however censurable (like other unnamed types), "is most pleasant in everyday life" (240b5). These two types represent the flattery of psyche and body respectively. They differ from the lover in that their desire is for money or material advantage rather than for corporeal erotic pleasure. It is thus their "profession" to give pleasure to the youth, whereas the lover is literally an "amateur": he does not know what he is doing, because he lacks the technical detachment of logos. The flatterer and courtesan remind us of what the non-lover advises the youth to be. In the inconsistent terms of "everyday life," there is a daimonic pleasure in the pursuit of the evils of flattery, but a divine pain in the pursuit of the evils of Eros. Love is higher than flattery, but for that reason, more inaccessible, and a greater evil for mankind. Flattery is pursued voluntarily; it is an "acquired opinion" or consequence of speech. But love is a form of necessity: it enforces man's bondage to nature. Flattery is the rhetoric of the non-lover, whereas the lover would appear to be reduced to silence, unless he transcends the object of immediate desire, or becomes a "friend" in the sense either of citizen or philosopher. The net result, however, is once again that Eros requires, for the transformation of fulfillment, a component of moderation or sobriety represented in the *Phaedrus* by the non-lover. Neither lover nor non-lover can be consistently or completely understood in isolation of each other, because the wholeness of man encompasses both dimensions of existence.

Thus far, in describing the damage to the youth's mind, body, and possessions, the concealed lover has referred directly to the lover's character or psyche, but not to his body. The lover's psyche has been presented to us as under the control of corporeal desire, but these psychic manifestations of the body have been concealed by rhetoric. But now, in referring to the discrepancy in age between lover and beloved (240c1 ff.), the concealed lover faces a more difficult obstacle to the success of his deception. A lover may pretend to be a non-lover, and an older man may disguise his psyche with the rhetoric of youthfulness. But not even cosmetics can adequately transform an old body into a young one. A difference between the psyche and the body is that, whereas the former need not age (the extreme case being that of the imbecile), the latter must. In abstract terms, the body is bound by temporal and historical chains as the psyche is not. We may think the thoughts of our youth (or of the past), but we cannot relive its corporeal determinations. It seems a fair assumption, then, that the youth whom the concealed lover addresses, will perceive the difference between their ages. Necessity is corporeally manifest: the same necessity that drives the concealed lover toward rhetorical seduction ought therefore to contradict that rhetoric, or to preserve the beloved from its effect. Once again we see the defect of consistency; from the viewpoint of the body, there is no difference between the non-lover and the lover. The two differ with respect to their psychic response toward corporeal desire. The concealed lover, in calling attention to his own body, is at a deeper level of necessity arguing for the irrelevance of the body, and so against his own intentions. If "equality of age leads to equal pleasures and thus to friendship through similarity" (240c2-3), the concealed lover and the youth can become friends, if at all, only through their psyches, which achieve a similarity of age by loving the same speeches. For example, both can appreciate the force of the "old saying" (240c1) that age delights in the same age.

The most perfect friendship between young and old would then be conversation, or the transformation of the divine Eros into "divine philosophy" (239b4).

We can therefore appreciate the reflexive scope of the concealed lover's words when he says, in conjunction with his indictment of age, that "necessity is said to be a burden in every way for everyone; this is especially so in the case of the dissimilarity [of age] between lover and youth" (240c4-6).[24] The balance of the paragraph, more directly than hitherto, speaks of the harm that erotic desire brings to the lover himself. The necessity which goads him on toward physical pleasure (240c7 ff.)[25] yields an at least equal amount of pain. Having been enslaved by desire, he becomes the servant rather than the master of youth (240d3-4). Once again we may see here a critical reference to the *Symposium*; the desire for what one lacks, when defined in terms of corporeal beauty, produces a bondage or enslavement that cannot be broken without "divine" assistance. Eros alone does not transform the love of corporeal beauty into the love of speeches, not to mention the love of "beauty itself." Apart from this, the lover is himself, as a consequence of his age, ugly. The youth must feel extreme pain from viewing the ugliness of his lover's body, but the lover must necessarily perceive this pain as he "looks at, listens to, or touches" the beloved (240d4-7). This shared pain is even more necessary in those effects of age which the concealed lover tactfully refers to as "the things which it is not pleasant to hear about in speech, let alone being constrained to cope with in deed" (240d7-e2). The concealed lover would appear to have been carried away, by reflecting upon the painfulness of his own situation, into exaggerating the necessity of the lover's decrepitude. Even

24 It is interesting to note that this is the seventh of thirteen references to ἀνάγκη in the second section of the concealed lover's speech. There is only one mention of ἀνάγκη in the first or defining section: logos is less bound (i.e., obstructed) by necessity than is praxis.

25 At 240d2, the lover is said to be compelled to "see, hear, and touch" the youth's body. Note that hearing, the middle term, leads away from the body toward conversation.

should this be so, however, it demonstrates convincingly the psychic pain he must suffer from observing the difference between his body and that of his beloved. And this in turn leads to the infliction of mutual pain through speech rendered base by suspicions of disgust and infidelity (240e2-7). Once again we see the problematic effect of the corporeal Eros upon the possibility of an ascent via logos. The passion of the lover is here described as a necessity that leads to physical rather than psychic intoxication (240e5); in the terms of the *Symposium*, to an aging and drunken Pausanias rather than to Socrates.[26]

It is therefore more than likely that the cessation of the lover's Eros (240e6) will be due to physical exhaustion rather than, as the concealed lover claims, through the acquisition of "intelligence and moderation in place of Eros and madness" (241a3-4; b1). Even on this assessment of the situation, however, the fact remains that the presence of psychic virtue is made dependent upon the absence of corporeal Eros.[27] And the termination of physical desire is not transmuted into psychic friendship between lover and beloved, but into what Hackforth presciently translates (surely not under the influence of Sartre?) as "bad faith" (240e9: ἄπι-στος). In other words the "virtue" of the lapsed lover is a selfish or vicious imitation of divine philosophy. His newly acquired moderation imitates noetic moderation; it is so distorted by the shameful memory of previous passion as to renege on promises of future goods (240e9-241a2; 241a6 ff.). The former lover conceals his self-disgust from himself, to say nothing of his other inadequacies, under the pretense that he is no longer himself, i.e., that he has become a new and better man (241a6-b5). But his shame prevents him from asserting this transformation (241a7), which is to say that it has not genuinely taken place. If it had, he would at least have tried to heal the damage done to the youth's character, assuming that his previous promises were too dishonorable to fulfill. Instead, he admits that his old appetites, and so his old

26 Cf. *Symposium* 183b-c; this point is also noted by Robin (*Phèdre*).
27 Cf. the position of Cephalus in *Republic* 329 ff.

character, are still very much present; thus he is compelled (ὑπ' ἀνάγκης) to run away, which is to say that he is still under the necessity of Eros (241b3-5). At best, the lover is now continent rather than virtuous; but his continence is due to necessity (in the form of age) rather than to choice. The youth, having through his own ignorance gratified one who was "mindless by necessity" (241b7), is now compelled to pursue the lapsed lover with complaints and threats. The dubious nature of the acquired "intelligence" of the lapsed lover is obvious from this sentence, which concludes with the advice that the youth ought "much rather to have gratified a non-lover who possesses intelligence" (241c1).

The concealed lover pretends to be an intelligent non-lover. Instead, he is an intelligent or relatively moderate lover, who is capable of anticipating the fate which awaits him if he cannot moderate his passion. But he is not sufficiently intelligent to avoid praising moderation in terms which lead away from "gratification" (241b7: the word employed by Lysias' non-lover is now revealingly extended to cover his own desire) toward friendship or philosophy. If the youth were to take his speech seriously, there would be no reason for him to gratify the concealed lover. The fact is that the erotic desire for corporeal gratification is in itself "mindless" or "silent." In the terms introduced by the concealed lover, it is *the* human manifestation of necessity, rather than of an acquired opinion. But the silence of necessity means that it cannot serve as, or furnish us with, an acquired opinion about, or interpretation of, itself. Those who begin with the fact of necessity are therefore either reduced to silence, or are free to advocate *any* opinion as an interpretation of necessity, which, since it lacks any criterion for preferring one opinion to another, is merely a concealed version of silence. A philosophical interpretation of Eros cannot simply point to the necessity of corporeal desire, but must articulate the response that man ought to make in the face of necessity. This is merely to say again in different words that the necessity of the psyche is different from the necessity of the body. The desire to speak about desire is not here the same as the desire about which we speak. For this reason, the connection between corporeal Eros and philosophy is by no means as perspicuous as would appear from the surface argument of the *Symposium*. Surrender to love necessitates, as the concealed lover puts it, a surrender to faithlessness, distemper, jealousy, pain, damage to property, body, and psyche (241c2-6). However exaggerated the charge may be, there is something true about it, and no account of Eros is adequate which cannot account for that truth. So much, then, for the non- or concealed lover, whose function has been to suggest the limits or dangers of an Eros not guided by the divine madness. We cannot understand love unless we understand its opposite; and the division of Eros and non-Eros is the result of an implicit diaeresis of the psyche. In the *Symposium*, the psyche did not escape from genesis, which is to say that its account of immortality was radically defective. In the *Phaedrus*, Socrates will try to remedy this defect, and thereby to provide us with the basis for a comprehension, if not a complete diaeresis, of the psyche.

The speech ends with an invocation to knowledge (241c7), but not quite as it began. Instead of a diaeresis, the concealed lover breaks into poetry, thereby warning Socrates to end his speech without having actually finished it (241d1-3). We may take the warning as a prophecy that knowledge of the psyche indeed depends upon poetry, but in a way which requires the concealed lover to remove his disguise, or at least to substitute one disguise for another.

CHAPTER THREE:
The Lover

I.

Socrates declines to praise the non-lover, as Phaedrus had expected him to do. "Didn't you perceive, blessed one, that I am now speaking epic rather than dithyrambs, even though [engaged in] blaming?" (241e1-2). Presumably Phaedrus' appreciation of rhetoric does not extend to a fine ear for poetic meters. One may also assume that he did not "perceive" the praise of the non-lover implicit in the criticism of the lover. This praise, as we saw in the first two chapters, amounts to a preliminary version of a portrait of the philosopher, namely, a portrait that abstracts from madness. Furthermore, dithyrambs are characteristic of Bacchic possession or Dionysian madness; epic meter is used to sing of heroes and great warriors, and is sober by contrast, perhaps the most sober of all poetic meters.[1] Socrates would therefore seem to be sobering up, aging, or becoming more manly in the course of criticizing the lover.[2] This would suggest that Socrates must be altogether sober in order to engage in explicit praise of the non-lover. Socrates, however, puts a different interpretation on the matter. The switch to epic, the meter of praise, even though he has been indulging in blame, is taken as a sign of greater enthusiasm to come, should he proceed to praise the non-lover

1   Hence, according to the Athenian Stranger in the *Laws* 658a4 ff., it is preferred by old men.
2   And this corresponds to the fact that the concealed lover's speech reached its climax in discussing the consequences of the lover's age.

(241e3-5). By combining these two observations, we may infer that Socrates refuses to engage in sober enthusiasm; to look ahead for a moment, what is required is enthused sobriety. In still more sober terms, Socrates does not object to explicit criticism of the lover, but he refuses to engage in explicit praise of the non-lover. Eros is essential but incomplete; as we learned from the *Symposium*, Eros is the "incarnation" of incompleteness. For this reason, a "logical" or entirely sober analysis of Eros, whether with respect to its function or deficiencies, would be inappropriate, and even dangerous. If Socrates were to cast the technē of Eros into speech modeled after *epistēmē*, the result would be something like the Megaric logic of sophistry, or a nominalistic theory of meaning wedded to a logic without the laws of contradiction and excluded middle. Since Eros is radical incompleteness or continuous change from one opposite to another (*Symposium* 203d8 ff.), it has no *eidos*, and therefore cannot accurately be represented in logos. Every statement S about the form of Eros would entail non-S, nor could there be any synthesis of these opposites that did not immediately negate itself. Instead, Socrates speaks of Eros in rhetorical, poetic, or mythical (241e8) language. Myth serves to *recollect* or unify the discontinuous manifold of the positings and negations of Eros. As we shall see later, this recollective function of myth is also employed in the noetic apprehension of hyper-Uranian beings, and hence in diaeresis as well.

Socrates blames Phaedrus for having intentionally cast him into the clutches of the nymphs (241e4). In order to avoid a still greater compulsion, he abandons his myth, and is prepared to cross over to the other side of the river (241e8-242a2). We are told merely that, to every blameworthy attribute of Eros, there corresponds an opposite good of the non-lover (241e5-6). In general, this means that the non-lover will assist the youth in acquiring manliness, moderation, and intelligence. By his resistance toward compulsion, his moderation with respect to enthusiasm, and the intelligence of his mythical critique of Eros, Socrates would seem to be himself an outstanding example of the non-lover. As we now know, of course, the "non-lover" is in fact a kind of lover;

more accurately, there are kinds of "non-lovers," of which we have had two different examples. And this implies that the division of "lover" and "non-lover" is in fact impossible: Eros is not a kind that can be sorted out by diaeresis, which is another way of observing that it has no eidos.

After the first speech, Socrates says that it had a "daimonic" effect on him, not because of the speech itself, but because of the sight of Phaedrus' shining enjoyment. This visible love of speech, which Socrates shares, if only here as a passive viewer, is called by him Bacchic, and Phaedrus is described as "divine" (234d1-6). After the second speech, when Phaedrus protests against Socrates' threatened departure, Socrates again calls him "divine with respect to speeches…and simply wonderful" (242a7-8). And again, the force by which Socrates yields to, or shares in, Phaedrus' divinity, is not itself called divine, but daimonic (242b8-9). Phaedrus, who merely repeats the speech of Lysias, is obviously silent in comparison with Socrates, who, although he attributes his own speeches to other authors, is the model of a discursive man. Phaedrus, as the silent, corporeally beautiful cause of speech, is like a heavenly body, or a god, whereas Socrates, who is himself moved to speech by this divine vision, is daimonic, or intermediate between the divine and the human. This difference between Phaedrus and Socrates prefigures the divine gift by which some humans are inspired to philosophize. At a lower level, it also suggests the difference between the two kinds of "non-lovers" we have studied. The calculations of utilitarianism are in the service of hedonism, whose silent enjoyment is paradoxically like the silence of the heavenly or cosmic gods; whereas the dialectic of the concealed lover turns into philosophy, whatever its initial impetus.[3]

The "divine" Phaedrus orders Socrates not to depart by

3   There is a similar situation in the *Philebus*, where the beautiful and silent Philebus, partisan of Aphrodite, "causes" Socrates and Protarchus to engage in an elaborate conversation about pleasure and intelligence.

pointing to the sun, paradigm of cosmic divinity. It is high noon, the hottest and brightest part of the day, when the sun "stands steady" (σταθερά) at the peak of its ascent (242a3-5). In other words, time will "stand still" during Socrates' second speech, which is a divine revelation in a much more explicit sense than his first speech. This revelation is a necessary prelude to a "temporal" or discursive conversation (242a5-6) between Socrates and Phaedrus. The second speech deals with two forms of timelessness, the divine madness and the immortality of the psyche. And although Phaedrus is the "cause" of both speeches, in the second instance there is an additional factor, Socrates' *daimonion*, here described as a voice from heaven, or as a supplement to Phaedrus' silence (242a8-b5, c1-2).[4] Thanks to these two forms of necessity (242b2, c2), Phaedrus' silent beauty and the daimonic messenger from heaven, Socrates will avoid war with Phaedrus (242b6: οὐ πόλεμόν γε ἀγγέλλεις), and "give birth" to another speech about Eros (242b4), or himself exercise the gift of prophecy (242c3: εἰμὶ δὴ οὖν μάντις μέν). In the *Symposium*, Socrates avoids war with the hybristic but "soft" Agathon by repeating the erotic lessons given him by the prophetess Diotima, lessons which were not supplemented by daimonic assistance. More precisely, in the *Symposium*, Eros himself represents the daimonic, whereas in the *Phaedrus*, Eros is divine and Socrates (through his daimonion) is daimonic. Eros and Socrates both move one step upward in the *Phaedrus*.

In the *Symposium*, visibility was obscured by darkness, or the movement of genesis. To the clarity and "timelessness" of the *Phaedrus* corresponds a higher status, not simply for Eros, but for the psyche. As we shall see later, the movement of genesis is replaced by the movement of eternity in the psyche itself. In the passage before us, Socrates, after referring to his own "trifling" power of prophecy, says that the psyche, i.e., the human psyche

4   Socrates says that only Simmias of Thebes has inspired more speeches than Phaedrus. This is a hint as to the rhetorical status of the discussion of immortality in the *Phaedo*.

altogether, is mantic (242c7). The Socratic daimonion is then a special, no doubt intensified, expression of a fundamental human capacity for illumination which goes beyond the discursive function
of reason. Its source, called "divine," illuminates or guides discursive reason, but by that token, is accessible to speech. The daimonion presents itself to Socrates as a voice, forbidding him to
depart before he has expiated his sin against the divine. And
Socrates "clearly understands" his sin (242c5-6); the illumination
provided by the divine prophecy can be discursively stated. But
the perception of sin is not simply an attribute of discursive intelligence; Phaedrus, for example, does not perceive "what"
Socrates is saying (242d2-3). He does not grasp the significance
of the quotation from Ibycus because he himself is one who
prefers human to divine honor (242d1). This would seem to cast
doubt upon Socrates' claim concerning the prophetic gift of the
psyche; in order to remove that doubt, as well as to expiate his
sin, Socrates will deliver his second speech.

Socrates now attributes his sin to the necessity imposed by
Phaedrus, but we recall that he invoked divine inspiration at the
beginning of his first speech. The "spell" cast by Phaedrus, as
Socrates now calls that necessity (242d5, e1), was previously identified as a combination of inspiration by the Muses and compulsion by his friend (237a7-b1). Socrates suppresses the divine
contribution to his sin because he is about to identify Eros as a
god, and at the same time to deny that the divine is evil (242d9
ff.). Whereas previously we were made aware of a disagreement
or disharmony among the gods, the second speech begins, thanks
to the quotation from Ibycus, with a distinction between the
goodness of the divine and the evil of the merely human. To
honor the human instead of the divine is to accept the autonomy
or sovereignty of the human, and this, as the context implies, is
the source of sin. The point is emphasized by Socrates' insistence
upon the terrible character of impiety, in contrast to Phaedrus'
skepticism. When Socrates asks if "there is anything more terrible" than the foolish and impious defense of the non-lover, Phaedrus replies, "no, if you speak the truth" (242d7-8). And when

Socrates asks, "don't you believe Eros to be [the son] of Aphrodite and a god?" Phaedrus answers, "he is indeed said to be" (242d9-10).

As the dramatic and rhetorical structure of the *Phaedrus* makes clear, Socrates "sinned" voluntarily in his criticism of Eros, just as he is now invoking poetry or rhetorical concealment in order to expiate his sin. One might suspect that Socrates was franker in his first speech than he will be in his second. In that speech, in any case, Socrates attributed evil as well as good effects to Eros; indeed, the emphasis is almost entirely on the evil effects. If the first speech is correct, either one must deny that Eros is a god, or else surrender the principle of the *Republic* that evil does not adhere to the divine. In the *Phaedrus*, Socrates refuses either alternative. Therefore, the question arises as to why he allowed himself to submit to "necessity" by delivering the first, sinful speech. This question, as I have shown at some length, can only be answered by perceiving the connection between the *Phaedrus* and the *Symposium*. And this in turn means that the first two speeches of the *Phaedrus* are not superfluous epideictic appendages, but an integral part of the dialectical structure of the work. In short, Socrates' second speech will refute the attribution of evil to Eros by insisting upon his divinity (242e2-3), i.e., by submitting the daimonic Eros of genesis to divine fate.

In obedience to this necessity (243a3), Socrates must now purify himself from the impious consequences of the corporeal necessity of Phaedrus' beauty, or from merely human speech. The two speeches criticizing Eros were marked by a "refined foolishness" (242e5: ἡ εὐήθεια αὐτοῖν πάνυ ἀστεία), which reminds us of the phrase "boorish wisdom," employed by Socrates at the beginning of the dialogue to criticize the demythologizing use of physics (229e3). Socrates tacitly connects these two passages by identifying his sin as "against mythology" (243a3-4), or speech about gods and heroes. Socrates, despite his initial criticism of Phaedrus, had joined Lysias in the activity of "demythologizing" or "rationalizing" stories about the gods. In his initial statement, Socrates did not deny the possibility, but only the utility, of demythologizing. A physical analysis of myth is irrelevant to one who is concerned with the task of knowing himself (229e5 ff.). If, however, we employ a "human" rhetoric, rather than an "inhuman" physics, in the defense of utility and sobriety, the results, although incomplete, are neither superfluous nor evil. The foolishness of the previous speeches was "citified," or necessary for living in cities. But it was not "wise," and this is to say that it was incomplete. The study of nature, in itself "countrified" or incompatible with being civilized, must combine with political refinement in order to preserve the distinctively human way of life.

The sin or defect in the anti-erotic rhetoric consisted in the exaltation of what was neither healthy nor true (242e5-243a1). In order to purify himself, Socrates must have recourse to the medicinal rhetoric which administers truth in a healthy dose of myth or poetry. Purification depends upon health-giving, rather than upon unqualified, truth. Just as poisons have their beneficent use in medicines, so too do certain kinds of falsehood. Thus the "ancient purification," known to Stesichorus but not to Homer, which Socrates employs, amounts to the confession of previous falsehood. Stesichorus was wiser than Homer because he understood that his loss of sight was caused by his having slandered Helen (243a4-6). By associating himself with the repentant Stesichorus, Socrates not only criticizes Homer, but establishes that both poets lied about Helen, or that the most important Greek myth is at least partly false. Instead of engaging in a non-poetic archaeology like that of Thucydides, Stesichorus recovers his vision by a poetic confession, just as Socrates is about to prevent himself from being blinded by recounting the myth of the psyche.

The blindness of the poet may be healed by recourse, not to scientific accounts or logoi, but to a different kind of poetry: medicinal rhetoric.[5] Homer's eyes were veiled; hence he substituted

5 For a contrast between blindness and philosophy in a "scientific" context, cf. *Timaeus* 47a2 ff., esp. b2-5.

a kind of dreaming for the perception of what is truly present. His "defect" in wisdom prevented him from understanding the unhealthy consequences that accrue to those who are drugged or charmed by their dreams into keeping their eyes closed. Perhaps Stesichorus was able to recover his vision because his dreams were less beautiful than those of Homer. Perhaps his vision of Helen was not sufficiently intense to keep him from regretting the vision of the waking, "real" life. His music, like the art of the physician, enabled him to grasp the cause of his blindness (243a6-7), and may therefore be called more sober than the music of Homer. The palinode of Stesichorus is the cry of a poet who denounces his art, but cannot discover a superior mode of speech. Socrates, in keeping with his prophetic gift, exercises foresight, and therefore avoids the need for hindsight. Not only does he escape blindness, but he manages to express his criticism of Eros as well. In the first case, foresight took the form of a veil of shame (243b4-7); in the second, it takes the form of an attribution of the speech to Stesichorus (244a2). Despite his bared head, Socrates is still veiled over by irony or medicinal rhetoric.

It would be an act of philosophical impiety not to understand the serious teaching of the playful introduction to the central section of the *Phaedrus*. We would then take Eros with as little seriousness as does Phaedrus himself, who does not care about gods or daimons, but only about rhetoric. Nothing would please him more than to have Socrates deliver a speech contradicting the doctrines to which he had previously given his enthusiastic acquiescence (244b8-9). Phaedrus is more interested in logical technique than in the content of speeches. He is unaffected by impiety, but he has also failed to grasp the theoretical significance of the criticism of Eros. As Socrates makes explicit, a lover of noble and gentle character would perceive the vulgarity of the anti-erotic speeches (243c1-d1). Their defects are invisible to the violent lover as well as to the non-lover. Neither of these will perceive the "democratic" (243c7; cf. 227d1-2) or "slavish" (243c8) character of anti-erotic love. Phaedrus is both dubious of and shocked by

Socrates' comments here, as his oath indicates.[6] But he is too "re-fined" to behave like the sailors with whom Socrates implicitly associates him (243c7: ἐν ναύταις). Besides, Socrates washes out the salty taste of his insult with the fresh water (243d4-5) of a sug-gestion that Phaedrus ask Lysias to deliver another speech: "one ought, all else being equal, to gratify a lover rather than a non-lover" (243d5-7). Phaedrus is delighted; the pleasures of rhetoric will easily repay the slight discomfort at having to listen twice to the praise of the lover. In fact, Phaedrus promises to "compel Lysias by every necessity" to respond in kind to the speech Socrates is about to deliver (243d8-e1). Phaedrus' love of rhetoric, stronger than his love of money, is sufficient to keep him close to Socrates, and thus to the theme of Socrates' speech. Thus, al-though Phaedrus is close to forty at the time of the dialogue, he is transformed into a youth by the youthful nature of his Eros (243e4-8; cf. 257c8, 267c6, 275b7).

II.

Socrates begins his recantation by informing the "beautiful youth" that Phaedrus was in fact the author of his first speech.[7]

6   Most translators are cavalier in their treatment of details like oaths. Hackforth, for example, translates Phaedrus' reply as "Indeed, Socrates, he well might," a tribute to the demythologizing rigor of English philology. At 229c4, Phaedrus also swore by Zeus (trans-lated by Hackforth as "pray tell me") in demanding to know whether Socrates actually believes in the truth of mythology. The oaths show outrage, not piety.

7   The word λόγος generally means "speech" rather than "scientific account." Socrates identifies his speeches as myths (241e8, 253c7), or as a poetic and hence inspired species of logos. Hence the signif-icance of 243a3-4; Socrates' first speech sinned against mythology: i.e., it was "demythologizing." The second speech will expiate that sin. Robin (*Phèdre*), p. cviii, is wrong to say that Socrates' second speech "ne commence pas par être un mythe," but he is certainly right about the change in style from the discussion of immortality to that of what the psyche is like.

That is, Phaedrus was the cause (238d5) of the inspiration (237a7 ff.) by which Socrates gave his sober critique of "Eros and madness" (241a4). Socrates thereby casts doubt upon the authenticity of the inspiration attributed by him to the Muses. If the Muses lied in his first speech, as they lied to Homer and Stesichorus previously, one is forced to wonder whether they deserve our unqualified trust, despite Socrates' apparent frankness. If Socrates lied about the gods, then we are forced to wonder about his piety, to which the appearance of frankness is linked. Our wonder, however, is not incompatible with the pious observation, despite Hackforth's warning against "Neoplatonic subtlety,"[8] that Socrates, in beginning his second speech, gives the full names and residences of both Phaedrus and Stesichorus. "Phaedrus, son of Pythocles, of Myrrinous," contains echoes of the Pythian oracle at Delphi, as well as of myrtle-leaves; in place of this, we are given the "well spoken, desire-exciting" speech of Stesichorus, son of Euphemus, of Himera (244a1-3). The ironical significance of these names suggests that a profane revelation is about to be substituted for a sacred one. In any case, Socrates, in presenting the "palinode" of Stesichorus, begins as follows: "one must say this, 'it was not a true speech' that, in the presence of a lover, one should rather gratify the non-lover because the lover is mad whereas the non-lover is sober [temperate]. If madness were altogether evil, it would have been nobly spoken..." (244a3-6). Socrates praises the manic rather than the erotic aspects of love. He begins at once with the characteristic of Eros by which we are raised *above* the desire for the body, and strictly speaking, even for the friendship of the beloved as a person. For the utilitarian non-lover, Eros is a means to the ends of pleasure and material

---

8   P. 56, note 1. In the study of Plato, and especially of a dialogue on madness, Neoplatonic subtlety is far preferable to Anglo-Saxon stolidity, which leads to a refusal to perceive an entire dimension in Plato. Cf., however, Thompson, *loc. cit.*, who, like many 19th-century scholars, is far more sensitive than 20th-century philology to the nuances of the dramatic and rhetorical structure of the dialogues.

gain. For Socrates, Eros is a means to the end of divine illumination. He begins his erotic instruction with a more radical analysis
of the stage in which Diotima's instruction terminated. Diotima's
divine revelation was presented exclusively from the human perspective; Socrates will speak from the perspective of the divine
itself, or as much from that perspective as his mantic art permits.
Hence the greater "clarity" in the dramatic setting of the *Phaedrus*,
which contains a greater, higher, or more synoptic revelation than
the *Symposium*.

Socrates continues: "the greatest of goods has come to us
through madness, namely, [the kind that] has been given us as a
divine gift" (244a6-8). Despite the poetic mode of Socrates' discourse, his palinodic revelation is distinguished from the songs
of Homer and Stesichorus by its frequent use of diaeresis. Even
as a prophet, Socrates proceeds by division, collection, and definition: by "counting and measuring," but in a sense that includes
the numbers of poetic as well as of mathematical music. Whereas
the concealed lover began his speech with a diaeresis of the
monad *desire*, the Stesichorean Socrates begins with a diaeresis of
the monad *madness*. This is the nub of the recantation (as well as
of the difference between the *Symposium* and *Phaedrus*). At the
same time, the structure of Socrates' second speech is diaeretic,
in the technical sense, only with regard to the first step. Once
madness is divided into divine and non-divine, Socrates proceeds
to inspect each of the four kinds of divine madness, or (presumably) to exhaust the species without separating it off from other
species. The typical diaeresis has the form:

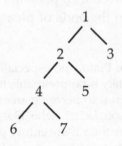

whereas the division employed by Socrates will be:

with an elaborate digression between 6 and 7. The poetic version of diaeresis, although following a quasi-mathematical structure, would seem to differ from the epistemological diaeresis by making more distinctions within the species separated out for inspection. *It is more subtle than the epistemological diaeresis.*

The first kind of madness to be inspected is the prophetic. Socrates cites the prophetess at Delphi, the priestesses at Dodona, and the Sibyl (together with unnamed "others": 244a8-b3). In keeping with previous references to Bacchic revels, nymphs, and Muses, all the examples of divine prophecy are feminine. Socrates does not mention either himself, despite references throughout the dialogues to his prophetic gift (and here at 242c4), nor the human psyche, previously identified as mantic at 242c7. The examples in the *Phaedrus* (as well as Diotima in the *Symposium*) suggest that there is something feminine or passive in the prophetic power of the psyche.[9] The prophetess receives the divine message, or is fecundated by it, and gives birth to a verbal revelation (like the

9   It is useful to cite the *Theaetetus,* apparently a "mathematical" or "epistemic" rather than poetic dialogue, to support the observations in the text above. Socrates refers to his prophetic powers in that dialogue (e.g., 142c3), which are obviously linked to his maieutic technē (cf. 151b4). Note 154d3 ff., where Socrates swears "by Hera," a woman's oath, and 155d1 ff.; in the latter passage, Theodorus is also said to be a good prophet, and speech is identified as Iris, the messenger of Zeus: i.e., the divine interpretess of wonder, in which philosophy has its beginning.

poet). In addition, she may fulfill the maieutic function of testing the genuineness of pretenders to the title of "prophet." The danger of the false prophet is political as well as private (244b1-2); there is a connection between madness and the many noble accomplishments of the Hellenes. No doubt Socrates is here alluding ironically to the irrational custom of recourse to oracles, especially in deciding the lines of political conduct. But there is a more serious, and more important, point, consonant with the praise or affirmation of madness. This is exhibited in the emphasis upon the noble or beautiful (244b1, c1, c3, d3) as opposed to the shameful or ugly (244b7, c4). The ancients were right to name prophecy, the most beautiful technē, with the word for madness (244b6-c2). This correct, i.e., sober, act of naming was accomplished by a "weaving" of madness and prophecy into a discursive harmony (244c2: ἐμπλέκοντες). Nobility or beauty is tacitly understood in this context as success, more specifically, as political success, and so in the sense of utility. The successful or useful is part of what we mean by political nobility; the doing of splendid deeds is contingent upon wealth, office, social standing, martial triumph, and the like—goals for which the Hellenes were accustomed to consult oracles. But the accomplishment of these goals, or the knowledge of the future, is in the lap of the gods. That which directs us toward the noble or beautiful, whether in the sense of worldly utility or divine excellence, is silent or alogical (like beauty itself). It is a kind of vision which serves as the necessary basis for sober discourse (like naming); Socrates calls this vision "madness" and attributes it to a "divine fate" (244c3; cf. 244a7-8).[10]

The men of today, Socrates continues, are "ignorant of beauty," and hence distinguish between madness (μανική) and

10 This cryptic phrase has varying significances in the Platonic corpus. E.g., in *Meno* 99e-100b it is opposed to nature and learning, whereas in *Laws* 642c, 875c it is associated with nature. Cf. also such expressions as θεία φύσει ["by a divine nature" – ed.] which in *Republic* 366c7 serves as a basis for justice.

prophecy (μαντική) by the addition of the letter "τ" (244c4-5). However, we may observe that the contemporary unweaving of the harmony or identity between madness and prophecy would seem to be necessary for the Socratic diaeresis of madness. If the harmony is more beautiful than the division, there seems to be a tension between beauty and truth (assuming Socrates' diaeresis to be true, or more true than the simple identification between madness and prophecy). The fact that this disagreement is symbolized by the minute sign of a single consonant testifies to the need for sharp vision rather than to the triviality of the tension. The palinodic rehabilitation of erotic madness thus suggests by its "infra-structure" that poetry (=madness) must be divided by *ordo et mensura* (=sobriety). This in itself does not contradict the explicit claim of the primacy of (divine) madness to human or dianoetic (244c6) sobriety.[11] Without the divine fate or gift, the nature of madness, and hence too the difference between mad and sober prophecy, would be invisible. But the latter difference is emblematic of the difference between apprehending and dividing noetic monads, to which I shall return in a later section.

The ancients, with their more highly developed poetic taste, called bird-lore, the main example of sober prophecy, οἰονοϊστική, i.e., an amalgam of οἴησις, νοῦς, and ἱστορία, or opinion acquired by noetic (here=discursive, human) investigation (244c7-8). The moderns call it οἰωνιστική, lengthening the "o" to make it more impressive (244d1). Socrates fails to mention that they also drop the "o" in the third syllable, which obscures the presence of mind (νοῦς) in the amalgam. We seem to have here another instance of modern "unweaving," or the separation of mind from

---

11 In the extremely sober *Timaeus*, where μανία is given a pejorative sense (86b2, d3; cf. 69d4), and which therefore illustrates the nature of sober myth, prophecy is called a gift from god to unreason: no one acquires the gift of prophecy while in his senses, but only when asleep, diseased, or enthused. All prophecies are to be interpreted by the ἔμφρων or σώφρον. ["sensible" or "moderate" – ed.]

"sober" or uninspired prophecy. To summarize: a more careful inspection of the phenomenon of prophecy shows us that it is not discursive or intellectual (in the human sense) in either its manic or sober species. The manic species is reminiscent of the divine *noēsis* by which we apprehend formal unities; the process of division, although sober rather than mad, should not be confused with such forms of division as performed upon the horizon by the arc of a bird's flight (or upon the bird by man, who wishes to "read" the future from the shape of its entrails). Still more soberly: sober division cannot appropriately be *named*, but must necessarily be *used*, in the praise of divine madness. The vision of the divine is at once a division between the divine and the human. Let us also notice in passing that, by asserting the superiority of divine madness to human sobriety (244d2-5), the division employs *ordinal* rather than *cardinal* numbers. Perhaps this corresponds to the unmentioned species of divine sobriety.

The first kind of divine madness, then, is the prophetic, which is directed toward the future manifestation of noble or beautiful accomplishments. Let us look again at the "mathematical" structure of the palinode:

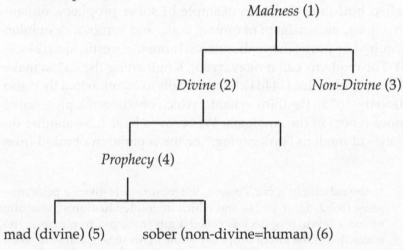

$$Madness\ (1)$$

$$Divine\ (2) \qquad Non\text{-}Divine\ (3)$$

$$Prophecy\ (4)$$

$$mad\ (divine)\ (5) \qquad sober\ (non\text{-}divine\text{=}human)\ (6)$$

The sub-division of prophecy into mad and sober seems to show the "mathematical" or diaeretic inadequacy of the divisions, or at least the rhetorical presentation of the divisions, of the praise of Eros. How can sober prophecy, which is explicitly attributed to human intelligence, be contained, or discussed, under the rubric of divine madness? Perhaps we might reply that sober prophecy is discussed under (4) merely to sharpen by contrast the discussion of (5). This in itself, however, would suggest an inadequacy in the diaeretic method altogether; namely, the incompleteness of the sub-monadic species when taken in isolation from each other. The manyness of the one, it seems, precludes our grasping each unit in that manifold as again a one; manyness adheres to, and thereby participates in, the noetic structure of the sub-monadic species. Here again we find an anticipation of what will later occupy us at length. Another response might be that "sober" prophecy is analogous to the "non-" or "concealed" lover; namely, that it is a concealed version of divine madness, or a less "energetic" (=inspired) and in that sense "sober" form of madness. On this assumption, even *ordo et mensura*, or dialectical counting, would be understood as a "gift of the gods." But why, in a praise of madness, does Socrates not explicitly assert this prestigious increment to the realm of the divine fate—if such is actually his opinion? So this suggestion, too, is unfortunately as opaque as the situation it attempts to clarify. Besides, if the gods count, must they not be expected to count accurately? The second kind of divine madness intensifies the difficulty raised by the reference to sober prophecy. For, although distinguished (=divided) from the sub-monadic species of prophecy, it is nevertheless called (a kind of) prophecy (244d7).

It would seem that a more accurate division of the material now being discussed might take this form:

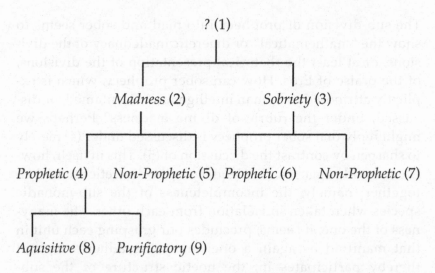

As I have indicated by the question mark in the first position, it is no longer evident what monad Socrates is actually dividing, if this is indeed an accurate (although incomplete) schema. "Madness" would then be the concealed form of the monad, which, it is a fair guess, might be the psyche. But if so, why this particular mode of indirection or concealment? For one reason, no doubt, to minimize emphasis upon the phenomenon of sober prophecy—and yet, it was precisely the present position of sober prophecy that led us to question the schema in the first place. I myself believe that Socrates is indicating, among other things, the impossibility of performing a genuinely rational diaeresis of psychic phenomena (if not indeed of all others). Suffice it to say that Socrates, to the extent that he discusses it at all, has absorbed sobriety under the rubric of madness. And rhetorically, at least, in a praise of madness, this has its own logic. More difficult, because not explained by the principle of rhetorical logic, is the division between the first and second species of prophetic divine madness. In the last schema, I referred to them as acquisitive and purificatory. As Socrates describes it, the function of the first species is to accomplish "beautiful works" (244b1-2); hence it is directed toward the future. The present situation (of the addressee, if not of the prophet) is one of desire, hope, or potentiality; the desire is

}84{

for a future determination. In the case of the second species, the desire for the future (purification) is directed by the past (sin), which is the primary cause of present afflictions (244d5-e5). The repentant sinner desires to be free from a past (and so present) determination, whereas the would-be acquisitor desires to submit to a future determination.

This observation suggests that one may be freed from the past, because it has already transpired, and so its determinations are effective and known. Wishes for the future, however, i.e., for future possessions or accomplishments, are not for freedom but for a restriction of our "possibilities." In somewhat different terms, because the future has not transpired, we cannot be free from or with respect to it; hence the notorious ambiguity or unreliability of prophecies about the future. This distinction has far-reaching philosophical implications, which it would be out of place to develop here. I should like, however, to make one further remark. Those who submit the past to the sovereignty of the future do not pay homage to freedom but to chaos. On the other hand, atonement for past errors makes the (in itself indeterminate) future a consequence of the present. In the Platonic dialogues, it is the primacy of the present which makes the past more significant than the future. This order of priorities is dictated, not by vulgar reactionism, but by Platonic *liberalism*, or a philosophical conception of freedom. Purificatory divine madness is medicinal (244d5, e2) or delivers us from known troubles (e3-5), whereas future-oriented prophecy, even if successful, delivers us to unknown possessions having unknowable consequences. Thus purificatory madness is prophecy which reveals, not the future, but mysteries (e2), or the timeless understanding of temporal disease and sin.

So much with respect to future- and past-oriented prophecy. The third kind of "inspiration and madness" comes from the Muses;[12] namely, poetry (245a1-4). In the *Ion*, poetry is also called

---

12 Cf. 245a1, τρίτη δὲ ἀπὸ Μουσῶν and *Republic* 597e6-7. The former phrase has a resonance of "third from the Muses."

"inspiration" or "possession"; the word used in the *Phaedrus* is there linked with "divine fate."[13] Poetry thus receives, if not a higher, certainly a more complex interpretation in these two dialogues than in the *Republic*. Once again, it is difficult to distinguish poetry sharply from prophecy. The obvious echo of the *Ion* reminds us that madness in general was called a "divine gift" at 244a7-8, whereas the phrase "divine fate," although probably intended to designate madness generally, is used in the context of the discussion of prophecy (244c3). Furthermore, the function of poetry is "to ornament the myriad deeds of the past for the education of those who are born later" (245a4-5). This ornamenting or making beautiful is something like the purification of the past, just as education (as always in Plato) is like a healing of psychic illness. Poetry and purificatory prophecy both "soften" the harshness of the past, or render it accessible to "a soft and pure [=untrodden] psyche" (245a2).[14] This, too, is at least the aspiration of prophecy proper, i.e., to make the future softer in the sense of beautiful or secure. Poetry is perhaps even more like prophecy than like purification in another respect: poetry is wishing about the past, and prophecy is wishing about the future, whereas the purification of past sins gives immediate comfort to the present. These references, together with Socrates' next remark, that poetic madness "awakens and makes Bacchic" the soft psyche, remind us that Socrates himself claimed previously to have been both possessed by Bacchus and inspired by the Muses. In addition, he identified himself as a prophet, whereas (at least thus far) there has been no mention of his access to purificatory madness. Prophecy proper and poetry may have a passive or "feminine" dimension that is not present in purificatory madness (although

13 *Ion* 536c2: θεία μοίρα καὶ κατοκωχῇ. ["by a divine fate and possession" – ed.]
14 Cf. *Symposium* 195c6 ff. and Rosen (*Symposium*), pp. 178 ff., for the connection between softness and poetry. According to Agathon, Eros "walks" on the softest of things, the human psyche. However, his own delicacy would perhaps leave the psyche as pure as though it had never been "trod upon." Cf. *Phaedrus* 268e2.

this possibility is contradicted at least by the *Symposium*, where Diotima "purifies" Socrates by initiating him into the mysteries of Eros).

These echoes and conjectures are no doubt themselves "poetic" rather than "mathematical." But they correspond to the poetic ambiguity of Socrates' palinodic division of madness, each section of which seems to reflect fragments of the others. The first three kinds of divine madness serve thereby to emphasize the ambiguity of the divine image as reflected in the tripartite mirror of time. The psyche that is awakened by prophetic or quasi-prophetic madness can scarcely be distinguished from the wishing, dreaming, or sleeping psyche. It must therefore be awakened once more from the specious or Bacchic wakefulness, or brought to self-awareness by a speech which is less than an epistemic logos but more than a lyric poem (cf. 245a3).[15] This is the function of Socratic myth, which adapts the methods of *ordo et mensura* to the revelatory functions of poetry, or illuminates by discursive articulation the synoptic illumination of divine madness. As Socrates says, technē without mania is inadequate for the visibility of poetry (245a5-8), and it is poetry that makes the psyche visible.

This is all that Socrates wishes to say about the forms of divine madness that terminate in "beautiful deeds," or what we might call the praxis of madness (245b1-2). The purpose of the Socratic palinode is to explain why we should not be afraid of kinēsis, or how the divine madness of love provides security against the frightening aspect of kinēsis which sobriety alone cannot furnish (245b2-4). The *Phaedrus* is thus the psychic counterpart to the sober myth of physics in the *Timaeus*. Kinēsis frightens us because it destroys. Those for whom everything is in motion normally attempt to overcome the fear of kinēsis by showing that it also generates. But this line of argument is subject to two fatal difficulties. First, the cycle of birth and decay gives no satisfaction to the immediate or individual human longing for steadfastness. Second, the equation of being and genesis faces the danger of theoretical

15 Cf. 241e1-2 and the remarks at the beginning of this chapter.

or internal incoherence: the ratios of motion must be stable enough to be counted and measured by the numbers of mathematics, but also by those of music. The problem of the stability, visibility, and enumerability of motion thus culminates in the problem of the nature of the numbers themselves, and therefore, of the method by which they are employed. We need both noetic and empirical or logistic numbers, and methods which are proportioned to the differences between these two.

The argument for sobriety was essentially utilitarian. Thus far, the palinode has shown us how vulgar or base such a utilitarian argument is, and precisely in terms of praxis. In place of corporeal hedonism, madness substitutes grandeur or noble action. But this, too, is fundamentally a mode or interpretation of the "useful." In moving from practice to theory, the notion of utility must be transcended; otherwise, we shall never discover a steadfast foundation upon which to construct our understanding of what is truly useful. "Useful" means "useful for…" and itself points to an end or purpose; if there is no end to these ends, then "useful" loses its meaning, or becomes indistinguishable from "useless." Socrates calls the end of utility "the greatest good fortune" which the gods have given us by way of madness (245b4-c1). His demonstration of this good fortune will be believed by the wise, but not by the clever (245c1-2). The reason for this, of course, is that "cleverness" is here a synonym for "sobriety." There is at least a hint of the difference between wisdom and cleverness in Socrates' link between vision of the nature of divine and human psyche, and "noetic apprehension of the truth" about the psyche's passions and deeds (245c2-4). His "demonstration" (ἀπόδειξις) is not dianoetic or mathematico-epistemic, as its palinodic form should by now have taught us. Instead, it points toward (and therefore from) the horizon within which dianoetic demonstration (and the noetic perception of form) receives its significance or orientation. As we shall literally "see" (θεωρεῖν), speech (including both logos and myth) is oriented by the vision of the hyper-Uranian beings. But first we need to grasp how it is possible for the psyche to ascend to these hyper-Uranian beings. The principle or beginning of Socrates' demonstration will therefore be the nature of psyche, or more specifically, that aspect of its nature which is ascendant, i.e., akin to the hyper-Uranian beings (245c4).

III.

We come now to perhaps the most notorious passage in the palinode: the connection between psyche and unceasing motion. In keeping with our usual method, we take our bearings by the context in which this passage occurs, and not by reflections on its relationship to other Platonic writings. Such a relationship, after all, is a function of the meaning of the passages it relates, and cannot be applied as a measure, existing in advance, to or of the passages themselves. But the procedure of abstracting this (or some other) passage from its context, and subjecting it to "logical" or "epistemological scrutiny" with the "tools of modern analysis" is inadequate and even dangerous. As we know from the *Phaedrus* itself, every argument in a perfect writing has a dramatic, poetic, or rhetorical function which is a part of its logic in two related senses. First, the dramatic function tells us what a person like the speaker would "ideally" say to a person like his interlocutor, given such and such specific circumstances and intentions. But secondly, the "poetic sum" of these functions is the perfect writing—and let us not hesitate to say, the dialogue as a whole, or the intention which Plato has chosen to portray under a determinate set of circumstances. It is only then possible, and indeed necessary, to submit the ostensible argument to the most minute dissection. But the "modern tools of analysis" are incompetent for this job in its full rigor, and precisely because they have been conceived in the light of a theory which is less rigorous than Plato's own analytic method. Plato believed it possible to speak with precision in the numbers of poetry or music as well as those of mathematics. Furthermore, Platonic mathematics can scarcely become visible, let alone understood, in the light of a logic of nominalistic conventionalism.

In the case before us, Socrates introduces the deathlessness of the psyche as a preparation for his discussion of Eros, or the fourth kind of divine madness. In order to see the non-moving or "steadfast" measures (the hyper-Uranian beings), the psyche must have some property akin to those measures. This necessity did not arise in the *Symposium*, which remains altogether within genesis, or does not provide us with the basis for a theoretical *physics*, i.e., interpretation of genesis or *metaphysics*, as we might say. We should not be confused by the fact that Plato presents his metaphysical interpretation of physics, which I shall abbreviate as his metaphysics, in the form of myth (*Timaeus*) or poetry (*Phaedrus*). The reason has nothing to do with Plato's lack of conceptual or experimental tools suitable for the construction of a mathematical physics in the post-Galilean sense of the term. These tools were no more possessed by Aristotle, who nevertheless attempts to give a logos about nature. Furthermore, Plato's "likely story" is in many ways closer to mathematical physics (founded by men who regarded themselves as Platonists) than is Aristotle's "discursive" account. Aristotle's meta-physics is therefore also discursive in a way that the meta-physics of modern mathematical physics is not. This modern meta-physics takes one of the following forms: (1) silence, based upon injunctions of various kinds not to speak "about" physics, but rather "to do physics"; (2) meta-scientific or methodological remarks about the operational concepts and methods of physics, which is equivalent to silence about meta-physics; (3) various revisions of German Idealist philosophies of history, with poetic or mythical talk of creativity, freedom, the autonomy of the axiomatic framework, and so on; or (4) empiricism, either of the naive Humean kind, or as rendered more "logically sophisticated," but in either case leading again to meta-physical silence (which is often broken by versions of no. 3).

Briefly stated (since the development of this point would take us far beyond the *Phaedrus*), there are essentially two kinds of meta-physics, the Platonic and the Aristotelian. The difference between them turns upon a different conception of what would constitute a rational account of the phenomena of physics understood (not without further ambiguity) as the domain of genesis. The Platonic conception demands a mathematical foundation for a discursive account of genesis, whereas the Aristotelian conception does not. But Plato did not regard a "mathematical ontology" as the equivalent to a mathematical foundation for physics. A "mathematical ontology" is nonsense, or a contradiction in terms, because a logos about being cannot be the same as, or reducible to, mathematical "speech," which is actually pseudo-speech, or (when made ultimate) silence. To give only the crucial cases: no ratio of numbers, or set of numerical properties, can exhibit the visible heterogeneity of such occupants of genesis as man, horse, tree, and the like, to say nothing of justice, beauty, or goodness. Numbers cannot speak about themselves, as was evident to Pythagoras and Plato, if not to their contemporary disciples. A mathematical foundation for a discursive account of genesis, on the other hand, would give a complete and consistent, i.e., determinate and discursive, account of the invariant structure of genesis—of its forms or Ideas—as well as of the relation of difference which obtains between this eidetic (=noetic) structure and its generated, aesthetic (=sensuous) instances. We would need, not simply a dianoetic account of the noetic domain, but a noetic account of the dianoetic domain. The first is indirectly possible (see section V of this chapter), but the second is altogether impossible. Hence the recourse to myth, poetry, or prophecy; the same procedure, incidentally, as is followed by the most "positivistic" of contemporaries, who always invoke notions like "mathematical elegance," "simplicity," and the like. By the same token, an adequate account of Platonic myth, as necessarily discursive or dianoetic, is necessarily inadequate, or (less paradoxically) incomplete; it cannot be completed without access to noēsis, and this completion can never be completely explained. An explanation of myth is therefore itself a myth.

The demonstration of immortality is therefore one in which we may *believe* (245c2: σοφοῖς δὲ πιστή); it is not, or does not terminate in, demonstrative knowledge (ἐπιστήμη).[16] A demonstration worthy of our belief or confidence, even though not "mathematical" or epistemic, is not to be confused with a false demonstration. A false demonstration leads to ignorance in the sense of false opinion. The function of the mythical demonstration is quite different, and may be said to belong to a separate species. When Socrates says that we must "know the truth" (τἀληθὲς νοῆσαι) about the passions and deeds of psyche by looking at its divine and human nature (245c2-4), the "looking at" (ἰδόντα) the psyche is distinguished from, and necessarily prior to, knowing the truth. We cannot apprehend the truth about psyche if our vision of it is false. The difficulty, however, is that the psyche itself seems to be visible only in or through its passions and deeds, and not prior to or separately from them. The difference between seeing the passions and deeds of psyche, and seeing the nature of the psyche itself, is obvious in the case of immortality. In the terms of Socrates' demonstration, every passion and deed of psyche is a finite motion. But from the sum of finite motions, no vision or inference of perpetual (=infinite) motion is justifiable. The same is true with respect to self-motion. If every visible passion or deed of the psyche is an instance of psychic self-motion, we still know nothing about the invisible passions or deeds, to say nothing of the possibility of invisible motions external to, and serving as principles of, the psychic motions. On this basis, apart from the difficulty just mentioned, we could be certain of the immortality of the psyche only by watching its self-motion forever.[17] There would, then, be no demonstration, but only the enjoyment, of immortality.

16 A parallel discussion of psyche as self-motion in *Laws* 896a1 ff. is introduced by an assertion of the political need for religion (885b4) and is followed by the claim that there is an eternal war in heaven between good and bad (906a2). Note also the Athenian Stranger's warning (908d1 ff.) against ironical atheists, gifted by nature, who hide behind hypocrisy. Those who ignore everything in the dialogue but "arguments" will never grasp the real argument, which is conditioned by its dramatic context.

17 The reader will naturally remember that motion is elsewhere linked to genesis: what moves must have a beginning and end to its motion; cf. *Timaeus* 37d3-38b6 ff.

Immortality, if understood as perpetual motion, would seem to be the same as perpetual temporality, or the unending circle of passions and deeds. The visibility of psychic passions and deeds, as temporal experience suggests, is dependent upon the body. This point bears upon the problem whether Socrates, in his demonstration, is speaking of the individual or the cosmic psyche.[18] As he puts it, "psyche altogether is immortal. For that which always moves is immortal…" (245c5). The sentence ψυχὴ πᾶσα ἀθάνατος could perhaps be understood to mean "every psyche is immortal." This would mean in turn that every psyche is a perpetually moving circle of passions and deeds; we should then have to determine how passions and deeds are identifiable as *mine*, independently of the body. If the sentence in question refers to cosmic psyche, this difficulty at least would not arise. The immortality of psyche would then correspond to the life-span of the cosmos; its passions and deeds would then always be visible to one embodied psyche or another, which, by looking at its own passions and deeds, might infer, not its own (personal) immortality, but unending psychic motion as the impersonal principle, whether cosmic or ontological (in accordance with either the *Timaeus* or *Sophist*). In addition, this interpretation would remove the apparent disagreement between the *Symposium* and *Phaedrus*, or make evident that each discusses a different dimension of essentially the same situation. So much for a preliminary statement of the alternative interpretations of this statement.

If, however, the passage intends to demonstrate the immortality of the individual psyche, there is still another difficulty to which it is subject. If the immortality of every psyche is dependent upon its perpetual motion, how are we to distinguish between "perpetual" and "total" motion? If any part of the psyche is at rest, that part would seem to be dead. Now total motion may be divided into two kinds: the kind in which each motion m is always other than its predecessor $m-1$ and the kind in which the motions, as perpetual, preserve a

---

18 For some discussion of this problem, cf. Hackforth, pp. 64 ff. and Stenzel, p. 15.

continuous ratio or shape. The first kind of motion is criticized regularly in the dialogues as equivalent to chaos[19] and cannot be the kind Socrates is here alluding to, since it would exclude the possibility of personal identity. The second kind of motion may be designated for convenience as *circular*. However, the circularity of circular motion is not the same as the sum of its constituent motions. The shape of circularity is not itself a motion. Each motion m in circular motion is "always" (for the duration of its existence, assuming this to be discernible) becoming other than itself, or $m+1$, and "always" ceasing to be its predecessor, or $m-1$. The circularity of circular motion, however, is always the same, as can easily be seen when we realize that the circle, as perpetual, has "always" already been described. But even further, the circularity of one circle is identical with the circularity of any other circle. If, then, each individual psyche is immortal or always moving in the sense of circular motion, it would be impossible to distinguish one mortal psyche from another. Inasmuch as the circularity of the circular motion is itself at rest, the individual psyche would be immortal *only as dead and anonymous*. To summarize the preceding pages: the attempt to demonstrate the immortality of psyche by means of the principle of perpetual motion is not (it seems) suitable for demonstrating personal immortality. The "personality" of the individual seems to depend upon his temporal or corporeal existence or experience, whereas his "identity" seems to depend upon an absolutely impersonal shape or bond, which is similar to, if not identical with, geometrical and arithmetical forms or properties. There is apparently a disjunction in the nature of man, most obvious in the difference between psyche and body, but also implicit in the difference between the cosmic and the individual psyche, which Socrates refers to at 245c2-3 as the divine and human psychic natures.

This is the ambiguity of the opening sentence as I understand it. In a writer of Plato's skill, we may reasonably assume that the ambiguity is intentional, especially since it is obvious and could

19 Cf. *Theaetetus* 156a2 ff., where total motion is discussed as a myth (c3-4) and in terms of doing and suffering.

easily have been removed. All the more reason why it would be foolish to decide upon a single "correct" interpretation at this stage of our analysis. Whether Socrates refers to the cosmic or individual psyche (or both), the attribute required by psyche in order that there be a relation between it and the hyper-Uranian beings is immortality. Since the psyche, as a living being, is itself infra-Uranian or a resident of genesis, and consequently in motion, the form of psychic immortality is identified as perpetual motion.[20] The perpetuity of the motion is distinguishable (if not separable) from the motion itself, and serves as the bond or form of that motion. To repeat an earlier phrase, this (perpetual) shape gives security to the motion of life, and so provides us with security against the fear of motion understood as death. The next sentences refer to the perpetuity of psychic motion (or to its identity, but not to its personality), which is now shown to be self-motion. The reason why the psyche moves perpetually is that only those motions cease which have an external cause. That is: the external cause is not part of the nature of the moving entity, and hence cannot be controlled by it with absolute security. "Only what moves itself never ceases moving, since it cannot abandon [=cease to be] itself; but this is rather the fountain and principle of motion for whatever is moved" (245c7-9).

So far as psyche itself is concerned, perpetual motion means perpetual life (245c7). However, as perpetually alive, psyche is

---

20 The mss. reading τὸ γὰρ ἀεικίνητον is in my opinion superior to the reading of Oxy. 1016, τὸ γὰρ αὐτοκίνητον. ["for the ever-moving" ... "for the self-moving" – ed.] As Hackforth puts it, "self-motion" is not an evident premise from which to infer "immortality." Robin (*Phèdre*), p. lxxvii, note 1, defends the papyrus reading; he observes that it is hard to understand why Plato would oppose (δὲ) "that which does not move itself" to "what is always moving." However, the line continues παῦλαν ἔχον κινήσεως, παῦλαν ἔχει ζωῆς, ["when it ceases from movement, it ceases from life" – ed.] and so explains that what does not move itself cannot be, or is opposed to, the always moving. I agree, however, that the text is crabbed and obscure; but Plato often presents important issues in just such a style.

further identified as the principle of motion for all things, i.e., *whether living or not*. This strongly supports the view that Socrates is speaking of cosmic psyche, which, as self-moving, moves the body of the cosmos as a whole, and so too those moving but non-psychic beings. Differently stated, the individual psyche can only be the principle of motion in those previously unmoving things it causes to move; it cannot be the principle of motion for everything that moves. Apart from this, it is easy to see why Socrates, casting about for an immortal characteristic of psyche, might choose perpetual motion. But it is not clear how he knows that the motion of psyche *is* perpetual. The question is of course merely begged by the response that perpetuity is an attribute of self-motion. For one must then ask how Socrates knows that the psyche is self-moved. The argument from the first mover or principle of motion is not self-evidently an argument for a psyche, as is obvious from the fact that it has also been employed by materialists. Socrates asserts that psyche is the principle of motion; he does not prove it (245d1-6). Psyche might well be an epiphenomenon of the motion of matter. However, we must not hasten to give Socrates a black mark in logic. Socrates never claimed to be demonstrating "logically" the existence of psyche, but rather to give a demonstration within a poetic myth of the properties of psyche enabling it to achieve the fourth kind of divine madness. The present ἀπόδειξις is like a revelation, not an epistemic demonstration. It is therefore senseless to treat this passage as an ostensible or defective scientific proof. In the context of the dialogue, no one has denied the existence of psyche; hence no proof of its existence is required. In different terms, Socrates "reveals" a divine mystery about the principle in man which loves beautiful speeches. There is no doubt that, in the present passage, his identification of this principle with the principle of motion has not been substantiated. Socrates is here *re-mythologizing* the physical doctrine of motion, which is justified *ad hominem* by the fact that Phaedrus does not deny the existence or motive capacity of psyche. For Phaedrus, as for any Greek, psyche is life, or the principle of life. Socrates is mythically teaching Phaedrus that his love of beautiful speeches constitutes the most compelling aspect of his life, motion, or psyche, and that this love cannot be understood in materialist terms. The motion of the love of beautiful speeches (Eros) points toward a divine (hyper-Uranian) telos of that motion; since the telos is divine or immortal, so the motion must be, as well.

This is of course not to deny that the apodeictic passage in the Socratic palinode has implications for Plato's conception of psyche, apart from the use it serves in leading Phaedrus toward an understanding of divine madness. The *ad hominem* character of the passage is in fact a part, or illustrates an aspect, of the Platonic conception of psyche. But this conception cannot be reduced to a series of logical arguments, as is evident from the fact that the first premise of such arguments cannot itself be established by, or be the conclusion of, an (earlier) argument. Even as logically responsible philosophers, we must begin with the given. In this case, the given is the passions and deeds of the psyche. Still absent is a direct vision of the passive and active psyche; neither logic nor experience can supply it, and hence Socrates turns to poetry or prophecy, just as does Timaeus in the dialogue bearing his name. Physics or cosmology is a "likely story" because neither psyche nor cosmos is visible in its original (=whole) nature, but only through its passions and deeds.[21] In related if not equivalent terms, the principle of motion (ἀρχὴ κινήσεως) is visible in and through the motions themselves. To see the principle or bond of a given motion or class of motions is not the same as to see the "first principle." But further, Socrates' present demonstration implies that, even if we were to possess a complete discursive (dianoetic) or even mathematical account of the noetic structure of the cosmos, we would still not have seen (noetically) the principle of cosmic motion, because that principle is psyche or life, which is not equivalent to the discursive or

---

21 The same holds true for contemporary cosmology, with its quarrel between the "big bang" and "steady state" hypotheses. And it underlies the so-called "ontological difference" between Being and beings.

mathematical sum of the forms or formulae of motion. The principle of motion, as self-moving and ungenerated, is not the same as or formally analogous to the motion or motions of genesis. The form of a generated motion must be radically dissimilar to the form of ungenerated motion. The form of a generated motion must be double: the shape or noetic structure of the motion cannot be the same as the principle in the sense of the origin of motion. The origin is, to repeat, perpetual and self-moving motion, or psyche. The generated motion begins or is caused by the origin, and so, can be "measured" or described independently of its origin. As one finite motion among many, it belongs to a heterogeneity of shapes (kinds of motion), which may be distinguished from each other by their determinate differences, e.g., points of origin. The origin itself, however, has no point of origin. There is no point from which it could be measured or determined. We may, of course, call this perpetual motion "circular," but this contributes little if anything to our concrete grasp of the distinguishable form of circularity. The mathematical properties of a circle do not explain why a (or the) circle is in motion, perpetual or temporary. More precisely, they do not explain why a (or the) circle is a (or the) psyche, i.e., alive.[22] Therefore, in themselves they provide no security for the individual psyche against the fear of motion or death. The perpetuity of circular psychic motion is a necessary but not a sufficient condition for this security. As circular or immortal alone, the psyche is not individual (=personal); as circular or perpetual alone, motion is not psychic.

To summarize this reflection: the principle of motion is also the principle of genesis, but the motion of the principle is not a motion of genesis (245d1-e2). If it were, "the whole heaven and the whole of genesis[23] would collapse and come to a standstill,

22 For this reason, I regard the traditional post-Platonic identification of the psyche as a number to be in itself unintelligible. (For the relevant texts, see Merlan and Gaiser.) The criticism I make of the identification of geometrical and psychic motion is similar to Leibniz's criticism of Cartesian and materialist physics.

nor would there be any source from which, set into motion, it might come to be" (245d8-e2). Furthermore, the (circular) motion of the principle is not the same as its form (circularity), but the difference is not sufficient to enable us to grasp it discursively or determinately, and so to perceive the identity between psyche and perpetual motion. The assertion of this identity is mythical rather than logical or epistemic. The susceptibility of circularity to mathematical analysis indicates that mathematics, very far from being equivalent to discursive speech, is related to the silence of myth. Finally, since circles are mathematically identical, the immortality of the psyche, if defined by perpetual motion, cannot apply to the individual person, but may serve to characterize (or to contribute to the characterization of) how the individual is related to the hyper-Uranian beings. "One need not be ashamed" to say that self-motion is the "essential being and defining formula of psyche" (245e3-4: ψυχῆς οὐσίαν τε καὶ λόγον). But apart from the fact that absence of shame is not equivalent to presence of truth, the *ousia*, as is emphasized by its link to logos, is not the *on* or existence of the individual as individual. The circularity of psychic motion sets into motion an embodied psyche (245e4-6), but cannot be identified with, or reduced to, the motions of the embodied psyche; otherwise, the "necessarily ungenerated and immortal" (246a1) would be identical with the generated and mortal, and the world would collapse, never to rise again.[24] Or else the human would be reduced to the necessity of motion, and in effect, disappear.

23 I follow the mss. rather than Philoponus, who gives γῆν εἰς ἕν rather than γένεσιν. ["the whole earth would collapse into one" rather than "the whole of genesis would collapse" - ed.]
24 Cf. Robin's note on the contradiction between the ungenerated nature of psyche and the literal reading of the *Timaeus*. The problem is more complicated than Robin suggests, because he does not distinguish between the two forms of psychic motion. I add only that an ontological recipe is not the same as a mathematical analysis of motion.

IV.

So much for the "demonstration." Socrates now makes a curious distinction. "Concerning immortality of psyche, let this suffice; we must now speak as follows concerning its ἰδέα," i.e., its shape or nature (246a3-4). Following Socrates' own indication, we may make the following distinction. The perpetual motion, and in that sense the immortality, of psyche is subject to a kind of demonstration which resembles a dialectical logos. It is not a genuine logos because of the unproven (if non-shameful) identification between life and perpetual motion.[25] For example, life might be a particular internal determination of circular motion, brought about by a specific concatenation of moving particles, or the genesis of a certain kind of body. In any case, speech about motion is in itself not the same as speech about the human psyche, which is decisively characterized by self-consciousness in its various forms. Speech about psyche as the principle of motion is therefore different from speech about psyche as the principle of speech. The latter speech is reflexive as the former is not; the difference is like that between (mathematical) physics and (philosophical) psychology. The attribution of perpetual motion to psyche (whether as species or individual) does not confer personal immortality on the individual, whereas the attribution of self-consciousness or speech to psyche is necessarily a speech about the individual psyche *qua* person. If the individual, i.e., personal, or self-conscious psyche is in any sense immortal, it must be with respect to its speech; that is, the personal psyche must be able to speak to itself of its conscious achievement or acquisition of immortality. As we

25 Socrates' argument on this point is similar to, and the ancestor of, Aristotle's ostensible "proof" of the eternity of the human species, and so the world (cf. Skemp, p. 6). Arguments like these are "commonsensical" inferences *backwards* from the presence of men and motion, and in this sense inductions rather than demonstrations. Consider the medieval controversy as to whether Aristotle believed himself to have proven the eternity of the world, or to have provided a reasonable doxa.

have by now sufficiently emphasized, the demonstration of perpetual motion was not such a speech. Whereas Socrates at least pretended to be able to give a non-shameful version of that demonstration, he explicitly asserts that speech about the nature of psyche (as self-conscious, and so as speaking about its own apprehension of immortality) would be divine rather than human, or that it would surpass even his present inspired capacity. Instead of an ἀπόδειξις ["demonstration" – ed.], we shall be given an εἰκασία or image (246a5, a6). It would therefore seem to be easier to speak about psyche as a physicist or student of motion than as a psychologist or student of self-consciousness.

The likeness of the psyche to the "combined natural power of a team of winged horses and a winged charioteer" (246a6-7) presents us with a myth within a myth. In studying it, let us bear in mind that its principal function is to illustrate the effect of divine madness, and in that sense, of Eros, within the psyche. The perpetual motion of the horses and charioteer permits them to accomplish their journey to the surface of the domain of genesis, or to be in a *position* to view the hyper-Uranian beings. The structure of this motion, here likened to horses and charioteer, illustrates why the psyche is in a *condition* to view the hyper-Uranian beings. Motion has no eyes, but a charioteer does. The ambiguity of mythical speech is suggested by the fact that charioteers themselves have psyches; if we attempted to correlate each structural component of the likeness with an element in a discursive account of the psyche, we would generate an infinite regress. On the other hand, the ambiguity of myth is no excuse for a failure to attempt to understand it as carefully as possible. The "precision" of our analysis must conform to the nature of the myth. Myth has its own precision: for example, the psyche is here carefully likened to a charioteer and horses, a very specific image which evokes a range of meanings and resonances that some other likeness would not. Again, the terms of the likeness are carefully chosen; by specifying the horses and charioteer, Socrates silently calls our attention to the fact that he does not mention the chariot. Or again, if the charioteer is winged, why does he need horses (and chariot)? If we succumb to the poetic force of the likeness, or take premature refuge in the ambiguity of myth, we shall fail to ask, let alone to answer, questions like these. But in that case, we shall not have understood the myth. Differently stated, the poetic force of the myth is a harmony of its details; unless we grasp the details, we cannot properly be said to respond poetically to the myth. An accurate apprehension of mythic detail is not the same as the de-formation of myth by logos.

The first question that arises from Socrates' myth within a myth is why he chose the image of a charioteer. In my view, the main reason is obvious: it links the psyche to Apollo, the divine charioteer with whom Socrates is associated elsewhere in the dialogues, and thereby with the sun, itself employed in the *Republic* as the image of the good. The goodness of the psyche is evident in its relation to (ability to see) the hyper-Uranian beings. At the same time, the internal articulation of the image enables Socrates to indicate the base element in the psyche, which is divided within and against itself, because of the fact that it is embodied. The difference between the charioteer and the horses could be crudely and preliminarily expressed as the difference between the noetic and the corporeal dimensions of the psyche. The image of horses conveys pride, spiritedness, and desire; the difference between the "gentlemanly" (246b2: καλὸς τε καὶ ἀγαθός) horse and the horse of "opposite" nature corresponds to the two different possibilities of corporeally-oriented life, the pursuit of honor and the pursuit of physical pleasure (253d1 ff.).[26] When the desire for pleasure submits to the "gentlemanly" spiritedness (the two horses are at least partially reminiscent of ἐπιθυμία ["desire" – ed.] and θυμός ["spiritedness" – ed.]) or love of honor, the corporeal or equine psyche is accessible to the control of its noetic element. Finally, Socrates' silence about the chariot raises the strong possibility that it corresponds to the body. If this is indeed the case, it would presumably follow that the personal

26 They are similar to what the concealed lover called the innate desire for pleasure and the acquired opinion by which we aim at the best (237d6-9). Here, however, "opinion" is replaced by nature.

or self-conscious identity of the psyche is dependent upon its embodiment, as I suggested previously when discussing the identity of circularity in a multiplicity of circular motions.

So much for the general choice of the likeness; now let us begin again in a more detailed way. According to Socrates, the charioteer and the horses are connatural or "grown together." This strongly supports the union between personal psyche and the body, since the horses cannot be conceived except in conjunction with corporeal spiritedness and desire. The attribution of wings to horses and charioteer alike will shortly be explained as designating the "care" of psyche altogether for the cosmos altogether. More accurately, it will refer to the care of all *generated* psyches, as distinct from the uncaring because non-winged, but perpetually circular motion of the cosmic psyche. Let us first notice a distinction made by Socrates between psyches of gods, and those of "others" (246a7-b1). Both kinds come from, i.e., are generated by, predecessors or parents (which we may perhaps understand as a reference to the differentiation of cosmic psyche into particular psyches). The horses and charioteers of the divine psyches are altogether good; that is, they do not include a base or sensual horse. This means that the divine psyche is not connected to a body *in the same way* that the "other" (and so human) psyches are, or that their mode of genesis must differ from that of the other kinds of psyche. But the divine psyche is not altogether free from corporeality, as is obvious (and will become crucial later) from the fact that it, too, is a resident of the moving or generated cosmos, the (infra-) Uranian domain of genesis. It too contains the equine component, which, as entirely good, presumably corresponds to noble spiritedness controlled by intelligence. In other words, the divine psyche (despite its wings) does not ascend, or rather does not contribute to its upward motion, by the same kind of force (or vector of the same forces) as the non-divine psyche. Spiritedness replaces Eros in the gods. Divine or cosmic genesis is not erotic generation.

Whereas perpetual or circular motion was previously described as a psychic principle, we now see that there are at least three others: the principles of intelligence, spiritedness, and desire. The psyche would seem to be a composite of principles; the principle of their unification is thus far altogether mysterious or unmentioned. It cannot, as we have already observed, be the unity of circularity, although Socrates seems to imply that this is so. On the other hand, we do know that the principle of desire (the base horse) is the principle of the division between divine and non-divine psyches. It is this principle which makes the task of the principle of intelligence in the human psyche so difficult: our charioteer's task is "hard and troublesome from necessity" (246b4: ἐξ ἀνάγκης). Previously Socrates had spoken of psyche's "ungenerated and deathless" nature as "from necessity" (246a1-2: ἐξ ἀνάγκης). This interesting repetition suggests that the immortality as well as the mortality of psyche are derived from the same ultimate principle. But what is the specific nature of this common necessity? What necessity is common to perpetual motion and the motions of sensual desire, as distinct from the motions of spiritedness and intelligence? I believe that part of the answer is clear: immortality and mortality are opposite and so corollary attributes of non-intellectual or essentially corporeal motion; the first characterizes the circular cosmic motion and the second characterizes bodies generated within the cosmos. What still remains unexplained is the union between corporeal and intellectual motion, or life.

Socrates turns next to a discussion of this very question. At first glance it would seem that, contrary to 246a2 ("enough then about psychic immortality"), he is returning to the account of perpetual motion. But the distinction between mortal and immortal *life* (246b5: θνητόν τε καὶ ἀθάνατον ζῷον) concerns the personal or self-conscious nature of the individual psyche. Socrates begins with the following assertion: "psyche altogether cares for"—i.e., is interested in, and in charge of—"the non-psychic, and goes round all of heaven, being transformed into (γιγνομένην) a variety of forms" (246b6-7).[27] This is not so much an explanation as

27 Robin translates "C'est toujours une âme qui a charge de . . ." But this oversimplifies what seems to be a purposeful echo by Plato of the ambiguous ψυχὴ πᾶσα at 245c5.

an application of the principle by which intellectual and corporeal motions are united. In any case, this much seems clear: the task of tending the cosmos requires the cosmic psyche to be differentiated into forms corresponding to the total and particular aspects of the corporeal world. The perpetuity or circularity of circular motion, we may assume, serves as a bond to hold together the disparate motions of genesis, or to ensure the shape of the cosmos as a whole. No reason is given why this circular or bonding function of psyche should not be regarded as an epiphenomenon of the interaction of disparate motions. It cannot be too strongly emphasized that Socrates does not "explain" the origin of life by deducing it from a higher principle. The significance of the word "cares for" (ἐπιμελεῖται), when applied to "psyche altogether" (ψυχὴ πᾶσα[28] is used at 245c5 and 246b6) or the principle of necessary motion, is therefore radically unclear. To put this difficulty in another way, Socrates here blurs together the necessity of motion and the necessity of the form or nature of psyche as alive and intelligent. "When [psyche] is perfect and winged, it traverses the heavens and manages the whole cosmos, but one whose wings have fallen off is carried along [i.e., by the cosmic motion] until it can get hold of something solid, which it colonizes . . ." (246b7-c3). The possession of wings seems here to be attributed to cosmic psyche, or to what was previously described solely in terms of the perpetuity of its motion. This is to imply that the cosmic psyche possesses self-consciousness or personal identity, by virtue of its cosmic body. But the next phrase in the same sentence ("but one whose wings have fallen off . . .") seems to mean that there is a multiplicity of perfect, winged psyches engaged in the management of the cosmos. I believe that the latter interpretation is the only way to understand this sentence; hence Socrates is now speaking of "psyche altogether" as differentiated into perfect winged psyches (246b7). In other words, "psyche altogether," or the unity of circular or necessary and perpetual motion, does not

---

28 ["all soul" or "every soul"; Rosen translates this ambiguous phrase as "soul altogether" on p. 93 and "psyche altogether" on p. 105 – ed.]

in itself "care for" in the sense of being conscious of the cosmos; it has no wings not because it has lost them, but because only generated psyches have wings. (Note that the loss of wings is not equivalent to the complete loss of "care" or self-consciousness.) The differentiation of psyche altogether, or the emergence of care (or wings) is, once again, not explained. And this remains true even if one objects to my interpretation of 246b6 that it begins "psyche altogether cares for all of the non-psychic" and so must attribute care to cosmic psyche.

We are not told, then, what is the principle of caring or tending, nor how the cosmic psyche differentiates into a multiplicity of winged, but still incorporeal psyches. Finally, we have not yet been told why the wings fall off some of these psyches, causing them to unite with a body (presumably by the combination of their own random motion and the circular motion of the cosmos) to form a living and mortal being (246c2-6). Nor could we be told all these things, whether in myth or logos, unless Socrates were prepared to deduce the principle of conscious life from a "higher" (and non-living) principle.[29] And Socrates now makes explicit his apparent incapacity to provide such a deduction: "The name 'immortal' is not spoken by means of any rational account (οὐδ' ἐξ ἑνὸς λόγου λελογισμένου), but we imagine a god, whom we have neither seen nor adequately intuited (νοήσαντες), as a kind of deathless living being, possessing a psyche and a body, which have been united by nature for all time" (246c6-d2). This passage is subject to two different interpretations. According to the first, which is supported by the categorical nature of the assertion, no one, including Socrates, can provide a logos of immortality. As we have already seen, the "demonstration" of perpetual motion

29 The ontological recipes for the blending of psyche from elements like same, other, rest, motion, and the like, do not constitute the deduction in question. An ontological analysis of the formal structure of psyche is not the same as an explanation of the production of conscious life. Cf. the criticism of Hegel made by Schelling and Kierkegaard.

is a "pointing out" in the sense of a revelation rather than a logos. Now Socrates admits what I previously took pains to establish from the revelation itself; namely, that it cannot serve as a principle for the explanation of living or divine psyche. Differently stated, a logos depends upon a noetic apprehension of determinate form, and an adequate noēsis of psyche is unavailable to us. This says something important about the form of psyche. It is evidently either too complex or too indeterminate to be apprehended in noetic intuition. The present myth is thus a reflexive commentary on the nature of speech about psyche (or gods); we surmise or "divine" something of psychic form, and therefore something of its "formlessness," which prevents us, and always will prevent us, from encompassing it in discursive and determinate speech. In Pascal's words, we are "incapables d'ignorer absolument et de savoir certainement."[30] According to the second interpretation, there may be a logos, and hence a noetic apprehension, of psyche, but "we" have not yet achieved it, and Socrates' myth has as one of its purposes the preparation of our own psyches for this act of self-comprehension.[31] Such an interpretation would be preferable to those who claim that Plato regarded the psyche as a number, or who accept the recipes of mathematical ontology as an adequate account of the psychic Idea. I personally believe that the first interpretation is correct, both with respect to the Platonic teaching altogether, and the *Phaedrus* in particular. Within the *Phaedrus*, in any case, we are never given a logos of psyche, and are told that none is possible. The matter must rest with the pleasure of god (246d2-3).

Socrates turns next to the reason why some psyches lose their wings. The nature of the wing is to draw upward what is heavy to the heavenly region inhabited by the gods, and "somehow (πῃ) it

---

30 *Pensées* (ed. J. Chevalier, *Bibliotheque de la Pléiade*, Paris, 1954), no. 261, p. 1207. The phrase is preceded by the following words: "nous sentons une image de la vérité, et ne possédons que le mensonge." To the extent that myth is poetry rather than logos, it is a lie.
31 Cf. *Timaeus* 53d6-7.

shares most of all bodily [parts] in the divine, which is noble, wise, good, and everything of this kind" (246d6-9).[32] This suggests that the non-winged part of the psyche is most corporeal; that is, it lacks the divine attribute of self-consciousness, but consists entirely of the circular motion characterizing the corporeal or visible cosmos. But it also makes clear that the wing, even as sharing in the divine, is corporeal as well. Taking the present analogy together with our previous observations on the ambiguous differentiating process of cosmic psyche, the result would seem to be this: there are three kinds of "bodies" in the cosmos; first, the visible cosmos itself; second, the cosmic (and pre-conscious) psyche (which is analogous to the non-winged part of the body); third, the winged part of psyche, which stands for self-consciousness and care, hence for individuality. The "upward motion" characteristic of wings is thus different from the perpetual circular motion of cosmic psyche. Without anticipating future developments, we cannot fail to note that this "upward motion" is reminiscent of Eros as described in the *Symposium*. Perhaps it may be understood as a reminiscence of the previously divine condition, and a consequent striving to recapture it. If so, the *Phaedrus* would unite the doctrine of recollection and the acquisition of immortality, a union absent from the *Symposium*. Finally, we may observe that, on this hypothesis, there are two species of caring; the first or winged is divine in the full sense of governing the cosmos, whereas the second is divine in a secondary sense, or marked by the Eros for divinity. Again, the present myth offers an explanation for the variety of erotic appetites, but also for the possibility of the transformation of Eros into philosophy, that is, of one kind of caring into another.

32 Mss. B and T read κεκοινώνηκε δέ πη μάλιστα τῶν περὶ τὸ σῶμα τοῦ θείου ψυχή ["of the bodily things, the soul in a way shares most of all in the divine…" – ed.] . . . This would rather abruptly identify psyche as corporeal; the usual interpretation is to follow Plutarch in omitting ψυχή and to take ἡ πτεροῦ δύναμις as the subject. I am half-inclined to believe that the mss. are correct; Plato frequently gives us a clue to his more complex teaching by unexpected and apparently contradictory remarks. However, virtually the same results are reached by following Plutarch and working out the strands of the image.

The gods, then, and the divine psyche, whether cosmic or winged, all dwell *within* the cosmos, or are marked by corporeality, and hence by motion and time. It is therefore evident that an immortality based upon or rather simply equivalent to perpetual motion is, in itself, empty of human significance; further, there is a difference between the *eternal* motion of circularity, and eternity itself.[33] To move forever and unconsciously in a circle would seem more like a satire on, than an achievement of, immortality, and even more so if we are conscious of the farce. A satisfactory form of immortality cannot be an eternal imitation of eternity, but must rather be a genuine acquisition of, or conscious identification with, eternity. It should also be evident that there is something radically wrong in speaking of an eternal apprehension of eternity. Eternity is by definition atemporal, whereas consciousness that one is thinking, i.e., noetically apprehending, eternity, is a motion, circular or otherwise, dependent upon the personal identity bestowed by corporeality, and therefore temporal, or "a moving image of eternity." If the presence of circular motion within the individual psyche also characterizes (or contributes to the characterization of) the relationship between psyche and eternity as represented by the hyper-Uranian beings, this relationship would seem to be that of imitation. On the other hand, the corporeal nature of the wing, both as dwelling within the cosmos and as capable of lifting the heavy part of the psyche, suggests that the upward striving of the individual psyche toward eternity can never be unconditionally successful. In sum, the motions of the psyche, whether circular or ascending, can be at best instrumental to personal immortality in the sense of apprehension of, and thus identification with, eternity. Perpetual motion is therefore equally irrelevant to the essential nature of personal immortality. Perpetuity of the kind desired cannot be the same as perpetual duration, which is the temporal imitation of eternity; instead, it must be an escape from temporality altogether, and, as such, not moving or measurable.

33 I owe this formulation to Alexandre Kojève.

The divine nature, to repeat, is called "beautiful, wise, good, and everything of that kind." That is, the gods are themselves self-conscious or personal psyches, or subject to the same (or similar) corporeal bonds as men. This is also evident from the fact that the wing raises psyche to the cosmic domain of the gods; this domain is the "highest" part of, but still within, the cosmos. The psyche's wings are "nourished and augmented" (246e2) by the divine attributes just mentioned; again, they display motions characteristic of corporeal genesis. Socrates adds that they shrink and are destroyed by the "ugly and evil and the opposites [to the other divine qualities]" (246e3-4). It is curious that he does not explicitly mention "by foolishness" to balance "wise" in 246e1. Are we to infer that a psyche which is foolish, but beautiful and good, does not suffer from stunted growth and destruction? But this conjecture in passing. In addition, to be nourished, although contrary to destruction, is not the same as to be immortal. Whereas the reverse of divine attributes may destroy the psyche, it is not (so far as this passage is concerned) rendered immortal by their presence. I suspect this may mean that the immortal or circular (i.e., cosmic) psyche is neither divine nor the reverse, because it is not self-conscious. We are concerned here with the personal or Olympian gods, namely, those of the Greek (and specifically Athenian) city, which, incidentally, may account for the emphasis upon the political attributes of beauty and goodness: the "beautiful and good" psyche is that of the Athenian gentleman. The attribute of "caring for," now given an explicitly political signification, is again seen to be discontinuous with perpetual or circular motion. The previous differentiation of cosmic psyche is now identified with the Olympians, led by Zeus and his winged team, "who orders and cares for everything" (246e5-6).

Following and subordinate to Zeus are eleven companies of gods and daimons, the latter mentioned here for the first time in the myth (246e6-247a1). We must infer from this that the daimonic element is not present in the hegemonic psyche of Zeus, or that cosmic care (=government, order) is not erotic, at least in its principle, in the terms of the *Symposium* (which differ, we recall, from those of the *Phaedrus*). Socrates then says that "Hestia remains alone in the house of the gods" (247a1-2), whereas the rest of the twelve ruling gods follow Zeus in hierarchical order. If this is a reference to the scene on the east frieze of the Parthenon, then Socrates may be implying that Dionysus replaces Hestia in the heavenly processional.[34] The indirect allusion to Dionysus would then be a sober indication of the presence, within the dimension of care, of the principle of divine madness. The divine processional also seems to have astronomical resonance, but in a general rather than a particular sense.[35] The visible cosmos is governed altogether (and so circumscribed) by Zeus, leading his choir of gods and daimons in a motion which seems to mediate between the cosmological (or circular) and the psychic (or human). This motion seems to be distinguished from those of the gods in their passages or orbits within the heaven, on which each revolves, each doing his own work (πράττων ἕκαστος αὐτῶν τὸ αὑτοῦ: heavenly "justice"), and followed by whoever always wants and is able to do so (247a4-7). The "work" of the gods is evidently to care for the infra-Uranian motions of the cosmos, which are also circular, or correspond (approximately) to the strata or structural zones of the visible cosmos. Just as does Zeus for the whole, so the subordinate gods and daimons attach human significance to the various aspects of heavenly motion. Philosophical physics, it would seem, requires the integration of cosmological and politico-religious motions; hence its mythical form. Those who always want and are able to follow the gods, i.e., to perceive the psychic significance of corporeal motions, are the philosophers. By so doing, they join the divine choir, and are removed from the human domain of envy (247a7). The divine is in principle visible or common to all, like the light of the sun; one can "possess" the divine without trespassing upon the possession of the same vision by others who desire and are capable of it. Similarly, one takes nothing from the gods by viewing them; hence they are

---

34   Hackforth, p. 73.
35   Cf. Robin's note to 247a.

themselves not jealous of mortals who seek to know their motions.

Now Socrates seems to distinguish a third kind of divine motion: feasting and banqueting (247a8 ff.).[36] This motion differs from those by which each separately does his work; it collects the gods and raises them upward to the peak of the heavenly arch. Leisure is higher than work, although for the non-divine psyches, the ascent from work to leisure is excessively arduous (247b1-5). That is: it is easier for the human psyche to accompany the gods on their cosmic tasks of ordering the visible heavens than it is to ascend to the roof of the cosmos for a vision of the hyper-Uranian beings (247b5-c2). It is by seeing these that the gods are themselves nourished (cf. 247d1 ff.), and it is by following the gods upward that "the psyches called immortal" obtain the vision from which, as we may now assert, their name is derived. Philosophy or what is called immortality depends upon looking upward, first at the visible heavens, then at the gods, and finally, beyond the cosmos or genesis itself. The psyches, like the gods, attain to the highest position upon the back of the world, but thereby remain rooted within genesis, and share in its circular motion. Theory is thus presented in this myth as a kind of kinetic vision by which man achieves his highest perfection, but which at the same time is the boundary of life itself, or the mark of human limitation.

V.

We have now reached the dramatic peak of Socrates' palinode, and therefore of the dialogue itself: the vision of hyper-Uranian being. The image of a peak is especially appropriate here, not merely because of the allusion to height, but with respect to the difficulty of standing on a narrow and pointed surface. Just as Diotima devoted thirteen lines to the (largely negative) description

36 In the *Phaedrus*, there is a silent banquet of gods; in the *Symposium* there are human and divine banquets, and again, only the humans are depicted as speaking. The *Phaedrus* omits human banqueting.

of beauty itself (*Symposium* 211a1-b5), so Socrates allows no more than thirteen lines to his account of hyper-Uranian beings (247c6-e3). He prefaces this account with a solemnity equal to that with which Diotima informed him of the final revelation. In fact, Socrates indicates that the present myth, despite its conciseness, is superior to the revelation of Diotima. No previous poet has ever hymned the place beyond the heavens, nor will any be able to do it justice. "But one must dare to speak the truth, especially when speaking about truth" (247c3-6). To mention only the decisive point, it is here, and not in the *Symposium*, that we learn of the hyper-Uranian status of beauty itself. Again, it is in the *Phaedrus* rather than in the *Symposium* that we are given a poetic account of the psyche's nature or capacity to perceive such a being. The peak of the *Symposium* is thus, as it were, the prophecy of a prophecy; the dialogue does not in fact present us with a coherent and stable interpretation of Eros, who is himself incoherent and unstable.

If we take together the two dialogues, *Phaedrus* and *Symposium*, devoted to Eros, it is obvious that they tell us next to nothing about the so-called "theory of Ideas." In fact, there is no reference to such a "theory" in the modern sense of a systematic and determinate logos, and, although the words εἶδος and ἰδέα occur in the discussion, they are never given a technical definition, and with one possible exception (249b7), not used to stand directly for "Idea," whether in the sense of immanent or hyper-Uranian "real being." Interpreters therefore tend to follow one of two different procedures, and sometimes both. Either they read into these very brief passages the apparent teaching of the *Republic* on the extra-ontic nature of the good,[37] along with the doctrine of "separate" Ideas in the *Phaedo*, or they assume that the eidetic kinds of the method of diaeresis are identical with what Socrates here calls "hyper-Uranian beings." In either case, a doctrine not supported by the texts in question is illicitly employed in the analysis and

---

37 For an analysis of the relevant passage in the *Republic*, see Rosen (*Nihilism*), Chapter Five.

interpretation of those texts. The possible exception to which I just referred, in which Socrates seems to identify the hyper-Uranian beings and the forms of diaeresis, serves as the basis for a fundamental objection against the practice of conflation in question. For if the forms or kinds of diaeresis are identical with the "Ideas" in the sense of hyper-Uranian beings, then either the former are hyper-Uranian or the latter are not; and the same holds true, obviously, if we employ the diaeretic forms of the *Sophist*, *Statesman*, or *Philebus*. Since by any standards of interpretation it makes no sense to begin with a denial of the evidence, we cannot deny that the hyper-Uranian beings are indeed hyper-Uranian. This is normally or traditionally taken to mean "separated" in the sense for which Aristotle criticizes the Platonic teaching of Ideas. If the diaeretic forms are also hyper-Uranian, then they too must be separated. There is no evidence to support this conclusion in the dialogues, and scholars have tried to avoid it by positing a theory of historical development, according to which Plato moved from a belief in separate Ideas to the later interpretation of Ideas as logical or linguistic entities (to give the most popular contemporary view). This hypothesis, however, tells us nothing about the ostensibly separate Ideas of Plato's "middle" period, nor does it rule out the possibility that logical entities must themselves have separate forms. It tells us nothing about the meaning of "separate," which is another way of saying that passages like the one under discussion have never been subjected to exhaustive analysis in their own terms and in their own context, despite the plethora of "logical" analyses which have mushroomed in recent Plato scholarship.

The "analysts" have then for the most part been analyzing the forms of diaeresis. Our question is somewhat different. In the *Phaedrus*, we have both hyper-Uranian or (ostensibly) "separate" beings or Ideas, and diaeretic kinds. The prevailing view, and especially among the "analysts" (who have immodestly pre-empted that term to designate a contemporary form of linguistic nominalism), is that these two kinds differ, and represent two different stages of Plato's development. Yet we have both kinds in the

Phaedrus, which is officially classified as a "middle" or "separationist" dialogue. Second, the statement at 249b6-c4 seems to identify both kinds, and so to make both kinds unintelligible. It is an encumbrance, not merely to theses of two (or more) stages in Plato's thought, but to my own interpretation as well, as I am about to make evident. I cannot, however, give what I believe to be the correct analysis of this statement without presenting in some detail my interpretation of the hyper-Uranian beings. And in doing that, I shall indicate, as concisely and as precisely as possible, how I understand the relationship between the two kinds of form. This will serve, then, not merely as an exposition of 247c6-e3 (along with 249b6-c4), but as a preface to the discussion of diaeresis in the last third of the dialogue. Let me emphasize, however, that the main thrust of what follows is intended as commentary on the *Phaedrus*. Detailed studies of the *Sophist*, *Statesman* and *Philebus* (to say nothing of other dialogues) would be needed before one could competently offer a general interpretation of Plato's teaching of form. In a matter of such difficulty, it is senseless to be impatient.

I therefore take my bearings by the text, and in the following manner. The outstanding characteristic of the psyche's discarnate ascent to the roof of the cosmos is its *silence*. If we employ the usual Platonic terminology, the noetic apprehension of hyper-Uranian beings is synoptic and instantaneous, whereas the *recollection* of this synopsis, or the dianoetic classification of specific kinds by diaeresis, proceeds discursively and temporally; that is, by a division and collection which is a sorting out and re-assembling of what has been "previously" apprehended and is not itself the result of diaeresis. (This, by the way, is the key to my interpretation of 249b6-c4.) Let me state this more precisely. What Socrates calls "recollection" has two components; the first is the synoptic apprehension of noetic form, or the monadic unity which underlies our perception (sensuous or mental) of every determinate entity. This step takes place *in silence*. The second step amounts to the discursive attempt to talk about the noetically apprehended formal monad, which issues in the kinds of diaeresis, but not in a determinate description and definition of the noetic monad itself. I use the term *noetic monad* to replace the term "separate Idea." The noetic monad is separate in the specific sense that it is not accessible to discursive analysis of a determinate character, whether logical or ontological. I shall call them the ontological subjects of formal discourse, with the proviso that discourse is not "about" them, since they are always noetically prior to any statements of formal structure. The form of diaeresis is the formal or logical subject of discourse, but this discourse would be impossible if there were no ontological subjects.

In order to illustrate this bare statement, let us take the geometrical triangle as an example. Let N_t = the noetic monad "triangle" and further let D_t = the discursive analysis of triangular form. The difference between the two can be illustrated rather easily.[38] If I ask "what does Δ symbolize?" the answer is "a triangle." The picture is said to be a symbol of the "real thing," that is, literally, a token of identity or receipt for the real triangle. But Δ is in fact not just a token or receipt for a triangle; it *is* a triangle (in the way that 𓀀, a symbol for "man," is not itself a man). We normally try to express this by distinguishing between the sign and the referent; but the inked hieroglyph Δ functions as a sign by manifesting directly what it de-*sign*-ates. Thus if I ask, "what does 'triangle' symbolize?" the answer may be D_{t_k} or "a Δ" or something of the sort (where D_{t_k} stands for any one of several possible discursive definitions). The verbal sign "triangle" indeed refers to, and in this sense is a token or receipt for, Δ. Unfortunately, triangles come in a variety of forms: e.g., $\triangle \Delta \triangle$. If I now ask, "what have these symbols in common?" the answer is not D_{t_k}, because D_{t_k} is a symbol for Δ, etc., and not vice versa. In order to "see the point" or relevance of D_{t_k}, I have to

---

38 I have purposely chosen a geometrical figure for my illustration because such figures have special properties which make the point with unusual clarity. In my general formulation of the distinction between noetic and dianoetic form, I will not be restricted to geometrical form.

see first *what* D_{t_k} is pointing at. It is not pointing at this Δ or that Δ, nor $D_{t_{k+1}}$, but at N_t.

D_t "divides and collects" or articulates, and so separates, what in N_t is seamless. In N_t, the internal articulations of the form are not separate from each other, nor are they connected by symbols. The best illustration of what this difference means is to see that N_t is what it is, hence can give rise to no logical paradoxes arising from the symbolism in which D_t is expressed. What I am here (given the limitations of human speech) representing by N_t is not a symbol, nor a concatenation of symbols or linguistic expressions, but triangularity, or the form of (any) triangle. It is a principle of logic that contradictions are in words or strings of words, and not in things. If we make forms equal to linguistic or symbolic expressions, then there is no way at all to prevent them from embodying paradoxes, and things will literally fall apart; anything will then be sayable about anything, which is the same as silence. Even with a theory of types, we must terminate in form which is not linguistic or symbolic, and this form is noetic rather than discursive. To return to our example, there is just one N_t, but an unending series $D_{t_1}, D_{t_2}, ..., D_{t_n}$ (since none is or can be complete; for, as *complete*, it would cease to be discursive, but would be seamless, a unified manifold like triangularity itself). Thus one can call D_{t_k} a "logical construction," provided one remembers that the structure of that construction has an ontological subject (N_t) which is not a linguistic construction. Paradoxes of reflexivity (like the third man paradox, or the paradox of self-predication) arise when we try to specify the structure of D_{t_k} by means of another logico-linguistic construction, without realizing the difference between D_{t_k} and N_t. We are, in other words, seduced by our own notation (and therefore, by our ontological presuppositions, which gave rise to the notation).

To continue this illustration, let me indicate how it is that reflexivity paradoxes arise. Let D_{t_k} again be a discursive account of triangularity, and L_{t_k} a linguistic construction of the form of D_{t_k}. Then these questions arise: *First*: what is the relation between D_{t_k} and L_{t_k}? By hypothesis, we do not know that they are "related" by N_t, which we mistakenly assume is D_{t_k}. So we generate Φ_{t_k} or the "form" common to D_{t_k} and L_{t_k}. But Φ_{t_k} must have a "form" common with D_{t_k} and L_{t_k}, and so on, *ad infinitum*. *Second*: we ask "is the Idea of the triangle itself triangular?" But this, precisely on the thesis of logical constructionism, is like asking "does a string of logical symbols have itself the form it symbolizes?" If the answer is "yes," then symbolization is impossible. For let $D_{t_k} = T(a_1+a_2+...+a_n)$ where a_k is a symbolic representation of a property of triangularity. But $T(a_1+a_2+...+a_n)$ is manifestly not Δ in its form. If we inspect our illustrative shapes $\triangle$, Δ, $\triangle$ and try to say what they have in common, while letting $D_{t_k} =$ what we say, since D_{t_k} does not look like $\triangle$ Δ $\triangle$ it is meaningless to attribute triangularity to it, or to say that it manifests (=means) triangularity in a sense which "means what it says" or directly exhibits the form it bespeaks.

But this shows the difference between N_t and D_{t_k}. N_t is *what* (τί ἐστι) we noetically apprehend in looking at $\triangle\Delta\triangle$. Our visual language is somewhat misleading here; we ask, "does Δ look like $\triangle$?" But in looking at Δ and $\triangle$ we cannot visually see that they look alike unless we *first* apprehend N_t. Whereas whatever we *say* about N_t is always D_{t_k}. So the question "is the Idea of the triangle itself triangular?" requires some analysis. (1) Yes, the Idea of the triangle is triangular if "triangular" is an adjective symbolizing the apprehension of N_t. Similarly, the number "two" is dual, "oranges" are orangeish, etc. No paradoxes arise, but nothing is accomplished by posing the question in this sense; it is like a return to the most foolish aspects of medieval scholasticism. (2) No, the Idea of the triangle is not triangular if "triangular" means "has the geometric shape of a triangle." Because then the Idea of the triangle would look like Δ or $\triangle$ or $\triangle$, or what have you. That is, it would *be a triangle*, and not the form, whether understood as D_{t_k} or as N_t. In sum, N_t is the noetic monad and the ontological subject of D_{t_k}. But this can't be symbolized "N_t is D_{t_k}" because *it isn't*. Both $D_{t_k} = N_t$ and $D_{t_k} \in N_t$ are false. So far as discourse is concerned, N_t is a "blank symbol," which, it must be remembered, is not the same as the noetic monad it symbolizes. The noetic monad contains no logical or linguistic articulation, but only noetic articulation, by which we are enabled to discriminate between N_t and each other N.

So much for my introductory illustration of what I mean by "noetic monad." With this in mind, we can proceed to a general statement of the problem of hyper-Uranian beings. In order to talk about form, we must have something to talk about, whether this "something" be a separate Idea or the logical structure of discourse. If form is created by the act of speech itself, then we can literally say anything we wish, and therefore it becomes finally impossible to make a distinction between form and formlessness. In Platonic language, rational discourse depends upon a distinction within speech itself between genesis and *ousia*. But the *ousia* of a speech is not the same as a speech about that *ousia*. We make the distinction in speech, and so are committed to verbal symbolism for both dimensions, but the distinction is not itself merely verbal. Bearing in mind the previously discussed limitations of a symbolic notation, we may try to put the point once more as follows. If F is the form of proposition p, then the statement F' of form F must be formally identical with p, in which case F, as common to F' and p, is distinguishable from both utterances. Now F is not simply unspeakable, at least to the extent that we are talking about or referring to it, if only to show how nothing determinate can be said of it. But we must have seen F in p, in order to have uttered F'. F is not created *ex nihilo* by the logician. If we ask him for the form of p, he says "let me take a look," or words to that effect. The "look" which he takes, if it is successful, results in F', and we decide upon the success of that look by ourselves looking at F' and p. If the logician asks us, "what do you see?" we reply "F'" (or perhaps "F'''"), but whatever we say, what we have seen (if we see what the logician saw) is F.

The F which we and the logician see is the same in both cases. Even though we see it *after* the logician, namely, after he points it out to us discursively (whether with symbols and gestures alone, or with discursive interpretations in a natural language of his symbols and gestures), it would be senseless to say that we saw two different, temporal F's, or the same F moving around in time. For again, let F' and F" represent our respective assertions, whether to ourselves or to each other, of our apprehension of F. Granted that F' occurs at time T' and F" at time T", it makes no sense to say that F occurs at time T. The occurrence of F is identical with F itself; that is, F *presents itself* in a given temporal present, but its self-presentation is identical in any temporal present, and therefore distinguishable from each. The being of F, as an *ousia* (247c7: οὐσία ὄντως οὖσα), is *presence*, but not in the sense of temporal transience. No time T_n recurs, but the presence of F does. F' and F", seen respectively at times T' and T", exhibit or present an identical form F, which cannot be obtained as an equivalent to the sum of its temporal appearances, except in the sense that the "sum," or what the appearances share, is their "sum and substance," and so logically prior to any of them. F may be said to be hyper-Uranian in this specific sense. Whatever is infra-Uranian is temporal, or an instance of genesis, whereas F is neither temporal nor generated. On the other hand, "hyper-Uranian" cannot mean "separated" in the sense of "having nothing whatsoever to do with," since F appears, or presents itself, within F', which is itself infra-Uranian.

The visibility of F within F' is thus the paradigm for understanding the visibility of the hyper-Uranian beings, by what I have called "noetic apprehension," to the psyches capable of reaching, and therefore looking beyond while at the same time firmly rooted in, the heavens or cosmos. But the virtue of the paradigm (if it has any) is unfortunately also a defect. The force of the paradigm lies in its reference to the act of vision, through the use of determinate and discursive logical or symbolic notation. But Socrates asserts that the hyper-Uranian beings, although visible to mind alone, are "colorless, shapeless, and untouchable" (247c6-7), and the psyche, in apprehending them, is altogether silent. In other words, although we must physically perceive proposition *p* in order to assert the again physical (=infra-Uranian) statement F', our capacity to do this is dependent upon a nonphysical perception of F. *But everything we say about F is an*

infra-Uranian or discursive apprehension of it. Since F′ is the manifestation of the presence of F, it is not quite true that F is simply
unspeakable. And yet, talking about F is manifestly not the same
as noetically apprehending F. All talk about F (if it reaches a sufficient degree of complexity) seems to terminate in contradiction,
which is not true of the noetic apprehension of F. As I have emphasized, our symbol F is itself actually F′, and F′ is actually F″,
ad infinitum. We seem to arrive at the following paradox. We cannot say F′ unless we have seen F, but whenever we say anything
about F (including F′), we are no longer saying what we see.
Every assertion about F is an assertion about F′, and so apparently
discourse about logical form is in fact discourse about discourse,
or *meta-language.*

If we cannot apprehend F, then we cannot say F′. But whatever we say about our apprehension of F is not about our apprehension of, but about our vision of F′. This I take to be the
consequence of the distinction between noēsis and dianoia. And
we can make another inference here. Let us assume that diaeresis
is based upon a "recollection" of our discarnate apprehension of
F (as Socrates seems to say at 249b6 ff.). The recollection of this
apprehension as noetic or logically prior to diaeresis, must be formally the same as that apprehension. If it is F itself that we recollect, then noetic apprehension is possible for the incarnate as well
as for the discarnate psyche. But even further, the series of discursive divisions and collections which we are stimulated to
make by our re-apprehension of F, is not an exhibition of the
structure of F, but of some form F′. *The kinds or species of diaeresis
cannot possibly be identical with the hyper-Uranian F's.* They cannot
be formally distinct from those F's, since then they would not be
of the form F′, but of some other form, say non-F′. They cannot
be formally similar to or resemblances of F, since then the paradox
of the third man would ensue, namely, that F and F′ could be similar only by virtue of sharing a third form Φ and so on. There remains the possibility that F and F′ are not ontologically, but
nevertheless formally, identical. In other words, all form-statements are primed-statements (=F′), even those expressing the

structure common to form-statements of a given kind. But the kind exhibits the presence of a form (=F) which is not itself merely a statement. All primed-statements constituting F′ are then indeed "about" F, in the sense that F′ is formally identical with, or manifests the presence of, F. But they are *not* "about" F in the sense of producing its presence. F must *be*, prior to any of its manifestations, and we must apprehend F pre-discursively prior to manifesting its presence discursively. This, in essence, is what I take to be the logical sense of Socrates' mythic account of the psyche's silent ascent toward, and vision of, F.

In summary, if there is a "theory" of Ideas, in the sense of hyper-Uranian beings, it is not and cannot be a determinate, systematic analysis of their ontological status and logical shape. Every such theory about the Ideas is in fact a theory about the kinds with which diaeresis is employed. Such theories usually explain Ideas as numbers, separate or "real" universals, *a priori* concepts, or finally, as logical subjects or predicates. It is, unfortunately, easy to see that none of these can possibly account for Ideas in the indicated sense. It will be worth our while to examine briefly each of these suggested paradigms. To begin with, the account of Ideas as numbers or as quasi-numerical entities amounts to the substitution, except in the case of numbers themselves, of one form for another, or a part for the whole. Ideas may well have numerical properties, but the forms of non-numerical things are not visible as numbers. The "whatness" of a horse, for example, is not present, not sensuously apprehensible, as a number or ratio of numbers; and so, the difference between a man and a horse is not visible as the difference between two numerical ratios. Even if it should be possible to designate every Idea in a formula consisting of numbers and/or logical signs, the resultant formula would not show us the "look" of a man or a horse, but rather the numerical or logical formula *corresponding to* the form or look. The question would then arise as to the similarity between the formula and the form, and this question could not be answered either by pointing to a man or a horse, or by uttering another formula. The answer would have to be contained in a meta-formulaic discourse, which is a horse of another form, if I may be pardoned the pun.

In the same connection, efforts to account for participation, whether of things in Ideas, or of Ideas in each other, by a mathematical paradigm, will also fail. Let us take as an example the Idea of animal, and divide it as follows:

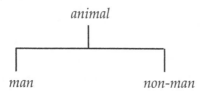

If "man" is contained in "animal" as one number is contained in another, there is a hierarchy of Idea-numbers, terminating in the number corresponding to the whole. This number has traditionally been designated as 1 (or as the One). But the following difficulties (at least) arise. If 1 stands for the entire noetic domain, it seems to be equivalent to the Parmenidean monad. That is, 1 is not visible as the sum of all numbers, but at best as the unit, through the multiplication (and not the division) of which all other integers are generated. The division of 1 would seem to generate, not separate eidetic monads, but *fractions* of Ideas. Thus, e.g., ¼ is not formally analogous to 4; granted that 4 (which, let us say, stands for "horse") contains 3, 2, and 1 (let us say "mammal," "animal," and "being") ¼ does not contain ⅓, ½, and 1/1.

But putting this to one side, the more serious question is how to multiply *or* divide the noetic domain 1. The traditional answer again is: by the *aoristas dyas* or indeterminate dyad. However, the dyad must itself be, or else be an instance of, the Idea 2, both as dyadic, and as second to 1. In this case, 2 is both outside and inside 1, *prior to division*. If on the other hand we say that the monad and the dyad are not numbers but the principles of numbers, then the Idea-numbers must be generated from non-numerical constituents, which violates the requirement that they be ungenerated, or irreducible to elements other than what they themselves are. But even assuming that we could generate Idea-numbers from the monad and dyad, the results would still be unsatisfactory. For first, granted that 4 contains 3, 2, and 1, "horse" does not contain the classes "mammal," "animal," and "being," but is contained in them. And second, granted that 4 contains 3, 2, and 1, how do we explain the *difference* between 4 as an eidetic unit, and 3, 2, 1? Surely the formal property of 4 is not exhaustively described by the phrase "contains 3, 2, and 1" (which is, incidentally, a phrase and not a number). For example, 4 contains two 2's; and again, "contain" is quite ambiguous, since, e.g., the sum of 3, 2, and 1 is 6, not 4. I might summarize these objections, which are meant to be representative rather than exhaustive, as follows: if the entire noetic domain is 1 or the monad, then it cannot be divided. But if it is not 1 or the monad, then it is divided *ab initio*, and cannot be united.

I can be very brief with respect to the thesis that Ideas are separate universals. To begin with, an Idea, as a specific kind, e.g., the Idea of horse, is necessarily a particular; namely, this kind rather than any other; F and not non-F. If universals were separate from their particulars, then the Idea-horse H would have to be separate from itself, and so yield H', which would then be similar to H, thereby generating the paradox of the third man. If it is objected that the particularity of a universal is not the same as the particularity of its instances, I reply that this is true ontologically but not formally. If h is an instance of the universal H, then by definition the form of h is H. Therefore the formal separation of H from h would entail separation from itself. Secondly and more generally, Aristotle's criticisms of the doctrine of separate form are in principle surely sound. If H is the form of h, it must be in h, and not somewhere else. But from the presence of H in h, it does not follow that we can speak directly of, i.e., bespeak, H, as we have seen previously.

This brings me to the thesis that Ideas are *a priori* concepts. Unfortunately, the thesis or paradigm is itself almost as ambiguous as what it purports to explain. We have to distinguish between "concept" in the sense of a conception by and in a thinking mind, and "concept" in the sense of noetic entity;

namely, one whose nature is to be conceivable, but which is what it is regardless of whether anyone is conceiving it. I believe there can be no doubt that the former is *not* what Plato means by "Idea." His Ideas are not thoughts, but "what" we actually (οὐσία ὄντως οὖσα) think about. As beyond the cosmos, the Ideas or hyper-Uranian beings could not be circumscribed "in" any mind, not even the mind of the cosmic psyche of the *Timaeus*. But "concept" in the sense of noetic entity is not substantially easier to understand. To conceive of F is to have it in one's mind (even if in the indirect sense that the thoughts of Aristotle's active intellect are accessible to the individual mortal). The image of the *Phaedrus*, on the contrary, is one of looking at something which is external to the mind of the individual psyche. Note, incidentally, that the externality of the hyper-Uranian being to the individual mind is not the same as the externality of a form to the instance of that form. In thinking the form of a horse, I do not mentally become the form, since then my mind would be a horse, formally if not ontologically. But if h is ontologically a horse, then it is formally H, i.e., formally a horse as well. Thinking is impossible if there is not some difference between mind and the forms which mind thinks. But "being" would be impossible if there were a difference between the form of an instance and the form which that instance instantiates. Hence the difference between an instance f and the form or Idea F cannot be explained formally.

This raises the last thesis to be examined here, which claims that Ideas are logical subjects or predicates; more simply, logical forms. Now I have already shown that they cannot be logical forms in the sense of formulaic (symbolic) expressions, separate universals, or *a priori* concepts. The only remaining possibility, so far as I can see, is that they are linguistic expressions, or discursive, immanent, particular and *a posteriori* meaning-expressions. In this case, however, we simply reject from the outset the notion of Ideas as hyper-Uranian beings. Ideas then become forms of speech, rather than forms of things. I am not going to submit this thesis to detailed analysis because it is not, and has never been taken to be, the teaching of the *Phaedrus*. However, for the sake of completeness, and because many have supposed Plato to be on the verge of such a teaching, if not actually to have stated it in the later dialogues, I will indicate its fundamental defect.[39] If logical forms are linguistic expressions, then either each such expression has a form, i.e., exhibits itself as a specific, self-identical form, or it does not. If it does not, then logical forms are formally indistinguishable from each other, or indeed forms "in name only." If it does, then either one can distinguish between the linguistic expression as the conveyer of the form, and the form itself, or one cannot. If one cannot, then the assertion F' is indistinguishable from the form F, which means that F, as an assertion, namely F', may be contradicted, or said to be non-F', with no standard accessible for distinguishing between the validity or appropriateness of F' or non-F' that is not itself an assertion, and so itself contradictable, *ad infinitum*. But if one can distinguish between the linguistic expression as the conveyer of the form, and the form itself, then either we generate an infinite regress (namely, if the form distinguished is itself a linguistic expression), or else form is not a linguistic expression. This is all that I believe needs to be said in the present context.

Now let me summarize everything that has been said thus far by restating in somewhat different terms why there can be no discursive theory of Ideas in the contemporary systematic, logical sense of the term. The reader should of course bear in mind that I am not saying "there are no Ideas." Instead, I am saying what Ideas are not, or if you prefer, what cannot be said about Ideas. Each Idea, in order to be self-identical and other than every other Idea, must possess a determinate structure as well as a unity. Let us call this unified manifold an internally articulated monad. If the monads were not internally articulated, then they would be noetic points, or indistinguishable from each other, and so, as noetic, lacking even spatio-temporal location. There would be one noetic monad, or rather, so far as any possible apprehension of or

---

39 For a detailed criticism of the thesis, cf. Rosen ("Mean").

speech about it is concerned, there would be none.[40] Since, however, the monads possess structure, or are internally articulated, they must have parts; and these parts must themselves be eidetic. If these parts are atomic, they must themselves be intelligible or not. If they are not intelligible, then the noetic monad has a structure consisting of unintelligible elements, and so, must be either unintelligible or other than its elements. If it is unintelligible, then nothing can be said about it; but if it is other than its elements, then form must be other than itself, which as we have already seen, is impossible or at least unintelligible and unspeakable. I therefore conclude that the parts are intelligible. But here we must be careful to draw the following distinction.

There is a difference between "intelligible" in the sense of "noetically apprehensible" and in the sense of "dianoetically (=discursively) comprehensible," literally, circumscribable, delimitable, definable. Let us first concern ourselves with the latter, which I shall call simply "discursive intelligibility." I argue that atomic elements of noetic monads are discursively unintelligible.[41] For each element, in order to be discursively intelligible, must be distinguishable from every other element, e.g., element e_1 of noetic monad M_1. But how can this be so, how can e_1 be distinguished from e_2, or more specifically, how can we distinguish M_1e_1 from M_2e_1 unless every e is itself internally articulated, and thereby possesses eidetic parts? This, however, leads to an infinite regress, and so, to the impossibility of determinately circumscribing or defining M_k from M_{k+1}. Notice that, even if there are certain elements common to every M, these common elements cannot be distinguished, either from each other or from non-common elements, unless they possess internally articulated structure, which cannot in each case be simply equivalent to the sum of common elements without reducing the common elements to

---

40 The formulation in this paragraph owes much to conversations with my late teacher, Alexandre Kojève, in 1960.

41 With this discussion, cf. the treatment of letters and syllables in the *Theaetetus* and elsewhere.

one element possessing unique, and therefore discursively unintelligible structure. Hence the structures of the common elements must contain as their distinguishing marks some non-common elements. Common element e_k must possess at least one element which is not possessed by common element e_{k+1} (even if it is an element of arrangement of elements). This means that the structure of common elements leads either to an infinite regress, in which case they cannot be distinguished, with the result that monads M_k and M_{k+1} could not be said to have anything determinate in common; or else, the distinctiveness of the common elements, and therefore the interwovenness of monads due to these common elements, terminates in, that is, is expressible as, *silence*. But this is to say that it cannot be expressed discursively at all, and even farther, that discourse, since it depends upon predicability, or the capacity to attribute X to Y (M_k to M_{k+1}), is impossible.

We therefore arrive at the odd, but in my view genuinely Platonic, conclusion that, if discourse is possible, then there can be no discursive (=formal, systematic, logical) intelligibility of Ideas. The intelligibility of Ideas is noetically apprehensible. We cannot state clearly and distinctly the structural elements of the monadic form M, by the apprehension of which we are enabled to state discursively (although perhaps not clearly and distinctly) the elements of M' (M and M' here corresponding to the earlier F and F'). It should also be emphasized that the necessarily discursive account of the discursive inaccessibility of Ideas, if it is conducted in technical or logical rather than mythical language, carries with it an ambiguity that, unless we are extremely careful (and perhaps even then) leads to vitiating paradoxes. I therefore repeat, our use of symbols like F, H, or M to represent Ideas is already an imitation or discursive image, and not the noetic apprehension of Ideas themselves. In other words, what we say about meaning is not the meaning itself. But the possibility of formally coherent speech about meaning depends upon the ontological distinction between meaning and speech, as well as the priority of meaning to speech. Let us bear in mind that it is wrong to speak of a "resemblance" between F and F'; the two cannot be formally or discursively distinguished (in the sense of determinately specifying their differences in structure), since every statement "about" that distinction necessarily makes use of their formal identity. Similarly, every effort to assert or bespeak F is at once and as such an assertion of F'. Hence the need for myth, poetry, or recollection, in order to remind ourselves of the ontological distinction between what we misleadingly symbolize to ourselves as F and F'. And thus, too, the great danger of removing ostensible "arguments" from the dramatic context of the dialogue, in order to symbolize them in logical notations and study their formal structure. In the case of the Ideas, we end up by studying our logical notation rather than the Ideas.

Our inability to bespeak form does not mean that we should be silent about it, but rather that we should remember the difference between form and discourse, and not try to formalize it. Formalizations are formulaic or discursive; and so, what they show is necessarily different from and prior to them. This is the ontological conclusion of the present discussion. There is also a formal conclusion: our discursive analysis of form, or what Plato calls the "kinds" of diaeresis, cannot themselves provide us with a coherent account of structure. To put this in the simplest possible form: the fundamental ingredients of formal structure cannot be distinguished from each other in determinate discourse, whether symbolical or natural, since the intelligibility of discourse is already dependent upon the interwovenness of those ingredients. Whatever we say about the "one" or "unity" is already a "two" or "manifold," and similarly with "same," "other," "limit," "unlimitedness" and the like. I can *see* the difference between "same" and "other," and even express it informally, but I cannot give a formally precise and complete account of that difference, or of "same" and "other" in themselves (καθ᾽ αὑτό). The elaborate formal constructions by which the main speakers in the dialogues occasionally attempt to give such accounts, are all incomplete, incoherent, or invalid. But this fact is precisely an (if not the) essential aspect of their pedagogic function, and we easily forget this if we detach them from the dialogues and study them as independent logical patterns.

Throughout this discussion, I have emphasized the need to distinguish between noetic apprehension and discursive vision or intelligibility. I should like to give a final example of what this entails, with reference to some recent discussion of how to avoid paradox in speaking about Platonic forms.[42] Consider the statement "Socrates is white." Let us assume that "white" is "a common name, applied in virtue of a relationship to an individual, the Form" or Idea of whiteness.[43] If I understand this correctly, it can only mean that (in my example) the person named "Socrates" is called "white" by virtue of the fact that Socrates himself is related to (i.e., participates in) whiteness itself, and so that the relation of names is valid because of the relation of things or beings, however different their natures, to which the names refer. The question therefore arises: by what are the things or beings related? The answer certainly cannot be "by their names," for then, if we changed the names, we would also change the relation, and so be able to make Socrates black simply by calling him such. Neither can the answer be "by logical properties of those names," since the names must themselves be related to these logical properties; the name "white," in short, is not White-itself. On this alternative, we are again faced by the question, "how are the names of logical properties related to those properties?" Sooner or later we must come to the terminus of questions like these by admitting that we "see," or as I prefer to call it, *apprehend* a relation or pattern, namely, Socrates' whiteness, which is not a name, or a linguistic expression constructed by a weaving-together of names, but which we cannot assert, whether to ourselves or others, except by the use of names or linguistic expressions.

---

42 The literature on this subject is infinite and inconsistent. I have found especially useful Allen (*Studies*) and Bigger. Of the older books, perhaps the best is Robin (*Théorie*).

43 R. E. Allen, "Participation and Predication in Plato's Middle Dialogues" in Allen (*Studies*), p. 46. The example of Socrates is mine; Allen speaks of 'F' in derivative and primary designation.

With this in mind, we are tempted to say that Socrates is related to White-itself by (the fact of) his whiteness. But this of
course gives rise to the question: "what is the relation between
Socrates' whiteness and White-itself?" Socrates' whiteness cannot
be identical with White-itself, because then, instead of having a
colored skin, Socrates would have the Idea of White-itself, which
is absurd. Second, Socrates' whiteness cannot be a "resemblance"
of White-itself,[44] like a mirror-image of a real object, or a copy of
an original,[45] without at the same time *resembling* the original. I at
least do not know what it means to speak of a "resemblance" between F and f in which f does not resemble F. The image of a mirror-image carries other dangers with it, incidentally, since a
mirror-image is actually an inversion of what it images, not to
mention the fact that a mirror-image of, e.g., a white skin is only
"skin-deep." As for a "copy," this word means something that resembles or is "similar to" a designated original, and the relation
of similarity is symmetrical. If f is similar to F, then F is similar to
f. In sum: the use of F in "primary designation" as synonymous
with F-ness or F itself does not explain how F-ness is present in
Socrates. Similarly with the distinction between "what has F" and
"what is F $(\alpha\dot{\upsilon}\tau\dot{o}\ \tau\dot{o}\ F)$"; for granting that the latter rather than
the former is the Idea, it cannot be the case that $\alpha\dot{\upsilon}\tau\dot{o}\ \tau\dot{o}\ F$ *is* the
F-ness, i.e., here the whiteness of Socrates, if we also assert that
Socrates' whiteness is a "copy" of White itself. And if we suppress
the notion of "copy" or "resemblance" then the assertion of the
identity between Socratic whiteness and White-itself is intelligible
only on the assertion of a difference between the two. For in addition to the fact that Socrates' colored skin is not the Idea of
Whiteness, to say "Socrates is white" in the sense of "Socrates has
X" means that Socrates is indeed colored white. But the Idea of

44 This I take to be Allen's meaning on pp. 53 ff. of the previously cited
    article, when he argues that particulars do not resemble forms, but
    are "resemblances" of them, like mirror-images of a real object.
45 H. F. Cherniss, "The Relation of the *Timaeus* to Plato's Later Dia-
    logues" in Allen (*Studies*) pp. 366 ff.

Whiteness is not colored white; the main point of the distinction in question was to avoid this consequence, or the paradox of the third man.

Now I come back to my distinction between apprehension and visibility. White-itself is apprehensible "in" (in the dual sense of "within" and "by means of") the visibility of Socratic whiteness; but it is not visible, either sensuously or logico-discursively. White-itself does not resemble (and is not resembled by) Socratic whiteness, which is a general term, nor does it resemble Socrates' white skin. Whatever name we give to White-itself (including "White-itself") is a misnomer (and *not*, incidentally, an "image"; the name "whiteness," however, *is* an image for the visible property). With this qualification, I suppose we may say that White-itself, if there is such a being, is a noetic monad, and the ontological pre-condition for the exhibition of the form "whiteness."[46] But such an assertion, despite its technical appearance, is more properly characterized as poetic or mythical rather than logical. And this is to say that logic arises by a specification which is also a *narrowing* of our apprehensive capacity. That does not, of course, make logic any less reasonable; it rather extends our conception of reason.

In his Stesichorean myth, Socrates exemplifies the divine madness in the highest degree. He is not talking "about" madness in the sense of meta-linguist or psychiatrist, but rather he is *talking madly*. What the excessively sober, infra-Uranian speaker calls "speaking the truth" is propositional or deductive discourse, which depends finally upon axioms, definitions, and deductive rules, which must themselves be "true" in a sense other than the "truth" of his propositional-deductive discourse. This other sense, called apodictic, evidential, *a priori*, and the like, may be understood by us as grounded in the noetic apprehension, not of "true speech," but of οὐσία ὄντως οὖσα, or what I translate as "the

---

46 Cf. Bigger, p. 91, who also distinguishes between the ontological status of forms and objects, but not, if I understand him, between ontological and logical monads or subjects.

identity of truth and being."[47] Discursive ratiocination, including both the formulation of principles (axioms, definitions, etc.) and the "diaeresis" by which we separate out the propositional consequences implicit in these principles, is infra-Uranian, and so generated, or differently stated, temporal-kinetic. But the apprehension of truth as the evidence of intelligibility, and so as the noetic skeleton of the forms of genesis, cannot itself be subject to the flux of coming-to-be and passing-away, which latter flux is, so to speak, the *negative* structure of each moment of genesis. This negative structure differentiates genesis into a continuum of moments, or supplies the spatio-temporal framework of difference, which is sufficiently visible to be measured and counted; but it gives no content to these moments, not even the numerical properties of which it serves as the sub-structure.

One may understand by "sub-structure" something like the ontological property of "otherness" as discussed in the *Sophist*. Here, however, it must be emphasized that the difference between one moment and another depends for its visibility or intelligibility upon the sameness that also differentiates itself throughout all moments of genesis as self-identity. Peculiar as it may seem at first glance, the difference of otherness is not the same as the difference of sameness. The otherness of man from horse is not the same as the eidetic unity or self-identity, different in man and horse, which in the same way permits their (different) exhibition of sameness. Again, the difference of one moment from another permits us to establish, and thereby distinguish, their respective magnitudes. But the specific magnitudes point to an identity in each moment which, precisely as the exhibition of sameness, differs from the negative structure of otherness by which moments are generated and pass away, receive and surrender an identity, are *identified*, and may be re-identified even after they have disappeared. Once more: the numerical identity of a moment of genesis is not the same as the moment *qua* generated flux. A failure

47 Hackforth says "true Being" and Robin "la réalité qui réellement est."

to make this distinction leads to the identification of sameness and difference, or to a suppression of the difference between formal and material difference, and hence to the dissolution of the former by the latter. This is another way to state the basis for the teaching of Ideas or noetic monads. The hyper-Uranian beings order and measure the flow of genesis. As the principles of order and genesis, they cannot themselves share in that flow.

This is what I thought it necessary to say in order to clarify what Socrates means by "hyper-Uranian beings." They are apprehensible only to mind, the governor of psyche; the "genus of true knowledge" (were it accessible to man) exhibits them in its own structure (247c8-9). That is, our knowledge is discursively true because of what we noetically apprehend; as Socrates puts it, the dianoetic component of the psyche is "nourished by mind and pure knowledge" (247d1-2). The discursive intelligence "cares about," or in other words desires erotically its proper nourishment, and (if guided by divine madness) is led upward toward the noetic vision which is appropriate to its need. This vision transpires on the roof of the world, and so, within the perimeter of genesis or time (ἰδοῦσα διὰ χρόνου). The psyche sees *through time* to the hyper-Uranian beings, even though it cannot existentially transcend (=fly beyond) temporality (247d2-3).[48] This diachronic vision is theory; as such, it is *post-erotic*, since it has achieved its desire or terminus. Hence Socrates says that the psyche "greets with affection" the being of diachronic vision, and is nourished by the sight of truth, or prospers therefrom (247d3-4). This ontological affection characterizes the "friends of the Ideas" as we might call them, or the *philia* of the philosophers. It is the mark of

48 Sinaiko, p. 65, refers to the psychic journey "to the place beyond the heavens" as "instantaneous, involving neither a lapse of time nor a change of place." This is not quite accurate, since the psyche does not go beyond the heavens. Sinaiko, however, realizes this, i.e., that the psyche does not depart from the moving cosmos (p. 66). What, then, is the meaning of "instantaneous" vision? Sinaiko calls it transcendent and remarks that (on the basis of the present passage) little can be said about its inner nature (p. 68).

their completeness, and therefore of philosophical immortality or circularity; the philosopher transcribes or encompasses the circle of genesis, and so passes through the union of the beginning and the end (247d4-5).[49]

Socrates then summarizes the content of diachronic (and so periodic) vision in a passage of extreme concision. The psyche sees "justice itself; she sees moderation; and she sees knowledge, not the kind that is present in genesis, nor which is differently in different things which we now call beings, but the true knowledge of what is true being" (247d5-e2). We may note in passing that nothing is said of courage, as might be expected from the reference to justice and moderation. Next, Socrates refers to "justice itself," but simply to "moderation." The greater emphasis suggests perhaps that justice has somehow a greater degree of self-identity at the level of theoretical vision. More obvious is the fact that Socrates does not name hyper-Uranian forms of things, but only justice, knowledge, and moderation. That is, he names passions of the psyche. Furthermore, we recall that Eros is neither just nor moderate; there is a difference between the striving or desiring and the possessing or apprehending components of philosophy. Finally, the true knowledge of true being can scarcely be the diaeretic knowledge of infra-Uranian beings; this again helps us to understand 249b6 ff., about which we have already had the occasion to comment.

This summary of periodic vision under the categories of justice, moderation, and knowledge is not merely concise, but also unsatisfying. We cannot help remembering Socrates' observation in the *Republic* (at 500d7) that moderation and justice are forms of the demotic virtue. But the significance of the present sentence becomes visible when we remember the role of the virtues in the two previous speeches. Lysias, we recall, does not allude to courage and mentions moderation once, obliquely, and as a synonym of "to be healthy." The concealed lover refers once to courage and twice to moderation; justice is not mentioned in

49   Cf. Alcmaeon, Diels, Fr. 2.

either speech. In other words, the anti-erotic speeches tend toward a conception of man as essentially "intellectual" in the sense of utilitarian or calculating on behalf of the body. In his Stesichorean myth, Socrates restores justice to psychic virtue, as a part of the fulfillment of the private desire for immortality, and hence as a consequence of divine madness. Thus, too, knowledge is restored from its base interpretation as corporeal utility to its noble interpretation as psychic immortality. The relative absence of courage from the speeches of the *Phaedrus* may perhaps most easily be understood by contrasting the private role of the divine madman with the public role of the soldier-philosopher in the *Republic*. The most important form of courage is directed against fear of death.[50] But the individual who has achieved immortality by his transcendence of the human or political can no longer fear death. Courage is for him then a superfluous virtue and is replaced by moderation. The political man, on the contrary, requires courage against death, whether inflicted by the enemies of the just city or by the nature of his own body.

Having feasted upon the hyper-Uranian vision, the psyche sinks down once more into its cosmic home (247e2-4). The winged horses are then taken to the manger, where they dine on ambrosia and nectar (247e4-6). By this gastronomic distinction, Socrates likens the equine component of the psyche to the Olympian gods, and implies that the principle of noetic vision is higher than the instrument of ascent. In addition to the distinction within human nature of body and psyche, there is a psychic dualism represented here by the difference between the horses and the charioteer (to say nothing of the difference between the horses themselves). There are, however, also four degrees of psychic excellence. The first and highest corresponds to the "life of gods" (248a1), or to the psyches capable of standing on the roof of the cosmos. The second-best psyche follows and is an imitation or image (εἰκασμένη) of the best or divine. This psyche cannot stand on

---

50 Cf. *Republic*, Bk. III, *passim*, and Aristotle, *Nichomachean Ethics* 1115a24 ff.

the roof of the cosmos, but may raise its charioteer's head "into the outer region," thereby completing the heavenly period with the gods, and viewing the hyper-Uranian beings, albeit with great difficulty, thanks to the commotion of her horses (248a2-5). In other words, this psyche differs from the best by virtue of a deficient noble horse. Its noetic capacity is apparently the same as that of the gods, but it cannot ascend high enough for this vision to be effectively employed. In fact, the third and fourth degrees of psychic excellence also seem to turn upon a deficiency of the ascensory principle, rather than upon any deficiency of noetic capacity. The third kind bobs up and down, because of the constraint of its horses, and so sees some of the hyper-Uranian beings, but not the rest (248a5-6). The "commotion" of the second degree of equine nobility comes presumably from the insufficient desire to ascend. But in what sense is the third-best psyche "constrained" from achieving its full height by the noble as well as the base horse (βιαζομένων δὲ τῶν ἵππων)? I risk the conjecture that Socrates is here thinking of the conflict in men between theory and practice, or what Aristotle calls the two forms of human excellence. The Eros of the noble horse is divided against itself, because there is a difference between noetic apprehension and virtuous (political) praxis. But I mention this in passing. The fourth and lowest kind of psyche includes all those others who long or yearn to follow the higher psyches upward, but are unable to do so. Their efforts at ascent turn into mutual competition, by which all are maimed (248a6-b5). The charioteer cannot function properly because of the radically defective nature of his horses: again, both the noble and the base horse. Hence his yearning for the vision of the divine being is unfulfilled. The fourth or lowest psyche must consequently feed upon "the food of conjecture" (τροφῇ δοξαστῇ) or opinion.

In sum, every psyche yearns for the noetic vision which alone provides the telos of perfection or circularity, and in that sense, immortality. Personal immortality has nothing to do, however, with perpetual motion; it depends upon the capacity of the best or noble part of the psyche to ascend to the roof of the world, and thus to be present before the vision of truth (248b5-c2). It is, then, not the charioteer but the horses which represent the personal (corporeal) aspect of the psyche. The noetic function of psyche is ordained by its nature to perceive hyper-Uranian beings; i.e., to grasp the ontological subjects of discourse about the things of genesis. The degree to which this function is discerned by the equine aspect of psyche defines its degree of nobility. The noble is the high or lofty, and the noble psyche loves, desires, or yearns after the high; hence its ascensory or winged nature. Hence the great confusion concerning the connection between reason and the good on the part of those psyches who fail to achieve the noetic vision.

Socrates now turns to the ordinance of Nemesis or necessity (248c2). This amounts to a mythical elaboration of the points just summarized. The law of necessity is the final stratum of order, and so is higher than the powers represented by the Olympian gods. It expresses here the degrees of noetic purity or psychic perfection, but in terms different from those employed in the previous section. Socrates is giving here the peroration to his discussion of psychic ascent, and so he employs the solemn language of cyclic immortality or reincarnation. In essence, he combines the second and third of the four psychic degrees previously distinguished, or rather speaks now of those psyches which are able to accompany god and see "something of the true things" (248c3-4). This new species is divided into two classes. The members of the first class are able to perceive something of the truth always; that is, throughout all revolutions of the cosmic circle. Hence they are always unharmed. The members of the second class retain cosmic or circular, but not personal, immortality. That is, they lose sight of the truth through some mischance (i.e., their equine instability leaves them, as we might say, necessarily subject to chance); this is equivalent to forgetfulness or loss of self-consciousness, and hence of personal continuity or immortality (248c5-7). We may note in passing that the psyches which undergo the process of reincarnation, in bodies corresponding to the degree of their fall from noetic grace, have once seen something of the truth. In this passage, Socrates has suppressed the fourth kind of psyche mentioned previously, namely, the kind that yearns for, but never sees anything at all of, the truth.

This kind is incapable of personal immortality at all, because such immortality is vision of the truth. Later, this kind will apparently be separated from the human altogether (see the beginning of section VI below).

According to the myth of Er, forgetfulness is an intrinsic component of immortality, conceived as reincarnation rather than as continuous self-consciousness. The function it serves, however, is different in the present passage. In the myth of Er, a forgetting of what may be called the extra-terrestrial, or the domain of psychic continuity, is a necessary condition for the unfolding of the psychic monad into historical existence. It is therefore as necessary for the philosopher as for the non-philosopher. In the present myth, forgetfulness defines the distinction between heavenly and terrestrial psyches, but it is described more as a liability than an opportunity. There are now degrees of forgetfulness; the excellence of one's life depends upon how much we remember of the extra-terrestrial. In the myth of Er, everyone forgets everything upon drinking of the waters of Lethe, and parallel to this is the fact that, in the choice of lives, everyone sees the same things. Were it not for this initial equality of vision, there could be no responsibility of choice. Here on the contrary, different psyches see different degrees of the truth. The major consequences of the difference between our passage and the myth of Er is that, in the myth of Stesichorus, terrestrial or historical existence is depreciated. According to the myth of Er, in order to become a perfect human, one must forget his divine heritage or vision of eternity. According to the myth of Stesichorus, perfection lies in remembering from the outset as much as possible of our divine heritage; as one might almost say, it depends upon forgetting as much as possible of the human.

We turn now to the order of psychic descent. During the ascent, there was a differentiation of psyches in terms of their noetic capacity. The parallel ascent in the *Symposium* emphasized speech and science, or seeing and talking. In the *Phaedrus*, the ascent is of seeing alone; one may suppose that speech is dependent upon embodiment. The order of psychic descent or embodiment covers nine degrees of progressively lower human excellence. It may also continue down into the animal kingdom, as Socrates indicates (248d1-2). The first and highest degree is that "birth which will become as a man a philosopher or a lover of beauty or [a practitioner] of some kind of music and a lover" (248d2-4). It is not clear from the Greek whether Socrates distinguishes these or lists them as three equivalent forms of the same degree. We cannot therefore be entirely sure whether there is one erotic form, or two non-erotic forms together with the erotic man of music. The structure of the lower degrees would seem to support the interpretation of three distinct kinds of human perfection. Also, the philosopher is normally distinguished in the dialogues from the musical or artistic practitioner. On the other hand, there is obviously a musical component in the philosophical nature, which also loves beauty and has been explicitly described as erotic. The evidence seems to favor our taking the highest degree as one complex human type, but the ambiguity remains. Altogether unambiguous is the absence of any explicit reference to science, or, more surprising in view of the cosmological themes, to mathematics, in the specification of the philosophical (or at least the highest) nature.[51] This is noteworthy in view of the emphasis placed upon science by Diotima; in her final revelation, philosophy is literally surrounded by the sciences. The difference between the two accounts is that, in the myth of Stesichorus, music replaces science. There is no reason to be surprised by such a substitution, since it is attributed to a poet; Socrates will allude to the study of nature later, and in his

51 Cf. Diesendruck, p. 52, who goes too far, however, in saying that the *Phaedrus* contains "gar keine Spur von *Mathematik*," or that Plato had gone "einen Schritt weiter," namely, beyond mathematics, as contrasted with his teaching in the *Republic*. Mathematics is silently present in the *Phaedrus*, with respect both to cosmic motion and dialectic.

own voice, in the discussion of rhetoric and dialectic. Finally, we should observe that the highest degree of embodied psychic ascent (as described by Diotima) differs from the highest degree of psychic descent: the way up is apparently not the same as the way down.

As is emphasized by the difference between the first and second degrees of descent, the philosophical or musico-erotic life is concerned primarily, and so far as we are told, exclusively, with the care of the individual psyche. The second and third degrees are concerned primarily with the care of the city. In the second degree, the psyche is incarnated as "a law-abiding king, or as a warrior and ruler" (248d4-5). We see here two different species of the practical imitation of the highest or theoretical man. I suggest that the species correspond very crudely to the regimes described in the *Laws* and *Republic* respectively. The warrior-ruler approximates to the guardian of the just city, who governs, not by laws, but by intelligence and courage. In the third degree, we find the statesman, the household manager, and the businessman (248d5-6). This category is concerned primarily with peaceful political activity; the military ruler is of greater excellence because, as Aristotle notes, he saves the city from destruction. The juxtaposition of war and money-making implies that the psyche exemplifies the apprehension of hyper-Uranian being more splendidly in war than in nonphilosophical peace. Somewhat more cautiously put, money-making is a characteristic of oligarchies and democracies, whereas kings and aristocratic warriors are primarily concerned with splendid deeds. Within the political domain, the Stesichorean ranking seems to place war above peace, perhaps because war is a more splendid subject for poetry. This ranking is unjust to the average citizen, but we have already noticed the relative absence of justice from the *Phaedrus* (except beyond the heavens).

We now descend another degree, from care of the city to care of the individual body; the city thus mediates between the psyche and the body of the individual. The fourth stage of descent contains the industrious or hard-working man, who is described as

a gymnast or doctor (248d6-7). So far, I believe, the general order
of descent is relatively straightforward and generally intelligible.
But the fifth or central of the nine degrees raises a pervasive problem of interpretation. In it, we find the mantic or telestic lives
(248d7-el): the only explicit reference to care of the gods is thus
placed below the three principal forms of the care of man. Of
course, the prophet may be regarded as an intermediary between
human and divine things, but this scarcely accounts for his relatively low position in the order of descent. There is a more obvious explanation, namely, that Socrates has a low opinion of the
mantic and telestic arts. But in the context of the *Phaedrus* such an
explanation raises more problems than it solves. After all, the
main function of the myth of Stesichorus is to explain psychic
mania, which was derived by Socrates at 244c1 from *mantikē*. We
have already seen the various ways in which prophecy plays a
central role at all stages of the *Phaedrus*; Socrates puts this beyond
all doubt by asserting at 242c7 that "the psyche is somehow mantic." And the mantic and telestic activities correspond to the first
and second forms of divine madness (244a8 ff., 244d5 ff.), which
would lead us to expect that they be given a considerably higher
position, perhaps second only to the highest degree. If, then, we
maintain that Socrates is here referring to vulgar or sober, rather
than to divine, prophecy, the question arises as to why he omits
mention of the divine form of divine care.

A very similar difficulty is raised by the sixth degree, which
corresponds to the poet or the practitioner of some other mimetic
activity (248e1-2). Poetic madness was the third of the four divine
species previously distinguished (245a1 ff.). If we assume that
Socrates intends to differentiate mimetic from divinely mad poetry, why does he do so in the present context? According to
Socrates' previous statement, it is a sign of contemporary man's
ignorance of beauty that he distinguishes between prophecy and
madness (244c2 ff.). Do not the fifth and sixth degrees of psychic
descent testify to the ignorance of beauty of Socrates *qua* Stesichorus? The least we can say about this is that there is a discontinuity between the structure of the Stesichorean myth as a whole,

and the order of psychic descent which serves as a part within that whole. The myth as a whole is divine, whereas the order of descent is secular. But why should a divine, and hence mad, discourse pronounce a secular, and hence sober account of the descent of the psyche? Given that this descent is equivalent to its progressive secularization, if we explain the absence of divine prophecy and poetry as a consequence of that secularization, then the same must be true of philosophy as well. Or else the function of the account of descent is to contradict the excessively poetic claims of the myth as a whole, and to suggest that there is just one kind of "divine" life for man: the life that transcends the polis. This life is not easy to identify, but here it is described as a friendship for wisdom and beauty together with musical eroticism. If it is accurate to call the highest human life "divine," we must notice that it has no explicit connection with the gods (who are followed by the discarnate psyche), whose care would seem to mediate between care of the body and mimetic art: a kind of care of the whole cosmos.

When man falls from heaven, or when his psyche is embodied, he seems to lose "touch" with the divine, which he can only remember, but before which he is no longer genuinely present. The four forms of divine madness would seem to correspond to four degrees of divine remembrance. But three of these, mantic and telestic prophecy and poetry, are apparently unreliable, or so their low position in the order of lives would suggest. Perhaps only philosophy is genuinely trustworthy, because it alone of the four forms is *reflexive*; it alone gives an account of itself as a form of divine remembrance, and by extension, it alone explains the remaining three forms. This is another confirmation of the fact that the myth of Stesichorus cannot stand on its own terms, but must submit to philosophical or reflexive analysis and interpretation.

Stesichorean poetry is obviously not "mimetic" in the crude sense of that term. It might perhaps be said to imitate the forms of psychic experience, but in so subtly indirect a manner as to require a different term than "mimesis" for its designation. For example, the mimetic poet as he is usually described in the dialogues is one who disguises himself *as* what he imitates. In this respect, the mimetic poet resembles the sophist, to whom we shall return in a moment. Both are alike in that both imitate philosophy by caring for, or professing to wisdom about, everything. Let me give a very simple illustration of what this means. We frequently refer to art as a "mirror of reality," by which we mean that art helps us to understand life by imitating its total complexity in reduced or humanly perceptible form. Since the imitation is said to reproduce the complexity of reality, no interpretation of a work of art is satisfactory which does not explain reality as well as its artistic image. But this is manifestly impossible, or equivalent to the view that, precisely because of its mimetic nature, a work of art encompasses as many interpretations as the reality it imitates. Hence it is concluded that there is *no* satisfactory interpretation of a work of art, or that the only satisfactory interpretation is to perceive and enjoy it. We "understand" a work of art (according to this thesis) by understanding that it is incomprehensible, or that the function of mimesis is the artistic substitute for an impossible interpretative understanding.

In poetry (or any art) understood as mimesis, the artist succeeds by disappearing; that is, he imitates human existence so accurately (and hence not in the sense of a photographic copy, which is altogether unable to convey the motion and transformation of life) that in perceiving his imitation, we have the illusion that we are not simply perceiving, but understanding the truth about existence in a way that no discursive or scientific account could equal. But this is not the case with the Stesichorean myth, if only thanks to its position within the dialogue as a whole. The problem is no doubt complicated by the fact that there is a mimetic aspect to the Platonic dialogue itself. But the dialogue calls attention to itself, thanks to the disjunction between its mimetic and discursive or philosophical aspects, in the way that a mimetic poem does not and ought not to do. The dialogue is self-reflexive, or prevents us from being simply immersed within our perception of it, whereas the poem fails as a work of art if it does not absorb us from the outset as a version, and indeed a superior version, of reality. Interpretations of works of art subsequent to our immersion into or perception of them, soon become indistinguishable from philosophy, as soon as we move beyond technical analysis of perceptible elements to a discussion of what the work "means." Hence the temptation is very great for the sensitive perceiver to insist that "the work means what it says" (a form of aestheticism that we also find in contemporary epistemology), or that it does not "mean" but "is." On the basis of considerations like these, I suspect that Socrates' Stesichorean myth belongs in the class of philosophical music rather than mimetic poetry.

Thus the discontinuity between the general treatment of madness and the account of psychic descent is a component in what I have called the reflexivity of the myth as a whole. In perceiving it, our attention is directed toward the myth as an external structure. Rather than being absorbed into our perception of that structure, we are guided to the need for systematic interpretation. Only on the basis of this interpretation are we then entitled to the perception that the myth is not mimetic but a kind of philosophico-erotic music. The difference between philosophical myth and mimetic art reduces finally to this: the tacit premise of mimetic art is that to understand existence is to exist—vividly, genuinely, deeply—whereas to explain existence theoretically is to cease to exist, and hence, to be unable to understand existence. The order of psychic descent is an order of increasing forgetfulness, not simply of hyper-Uranian beings, but of itself.

Thus far in the order of psychic descent we have moved from care of the psyche to care of the city, thence to care of the body, and subsequently to care of the gods. We have descended from man's care of himself to his care of non-human things or activities. Poetry or mimetic art is only partially an imitation of philosophy, because its care for everything is in fact non-reflexive, or a carelessness about itself. Philosophy, in caring for everything, cares for the psyche, because it is just the activity by which the psyche gives an account of (and to) itself. Mimetic art is too forgetful; it forgets the psyche. However, its comprehensiveness imitates psychic concern; hence it ranks higher than the specific *technai*, represented in the seventh degree by the artisan and farmer (248e2). These modes of life are marked by care for what may be called dead and living artifacts. In the eighth degree, we find the sophist and demagogue (248e3), or the corrupt imitations of philosophy and political rule. These rank lower than the mimetic arts because it is better to offer no interpretation of life than to offer a vicious interpretation. Mimetic art is an unconscious or non-reflexive imitation of the philosopher's erotic music or friendship for the beautiful. It should be observed that philosophy is "above" and art "below" political life; the love of beauty is selfish or selfless, but not political. For this reason, it is less comprehensive than the love of the good, and by no means identical to the love of truth. The difference between the love of beauty and the love of truth has already been implied by the fact that Socrates gave no mention of a hyper-Uranian beauty, whereas he did mention true knowledge of true being.

The order of descent concludes with the tyrannical life as the sole representative of the ninth degree (248e3). The tyrant, and not the sophist, is the complete perversion of philosophical self-concern into selfishness. The sophist, a playful imitation of the philosopher, loses touch with himself by absorption in discontinuous verbal facility (just as the demagogue is soon absorbed into the passions of the *demos* which he strives to lead). The tyrant loses touch with others by absorption into his own desire. Like the philosopher, the tyrant desires everything; like the poet, he imitates the whole by transforming it into a project of his will to power. Like the king or statesman, he cares for the city, but only as an instrument for the satisfaction of his desire. It would be no exaggeration, at least from the Greek viewpoint, to say that the tyrant's care for the city is in fact a care for his own body. The tyrant cares for himself as though he were a god, and his technē is strength. In sum, the tyrant embodies a distorted version of each of the lives above his in the order of descent. The corruption of each form of life is a species of tyranny; each man runs the risk of being tyrannized by his distinctive excellence, and so of forgetting himself precisely through self-absorption, or of forgetting what it means to be a perfect human being, a whole rather than a part.

At the beginning of my analysis of the order of descent, I observed that forgetfulness functions differently here than it does in the myth of Er. In the present context, it is said to be a consequence of mischance, and is linked with baseness or evil (248c6-7). The mischance in turn is occasioned by the psyche's inability to follow a god on his cosmic peripety, and thereby to see something of the true hyper-Uranian beings. This inability is intrinsic or natural, or due to the relative strength of the horses of the psyche. All psyches, prior to their fall, desire to rise to the roof of the world and thereby to see the truth. These facts, when taken together, raise a problem which the myth of Er explicitly resolves: the responsibility of the individual psyche for its kind of embodied life. If the order of descent is determined by a combination of natural incapacity and chance, there would seem to be no cosmic or ontological basis for human freedom and responsibility, and hence for justice. It would seem that life is the unjust penalty imposed on us by necessity (cf. 246a1-2, b4).

The problem is emphasized by the next step of the myth, in which Socrates introduces the related themes of justice and responsibility. "In all these [incarnations], he who lives justly receives a share of a better part [=degree of embodiment], whereas he who lives unjustly receives a worse share" (248e3-5). According to this assertion, justice, and so personal responsibility, are possible after the first incarnation, which itself, as we have now seen, is assigned by necessity rather than by the free choice of the psyche. But Socrates adds to the confusion: all but the philosophical psyches must spend at least 10,000 years in the corporeal domain, before regaining their wings. "The psyche that philosophizes genuinely [without guile], or that combines pederasty with philosophy" need spend only three revolutions of a thousand years each in the wingless state, if it chooses the philosophical life three times in a row (248e5-249a5). Let us be very precise: Socrates now seems to claim that the least forgetful psyches *choose* (ἕλωνται) their initial embodiment in the highest kind of human life. The Greek verb could conceivably mean "obtain" in a sense that does not assign personal responsibility. In either case, however, the possibility of free initial choice is raised only with respect to the philosophical psyche. As a consequence, the philosophical life has a kind of human dignity or significance which is lacking in the other, lower cases. But just as this dignity is linked to freedom, so it may be freely surrendered; hence the need for three consecutive choices of philosophy before the psyche is released from the body and allowed to return to the divine dwelling.

I want to make two further points in this connection. First, although Socrates says that a psyche which lives justly in one incarnation will receive a better fate in the next, he never suggests, and implicitly excludes the possibility, that a nonphilosophical psyche can be rewarded for its just life by promotion to the philosophical level. Second, we must notice the link between philosophy and pederasty. This reference reminds us that the entire discussion of divine madness was initiated with respect to an interpretation of Eros. Whereas Eros is attributed to the pre-embodied psyche as an essential component in its ascent toward the hyper-Uranian beings, in the psychic descent, Eros is mentioned only with respect to the philosopher. This makes initial sense, since only the philosopher "remembers" the precorporeal psychic appetite for the vision of the truth. In the lower or non-philosophical degrees of descent, the psychic Eros lacks reflexivity, and is absorbed by a specific object, or an imitation of perfection. The reason why the philosophical Eros is represented by pederasty is primarily because the philosopher generates in the psyche rather than in the body; his "children" are his recollections.

The non-philosophical psyches must submit to judgment after they have completed their first life. To repeat: it is not said that they "chose" this life, nor could they, in view of the fact that it was a consequence of forgetfulness. One might wish to blame this forgetfulness on the base or passionate horse in the pre-corporeal situation. But this is merely to raise the question of the responsibility for excessive passion. The details of the myth make it clear that all psyches intend or desire to reach the heights. If they fail, it can scarcely be the fault of the principle of reason. It does not seem to be just to distribute rewards and punishments on the basis of a natural or necessary mode of incarnation. Yet this is what Socrates does, following in his own way the Orphic teaching (249a5-b1). The complex but compelling mythical language is designed to overcome the ambiguities in the origin of justice. Apart from the philosopher, none of us chooses his initial incarnation; we are born into a life determined, so far as its main characteristics are concerned, by a mixture of nature and chance. However, as the myth indicates, within this life, each of us has the capacity to live justly or unjustly. It must be the case that what counts as "justice" differs from life to life, although it is not easy to conceive of the form justice might take in the tyrannical incarnation. In general, there is a difference between the justice of the philosopher, which is grounded in a memory of Justice itself, and the demotic justice of the non-philosopher, which must be entirely, or almost entirely, terrestrial.

After an interval of 1000 years, spent either in heaven or beneath the earth, the non-philosophical psyches are brought together in order to choose their second life, "whichever each one wills" (249b1-3). Presumably this choice is conditioned, not simply by what one learned in the first life, but also in the intervening period of reward and punishment. The initial psychic forgetfulness is thus partially overcome, and a basis for individual responsibility is established; namely, memory, or an imitation of the philosophical recollection. No doubt those psyches which have learned or remembered nothing are now translated into the life of a beast (249b3-5); perhaps this is the fate of tyrants. Socrates adds that psyches which were demoted to a bestial incarnation may rise again to the human level. The distinction between psyches capable of human embodiment and those which are not is the original vision of truth: "it is necessary for man to know how to speak in accordance with form (κατ' εἶδος), going[52] from many perceptions to one [=unity] gathered together by reasoning" (λο-γισμῷ: 249b5-c1). We have already met with this passage in discussing the hyper-Uranian beings. It is uttered in apparent support of the thesis that every human psyche (whether or not subsequently demoted to the bestial level) must have seen something of the hyper-Uranian beings (contrary to what we were told by the earlier passage of the myth), whereas the sub-human psyches "long for" this vision, but cannot attain it.[53] Bearing in mind the ambiguous status of this passage, we may say that rational speech is "recollection" in the double sense of memory and a gathering together of many into one. Only those psyches are capable of logos who were able initially to follow a god, looking up toward "what truly is" (249c1-4). We may therefore preserve the distinction, previously established, between recollection *qua* noetic apprehension and *qua* re-collective calculation or classification via discourse (=logos).

Now Socrates sharply distinguishes between the philosophical and the non-philosophical psyches: "thus it is just that only the intelligence (διάνοια) of the philosopher is winged; for she is always, as far as possible, near in memory with what, when a god is near them, he is divine" (249c4-6).[54] This is a noteworthy statement for several reasons. First, Socrates attributes winglessness, not to the psyche as a whole, but to the intelligence; previously, it was the horses who were winged, rather than the charioteer. He may well here be distinguishing between philosophical and

---

52 Reading ἰόντ' with Badham.

53 Cf. 248a6-b5. One cannot make a completely unambiguous identification between the fourth kind of psyche and the bestial psyche, because the former is said to live τροφῇ δοξαστῇ ["nourished by opinion" – ed.]. But the identification is far from impossible. There is something bestial about humans who have no recollection whatsoever of truth.

54 Robin correctly translates μόνη πτεροῦται ἡ τοῦ φιλοσόφου διάνοια as "seule, la pensée du philosophe soit ailée." Hackforth incorrectly renders the same phrase: "the soul of the philosopher alone should recover her wings."

non-philosophical Eros; that is, only the philosopher has a winged intelligence, and for that reason only he can overcome the quarreling of his steeds and ascend to the roof of the cosmos. If this is so, and his words support this inference, then there is no contradiction between this assertion and the fact that all psyches are said to be (initially) winged. Second, Socrates says here "is winged," and not "regains her wings" (as Hackforth, encouraged by the context, takes him to mean). Thus, the distinction between philosophical and non-philosophical intelligence is original, and not a consequence of the psyche's loss of wings (and consequently, it does not contradict the implication at 248e5-7 that all psyches eventually regain their wings). Still, if this point is sound, why does Socrates explain the wingedness of philosophical intelligence in terms of the memory, which refers to the fallen or corporeal rather than to the original, ascending condition? This consideration would seem to encourage us to translate πτεροῦται as "regains its wings," and as a result, we are tempted to translate ἡ διάνοια as "the psyche." The simplest solution to this perplexity, I believe, is to translate literally, and to take the comment on memory as an example of the capacity peculiar to philosophical intelligence. It is, then, just that only this intelligence recover her wings, because she alone had wings to begin with. The non-philosophical psyche regains its wings eventually, but for different reasons and in a different way than the philosophical psyche.[55] This corresponds to the difference between the second and third form of psychic excellence, introduced at 248 a1 ff.

Finally, Socrates attributes the divinity of a god to its vision of the hyper-Uranian beings. Divinity is achieved by the degree to which one's psyche reflects or recollects these transpsychic beings. In the case of man, it is dependent upon the correct use of the "reminders" (ὑπομνήματα) of perfect being (249c6-8). That is, the discursive *use* of recollection is different from the noetic apprehension of what I called earlier the ontological subjects of

---

55 A failure to appreciate this difference mars Sinaiko's account of the "philosophical" character of all human love (e.g., pp. 91 ff.).

discourse. Human perfection thus depends upon an *ekstasis* from contingent being and speaking, and he who exhibits the divine enthusiasm is rebuked by ordinary speakers as stirred out of his senses—a passage that every student of Plato should never forget (249c9-d3).

VI.

Socrates now summarizes the results of the speech about the fourth kind of madness. He who has previously seen true beauty (=the hyper-Uranian beings) is reminded of it by the perception of beauty within the cosmos of genesis. This reminiscence makes his wings sprout; he tries to fly upward but cannot do so. Instead, he spends his life looking upward, like a bird, careless of the world below, and so is regarded as mad (249d4-e1). He does not, as in the *Republic*, redescend into the cave; the "communion" of the best form of madness is with the hyper-Uranian beings (249e1-4). More precisely, as described in the *Phaedrus*, this communion is with recollections of those beings, and not with immediate apprehension of them. I have already tried to explain what this difference entails. To say that man cannot ascend in his lifetime to the domain of true being is to deny that the purely eidetic dialectic described in the *Republic* is possible. Discourse consists of "memoranda" of the Ideas. And although Socrates now claims that every human psyche saw something of the hyper-Uranian beings prior to its descent, for the majority, the vision was so fragmentary as to be easily forgotten after incarnation (249e4-250a5). Whereas the human psyche is erotic, only the Eros of the philosopher is *reflexive*, or recollects the telos of its appetite.

Those whose memory is reflexive or recollective are stimulated by the perception of a "likeness" of true beauty to the condition of madness with which we are now familiar (250a7-b1). The *parousia* of beauty differs from that of justice, moderation, and whatever else the psyche honors, by its incomparably greater splendor (250b1-3). The present account of noetic apprehension is "aesthetic" in the literal sense of taking its bearings by

sense-perception (250b1). Since the psyche is embodied, her perception is necessarily corporeal or mediated by the corporeal. And
the outstanding characteristic of corporeally mediated perception
is beauty. All human beings respond to the compulsion of beauty,
whereas comparatively few are compelled by justice or moderation. To this we may add that beauty is presumably also more
splendid and compelling than truth and goodness, which are
honored by the psyche but not mentioned here. The initial vision
of beauty is then described as a mystical initiation or orgiastic rite
which bestowed completeness and purity on those psyches that
accompanied the gods on their cosmic circuits.[56] This condition
of psychic perfection corresponds to the simple, indivisible and
blessed manifestations or appearances (φάσματα) themselves.
The psyche is purified by its vision of pure appearances of beauty,
which shine in the pure light that we may perhaps attribute to the
here unmentioned good (250b5-c4).

The philosophical Eros, or yearning for perfection, resembles
madness in two closely related ways. First, it seems mad to the
non-philosopher to neglect the human or political, and second,
it seems mad to strive after the perception of what transcends
the world of genesis. It is madness to regard the body as a tomb,
and so to regard life as death and death as life (250c4-6). But this
madness is in fact a divine sobriety, or a refusal to be deterred
by finite gratification from pursuing the genuinely human desire
for a speech about desire. The peculiarly self-transcending nature
of corporeal desire is implicit in the primacy of vision among the
senses (250c7-d4). It is by the vision of beauty that we are primarily attracted to the erotic object, and yet vision is the mode of
perception in which we are most separate from the body perceived. This *attractive separation*, as I shall call it, directs us toward
the beautiful shape or form of the body, even as it draws us toward the body itself. If the erotic appetite is transferred from the
body to the perception of the form, then corporeal sobriety is

---

56 Socrates says that "we followed Zeus, and others followed another
    of the gods" (250b7). Cf. 252e2 ff.

fused with divine madness. Hence the special philosophical significance of visually perceived beauty; the most compelling
property of the sensuous world is also the means for our possible
transcendence of the sensuous world (250d4-e1). As Socrates
says, we cannot see wisdom (φρόνησις) because there is no shining image of it, nor are any of the other beloved beings accessible
to sense-perception. But the beauty of the visible world, thanks
to its capacity of attractive separation, engenders the vision
within the psyche of the invisible world. This psychic vision is
wisdom.

The corporeal Eros leads us to perpetuate ourselves by generating children in the flesh, whereas the psychic Eros attempts
to capture in discourse the perpetual structure of genesis. This
erotic dualism corresponds to the dualism of visual perception,
or its power of attractive separation. Sexual love reaches its peak,
not in the act of physical intimacy, but in the generation of children: the violent attraction of Eros culminates in reproduction,
which is the corporeal analogue of recollection, or complete separation from one's own body. We love our children because they
are our own, but we love them more than ourselves. Even the
most selfish desire for perpetuity is transformed by the recognition that the self endures only through separation from the self.
Self-love, when completely developed, is transformed into the
selfless love of the perpetual, or what Socrates calls now "the
beautiful itself" (250e2: αὐτὸ τὸ κάλλος), which may refer to the
entire domain of hyper-Uranian beings, or (for the first time) to a
distinct Idea of beauty. He then proceeds to exemplify this process
of attractive separation or erotic transformation in terms of pederasty. I have elsewhere discussed the significance of pederasty
at length; suffice it to say here that it imitates philosophy because
it cannot generate children in the flesh, but leads man away from
the political toward a selfish cultivation of the psyche, toward
friendship and the love of beauty.

He who has forgotten the vision of beauty itself is driven to
copulate like a beast with the beautiful youth, although this bestial desire already contains the self-transforming instinct to

generate children (250e1-2).[57] The fundamental opposition at this lowest level of Eros is between piety and hedonism, by which Socrates distinguishes between care of the psyche and care of the body. The bestial pederast is driven by corporeal hybris to achieve pleasure in a way contrary to nature (250e5-6); this corresponds to the effort of the hybristic circle-men to conquer the gods, as described by Aristophanes in the *Symposium*. But he who is fresh from the vision of the hyper-Uranian beings responds to the godlike form of the beautiful body (251a1-3); that is, he is immediately separated from the attractive body by the transcendent force of the attraction itself. The sexual compulsion immediately transforms itself into the pious "recollection" of divine beauty; this recollective response precedes the carnal temptation, which is to say again that the way up is not the same as the way down (251a3-7). The lover experiences awe and reverence in his initial contact with the beloved; then the corrupting influences of the body manifest themselves. The lover is tempted to worship the body of his beloved, but this temptation is restrained by δόξα; he fears that he will be regarded as a madman.

Only after the deterioration of the initial response does an obviously sexual reaction set in (251a7 ff.). And what is most interesting, it is the sexual excitation that stimulates the roots of the psychic wings to begin growing again (251b1-7). The wings represent the desire for perfection or beauty itself, and not its achievement. They raise the psyche to the roof of the cosmos; this elevative function originates in corporeal desire. In other words, there is a difference between Eros and friendship (φιλία), as we have already discovered. To see the hyper-Uranian beings, and hence to recollect having seen them, is not the same as desiring to see them.

As the wings, invigorated by the warmth of corporeal perception, begin to grow, excitement is permeated with pain (251c1-5).

---

57 I believe that this passage is misunderstood by Hackforth, who translates καί in 250e5 as "or," thereby taking the preceding ἐπιχειρεῖ καὶ παιδοσπορεῖν ["and he attempts to generate children"– ed.] to be a pejorative reference to heterosexuality.

The cause of the pain is not the visual perception of beauty, but the psychic response to this perception. The corporeal excitation is transformed by the psyche into the growth and care of its wings. This transformation cannot be complete; the body demands the fulfillment of its own nature, and the quarrel between body and psyche is painful. The actual (visual) perception of beauty, as distinct from the erotic processes it engenders, brings joy to the psyche (251c5-d1). This joy arises from the direct presence of the beautiful boy, or from the psyche's memory of his beauty (251d6). The pain also has two related causes. In the presence of the boy, the wings begin to grow; in his absence, they wither again (251d1-6). The Stesichorean account of sexual desire in the potential philosopher thus separates it at the outset from pleasure. Corporeal hedonism is possible only for the psyche that has forgotten, or never saw, the beautiful itself. Whether we attribute this to Platonic asceticism or Socratic irony, erotic joy is here restricted to looking at "the one possessing beauty" (251e2-3), in the rather abstract phrase of the myth. The unmistakable references to sexual orgasm are transformed by the fact that they are given a purely visual significance (251e1-252a2). Desire is pain; release or joy is separation from, or overcoming of, desire by the perception of the form of beauty.

This account of the dialectic between the physiological and visual aspects of Eros is in some ways parallel to the representation of the two psychic horses. Now, however, no distinction is drawn between the noble horse and the charioteer himself. In the initial stage of erotic excitement, the recollective or noetic capacity of the psyche has not yet gained control over the spirited and passionate elements. Hence the ambiguity throughout this section as to whether Socrates is describing physiological or psychic processes. The key to the ultimate resolution of the ambiguity is the aforementioned distinction between desire and pleasure. This distinction is prior to the rejuvenation of the psyche's wings, and in fact a necessary condition for their beginning to grow again. Until this growth is completed, however, its processes disorient the lover, and his madness is indistinguishable from the enslavement of the physiological erotic (252a1-7). He neglects his family, friends, and property, and has no care for custom or good manners; in short, he behaves exactly like the lover who was criticized in the first two speeches of our dialogue. We can now see very clearly the contribution of those speeches to the central myth of the psyche. If the lover does not contain within his nature the passive or receptive component of the non-lover as well, the visual or separative function of Eros will not triumph over the physiological or attractive function. His madness will then be human rather than divine; in terms of the example, he will be a pederast rather than a philosopher. The "one who possesses beauty," rather than the beauty he "possesses," will then absorb the lover's Eros; his ailment, since it is now predominantly carnal, can be assuaged only by a carnal medicine (252a7-b1).

In sum: the initial erotic experience contains the means of its transformation into philosophical ascent, provided that the pathos (252b2, c2) is indeed sufficiently passive. The esoteric or hybristic (252b5-6) interpretation of Eros thus emphasizes his wings, or the power to rise from the human to the divine (252b6-9); but, as the image of the two horses shows, this power is actualized within man by his corporeal desire, and thus may be corrupted or enslaved by it. Neither the recollection of beauty nor the physiological desire is alone sufficient to account for the philosophical ascent. Both are necessary; hence the danger of philosophical madness, which can easily deteriorate into tyranny. The rarity of the genuine philosopher is due to the extraordinary difficulty in achieving a harmonious mixture of the two elements of Eros. But the promise of philosophy as human perfection is already implicit in the most fundamental activities of sensation and desire.

Human existence may be generally understood as the yearning after philosophy. Socrates previously described the degrees of this yearning in terms of the nine stages of psychic descent or incarnation. He now modifies certain aspects of his initial classification. In that classification, it seemed that only the highest form of existence is genuinely erotic (248d2-4). One may call this the

strict classification, or the radical distinction between the philosophical and all other forms of human Eros. In the present passage (252c3 ff.), Socrates returns to those psyches who, prior to
their incarnation, were able to follow in the company of some god
on the journey round the roof of the cosmos (246d6 ff.). The original description of the heavenly procession indicated that each of
the gods has his own divine work (247a6). This would suggest
that there are twelve different kinds of psyche attaining to the
highest vision; more specifically, there must be twelve degrees of
perfection within the highest of the four fundamental psychic
types (248a1 ff.). The first type includes the gods themselves. The
second type consists of those who are able to follow the gods continuously, despite the commotion of their winged steeds. The
third type obtains an intermittent view of true being, rising and
sinking alternately, but not capable of following the gods continuously. The fourth type never reaches the roof of the cosmos at
all. Obviously the second type must reflect the twelve-fold division of the gods. It is not entirely clear that this is true in the case
of the third type, but presumably there is some principle which
determines the divine procession into which the charioteer's head
makes its intermittent appearance. One might then expect that
there are at least twenty-four kinds of human existence corresponding to the degrees of heavenly vision (249e4 ff.). However, we
recall that the nine-fold division of corporeal existences contained
sub-divisions at every level but the last. Apart from the ambiguity
as to precisely how many lives are distinguished in this division,
it seems fair to say that Socrates has apparently selected examples
from a richer variety of kinds. It would seem that the twenty-four
variants on the twelve divine kinds are scattered through the nine
degrees of incarnation, which in turn articulate the second and
third of the four psychic types.

On the basis of our new information, the philosophical psyche
continues to be distinguished from the rest as a follower of Zeus.
He carries the burden of Eros with greater constancy than the others (252c3-4), and loves only those with Zeus-like psyches,
namely, those who are by nature both philosophers and leaders

(252e3), or what we may call natural philosopher-kings, as distinct from kings of the political (and philosophers of the professorial) variety. The second god to be mentioned is Ares; his followers are described exclusively in terms of their jealousy, and the violence with which they avenge supposed infidelity or injustice, even to the extent of sacrificing in blood themselves and their beloveds (252c4-7). With some hesitation, we may identify the followers of Ares as the warlike kings of the second degree of psychic excellence. This is indirectly supported by the brief reference to the third divinity, Hera, whose followers look for a kingly nature (253b1-2). This variant might plausibly be identified with the legal king of the second degree, who is contrasted with the warlike monarch (248d4-5). Only one more god, Apollo, is mentioned in this exemplification of the varieties of divine Eros, and nothing is said to identify the nature of his love (253b3). I offer the conjecture that Apollo, the god of lucidity, stands for the philosophical love of geometry or mathematics which was previously omitted from the description of the highest psychic degree. This initial description identified the highest life as that of "a philosopher, or a lover of beauty, or of some kind of musical and erotic man" (248d3-4). It now seems that the philosopher, as distinct from the second and third types, is identified with Zeus, and as I suggest, Apollo. Or otherwise put, the tripartite character of the highest man may be identified as combining the attributes of Zeus and Apollo.

Needless to say, these identifications are tentative and even playful. The serious point is that Socrates now joins the philosophical, the martial, the political, and (however we specify it) the Apollonian lives as examples of divinely inspired Eros. The highest form of divine madness thus contains the god of lucidity instead of Dionysus, the god of madness. But beyond this, the philosophical life differs from the other divine kinds in that it alone possesses a winged intellect (249c4-6). The exhibition of divine madness is therefore not restricted to philosophers; in fact, Socrates earlier mentioned three other kinds: the prophetic, the purificatory, and the musical madness (244a8 ff.). If there are twelve divine kinds of Eros, with a possible twelve additional sub-varieties (corresponding to the third psychic type), then the four kinds of divine madness have at least twelve species and perhaps twelve additional sub-species, scattered through the nine degrees of incarnation. Probably only the twelve divine species represent the divisions of the four kinds of divine madness, since otherwise, every degree of human existence would be divinely mad which does not square with the original distinction. In sum: there are three different enumerations of the kinds of divine existence in the Stesichorean myth. The first (which gives four kinds of divine madness) and the third (which gives four examples of twelve kinds of divine Eros) are compatible with each other, but the second enumeration differs from the other two in making a sharper distinction between the philosophical and the non-philosophical lives. And when we try to map the first and third onto the second, various ambiguities arise, turning upon the fact that such a mapping seems to transform all degrees of human existence into kinds of divine madness. In other words, *there is no clear and distinct division of human existence in accordance with kinds, as obtained by counting and measuring.*

The general significance of the tripartite enumeration of lives seems to be this: all men yearn for philosophy, and thus the highest elements in their existence may be understood as the mark of divine madness in the human psyche. But only the philosopher, with his winged intellect, is able to grasp reflexively the significance of Eros and madness. All men love something, and they divinize or worship the object of their love (252d5-e1, 253b5-c2). But only those men are truly divine whose love corresponds to a truly divine property, or who rise above the body to those things which are honored by the psyche. These things must be "remembered" (253a2-3) or inferred from sense-perception; and the most divine man is the follower of Zeus, or the one with the strongest memory. It is thanks to memory that man is able to perform the recollection by which he overcomes the divisions of human existence. This is why it is so amusing that the weak-memoried Phaedrus should have given his name to our dialogue.

In order to appreciate the metaphorical significance of pederasty, or what has sometimes been called Plato's "asceticism," it is sufficient to reflect upon the role of memory in the achievement of perfection and *eudaimonia* (253c2-6). The implicit denigration of heterosexual love is not intelligible as a "sociological" characteristic of the Athenian aristocracy, since it entails a criticism of orthodox political (and so religious) virtue and obedience as well. In a sense, public virtue is also based upon memory, as embodied in *nomos*, whether written or unwritten. If we consider political existence in terms of its comprehensiveness and respect for the origins, it may indeed serve as a preparatory imitation of the philosophical life. But political existence, precisely as a form of memory, or in its mode of comprehensive respect for the origins, is characterized by an absence of reflexivity. The unity provided by citizenship is always a form of division, as is primarily visible in the rivalry of cities, but also in the opposing interests of classes within a given city. The Eros upon which political unity depends is divisive in two senses; first and primarily, it is directed toward, and culminates in, the generation of bodies. Secondly, it emphasizes the division within human nature of the male and the female, a division that extends beyond the immediately sexual to all fundamental aspects of political or historical existence: war and peace, hunting and the domestic arts, pride and meekness, making and looking—the list might be extended indefinitely. I do not, of course, refer to some facile revision of the Pythagorean table of opposites, arranged as distinct traits of the two separate sexes. Each aspect of human life may be analyzed into its male and female component; this is the fundamental significance of the Platonic doctrine of Eros. The same is true of the pederastic Eros. But Plato chooses this form of love as the central, and in a way the only, example of his doctrine of Eros because its very "unnaturalness" allows, and even forces it to attain to a kind of reflexivity or consciousness of its goal as "higher" than the natural forms of human satisfaction. The praise of pederasty, whether or not in its "sublimated" form, makes sense only with respect to the praise of philosophy, and even there, it is an extreme exaggeration with a very special function. It is a low or corporeal reflection of a high or psychic desire for the unity which is not divided by acts of creation or generation in all of its forms. The pederast, taken in his pure form, cannot be prevented by absorption in his children, and so the city, from achieving a reflexive consciousness of the significance of recollection. Of course, the pederastic Eros may be deflected into poetry, rhetoric, or some other mode of generating. The dissolution of the corporeal Eros into diversity recurs continuously at each of its levels. We are dealing with a metaphor and with myth, not with a scientific or mathematical analysis of human nature. But the function of the metaphor is clear enough: to prepare us, as philosophers and not as perverts, for a transcendence of the body.

We may now return to Socrates' account of how the lover captures his beloved. In so doing, we return also to the mythical division of the psyche into three kinds (εἴδη), represented by the two steeds and the charioteer (253c7-d1). Both the good and the bad horse are winged; that is, desire, even in its lowest forms, is characterized by a nisus toward self-transcendence or completeness. The good horse is of an aristocratic appearance, and "a lover of honor marked by moderation and shame." These attributes make him "a companion of true opinion" who is led by speech and command rather than by force (253d3-e1). The bad horse is crooked and ugly, and includes among its proletarian features a snub nose (253e1-3).[58] This ironical reference to Socrates has the serious function of reminding us not to condemn the bad horse too hastily. He, too, has an essential function in the human economy. As the companion of hybris and imposture, he is deaf, and so must be controlled by force rather than speech (253e3-6). But this deafness and hybris constitute precisely the psychic bond to the corporeal world of genesis. It is our desire for things which

---

58 Cf. von Arnim's observation on 253e (πολὺς εἰκῇ συμπεφο-ρημένος) ["put together at random" – ed.] which he compares with *Republic* 561e, where the ποικίλος ["multifarious" – ed.]. or democratic man is described: "Diese widerspruchsvolle Mannigfaltigkeit des inneren Lebens, entspringt aber aus der πολυειδία des ἐπιθυμητικόν," [the diversity in form of the desiring part"-ed] p. 160.

guides speech to the love of the forms of things, or prevents the psyche from losing itself in rhetorical solipsism. In the most fundamental erotic sense, the bad horse is responsible for procreation, which is necessary for the possibility of philosophical existence. The good horse, "constrained by shame," does not leap upon the beloved; as the passage makes clear, he tries to avoid the beautiful boy altogether. It is the bad horse who forces the psyche to approach the beloved; that is, the "remembrance" (μνεία) of sexual pleasure attracts us to beautiful bodies and is the necessary condition for the recollection of beauty (253e6-254a7).[59] If the equine nature of the psyche were characterized by shame without desire, its preference for true opinion would not achieve the reflexivity that comes from the conflict between attraction and separation.

Thus Socrates explicitly says that the struggle of the two horses and the charioteer culminates in the psyche's agreement to approach the youth. This surrender to the charm of lust is then transformed by the vision of the beloved whom the psyche approaches. Only then, and not after the initial, pre-concupiscent perception of the beloved, does the charioteer remember the nature of the beautiful (254a7-b6). The perception of true beauty joined with moderation and holiness is then not the same as the love of honor joined with moderation and shame (253d6, 254b6-7). True moderation emerges dialectically from the conquest of lust by noetic perception. The struggle between the bad horse on the one hand, and the good horse and the now enlightened charioteer on the other, illustrates powerfully the process of separative attraction, or the foundation of noetic vision in sense-perception as inflected by desire (254b7-255a1). The charioteer is enlightened, not by the piety of the good horse, but by the hybris of the bad

---

59 Cf. Robin (*Phèdre*), p. ci, note 1. Robin takes πόθος at 253e7 to mean "regret" rather than "désir passionné," which, as he says, is inappropriate for the good horse. The passion of the bad horse may then be understood as necessary for the "longing" of the good horse, or for the "recollection" of true beauty.

horse. It is incorrect to say, as does Hackforth, that "in the case before us, the desire of the good horse cannot be discriminated from that of the charioteer: they both want precisely the same kind of satisfaction from the beloved" (p. 107). In fact, the charioteer is, at the first sight of the beloved, "filled up with the tickling or goading of desire" (253e5-6); that is, he is at first an ally of the bad horse. Each of the three psychic components plays its part in the transformation of carnal hybris by the "forethought" or recollection of the charioteer (254e5-7).

Socrates is now drawing to an end his Stesichorean praise of Eros. The description of the interplay between vision and desire in physiological Eros becomes therefore steadily less intricate; we are descending from the peak of the hyper-Uranian beings. The power of this section of the myth lies mainly in the extraordinary clarity of the image of the erotic psyche, divided against itself by the necessarily diversified expression of its desire for unity. That is, the rhetorical force of the middle section of the myth carries us upward by an evocation of divine psychic being. The rhetorical force of the present section carries us downward into the struggle between body and psyche, and down to the triumph of the body over the psyche. This descent culminates in the transition from the lover to the beloved. The lover who has apparently triumphed over his desire is now faced by the dangers of idolatry. His reverence for the beloved, whom he treats "as equal to a god," is the cause of further temptation for both (255a1-4). It remains to be seen whether they will triumph over or surrender to the temptation that arises from piety toward the body (cf. 256a1 ff.).

In other words, we are now in the midst of a description of Eros from the perspective of human rather than divine vision. The intentions of the lover, for all his reverence and the "truth" of his passion (255a2-3), are ambiguous. He does not yet have a reflexive grasp on, or recollection of, his memory of true beauty (cf. 254a6, b5, d3-4: the bad horse comes closest to ἀνάμνησις in the technical sense). Similarly, it is not clear whether the beloved is being corrupted by "age and necessity" or rising above the sober opinion that it is shameful to associate with a lover (255a4-b1). Even if fate prevents friendship among the bad, and guarantees good friends to the good (255b1-2), it may allow bad men to fall passionately in love with good youths. Neither does it follow that the erotic passion is the same as friendship; in fact, it is obvious that they cannot be identical, since passion is usually conquered by carnal desire. The youth may well be mistaken in his perception of the superiority of erotic to other forms of friendship; that is, his perception of the god within his lover is mitigated by the external consequences of the body, just as the god must be hampered by his corporeal dwelling (255b3-7). In any case, relations between lover and beloved lead next to a state of what can only be called unconscious narcissism for the youth. Their proximity "in the gymnasia and elsewhere" transforms the lover into a mirror, wherein the beloved sees and is enamored of his own reflection (255b7-d3). But this "counter-love" is only a mirror-image of erotic reflexivity (255d8-e1); the youth loves, but does not know what he loves.[60] Lacking this knowledge, he cannot speak, which means that he has not undergone the attractive separation of philosophical Eros. Thus far at least, there is no evidence that the beloved previously obtained an adequate vision of true beauty (255d3-6). The integrity of his wings is not yet evident.

The self-love of the beloved also reflects the corporeally encumbered passion of the lover, which the youth mistakenly calls friendship (255e1-2). Both are dissolved in the fountain of desire, or achieve a "unification" that imitates philosophical completion (255e2-4). At this point, according to Socrates, the dialectic of speech and silence commences within the psyches of the couple (255e4 ff.). If passion and narcissism are mastered by "the better part of intelligence" (τῆς διανοίας), or the separative vision of discursivity, then they will be joined in the philosophical life, and experience happiness and "noetic unity" (256a7-b1: ὁμονοη-τικόν). The perception of physical beauty will be transformed into the vision of true beauty; their bodies will then separate as their

60   Cf. Robin (*Phèdre*), p. cii.

minds unite. This unity is noetic and not simply psychic. The mastery of the excellent over the base steed does not erase the tripartite structure of the psyche (256b1-3). The achievement of psychic mastery produces what we may perhaps call an internal transcendence of mind. The greatest good is thus a unity of human sobriety and divine madness (256b3-7). Man rises beyond his finite and divided self when speech mediates between desire and noetic apprehension. The ensuing recollection is thus simultaneously a self-forgetting. In remembering what we saw on the roof of the cosmos, we necessarily forget that we are now residents within the cosmos. The ultimate goal of self-knowledge is knowledge that heals the inadequacies of the self.

Socrates describes only two instances of erotic friendship in the closing paragraphs of his Stesichorean myth. The first is the philosophical transformation of sexual desire into love of true beauty as reflected in genesis. This love brings together sobriety and madness in the form of self-mastery, freedom, and excellence; it is the existential pre-condition for the noetic ascent, and not that ascent itself (256b1-7). The danger implicit in this precondition is exhibited in the second instance of erotic friendship. This instance is coarser and less philosophical than the first, but it is still marked by the love of honor (256b7-c1). In a very general sense, we have descended from the first to the second degree of psychic incarnation. In the highest manifestation of the political life, sexuality attains a partial triumph over friendship. The love of honor makes one necessarily dependent upon praise from the many, or what they call happiness; this intoxication with applause is a kind of sexual union with the multitude (256c1-5). At the same time, the love of honor, as an imitation of the philosophical love of the best, pulls one upward, away from the degrading embrace of the crowd (256c5-7). The Eros of the natural king is to this extent pederastic; namely, it leads to the generating of deeds and speeches rather than of children in the flesh. Needless to say, this is not a complete account of political Eros. We are concerned here only with the way in which it marks a deterioration from, and is thus related to, philosophy. The beloved friend of the lover of honor is, then, honor. The love of honor both reminds him of his human-ity and raises him above it. Hence he possessed a defective ver-sion of psychic transcendence and the possibility of becoming winged (256d3-e2). In itself, however, this life does not sprout wings (256d4); although not rooted in the subterranean pathways of the lower lives, it is still too much bound up with the surface of the earth (256d6 ff.).

And so Socrates closes his magnificent second speech on love by returning to the beginning, the boy or beloved (256e3 ff.). The friendship of the non-lover brings only a human sobriety (σω-φροσύνη θνητῇ), or the servility that is praised as virtue by the many. Sexuality is inflected altogether toward bodies, or the "mindless" return to the earth which will some day be mistaken for Dionysian intoxication (256e4-257a2). The myth as a whole may be understood as an attempt to explain the erotic proportions of heaven and earth in man's psychic revolution. This revolution is composed of two different motions, one which is measured by the numbers of mathematics, and the other by the numbers of po-etry. Man, as it were, participates in two different kinds of eternity, or is the mortal bond between two domains of immortality. In order to grasp man's divine function, we must earn the friendship of Eros (257e3-4), which means that we must enter into the rela-tionship of attractive separation, the path toward reflexive con-sciousness that the dialogues call recollection. A description of the psychic odyssey, since it combines mathematics and poetry, or rather explains the poetic function of mathematics, must nec-essarily be a myth rather than an epistemic logos (257a4-5).

The myth is the sole discursive unification of madness and sobriety; it provides the horizon within which purely sober speech finds its bearings. As a song about the silent foundations of speech, it can be sung only by the divinely blessed lover; it is a divine fate or gift, and not an undirected intensification of human powers (257a6-9). The merely human, as represented by the Lysian speeches, although in itself it is directed toward the earth (257b1-3), is a necessary moment in the dialectical transformation of Eros. For without the earth, in gaining heaven we would dissolve the cosmos. Since sobriety is a necessary part of philosophy, the union of Eros and philosophy recommended by Socrates can be achieved only by a harmony of the three speeches. The task of "making" our lives is the process of fulfilling the lover and the non-lover through the right mixture of madness and sobriety (257b3-6).

CHAPTER FOUR:
The Language of Love

I.

In the great myth of Stesichorus, Socrates has ascended from outside the walls of Athens to the roof of the cosmos and back again. Although numbers were not absent from this celestial journey, it is obvious that poetry replaces mathematics as the key to the myth, especially if we compare it to the journey from the cave into the sunlight and back down again, in the central books of the *Republic*. The discussion of the good rests upon a connection between justice and mathematics, or upon equalities, identities, and determinateness—what can be "counted on," in the political and arithmetical senses of the term. In other words, the good, as the presence and intelligibility of order within the whole cosmos, may be approached by an abstraction from particularity or difference, and thereby from self-consciousness or the differentiating particularity of psychic self-experience. As the psyche achieves noetic unity with the good, it loses its own identity as a self (which depends upon discourse, and thence upon the body). Within the limits of feasibility, this is what happens to the individual as a citizen of the just city. The perfectly just citizen tends toward the limit of self-forgetfulness or mathematical monadicity. In general, the *Republic* deals with the nature and education of the psyche as engaged in abstraction from difference toward sameness. In the *Phaedrus*, and specifically in the myth of Stesichorus, we are concerned with the nature of psychic experience in the perception of sameness as difference. Instead of the good, the erotic psyche perceives true being primarily as the beautiful. The perception of beauty is rooted in self-recollection, or the private unity of consciousness as differentiated by corporeal perception. Therefore the *Phaedrus* takes place outside the city walls, and is concerned with justice only to the extent that it is a condition for the transcendence of political mathematics. Justice is relevant only as a condition for private perfection; perfection, as the perception of beauty, is private enjoyment.

Mathematics is the speech of the particular as universal, whereas poetry is the speech of the universal as particular. Nothing particularizes like love; hence the link between poetry and Eros. There is, however, a further distinction to be made. Socratic poetry is not the same as the non-philosophical poetry which for purposes of convenience, we may identify as the offspring of Homer. This was suggested at the very beginning of Socrates' second speech by his adoption of the persona of Stesichorus. Stesichorus' eyes were literally opened by a recognition of the nature of poetic lies about Helen; the return of his vision thus symbolizes the philosophical recollection of true beauty. Let us say that Socratic poetry is characterized by self-reflexivity, and so by a subordination to the end of the beautiful presentation of truth. This is, of course, not quite the same as the sober presentation of truth, whether beautiful or ugly. Beautiful speech is charming, as excessively sober or ugly speech is not. This charm serves two functions: to attract friends and disarm enemies. One might phrase this more charmingly by saying that beautiful speech, as employed by Socrates, replaces political acquaintance with philosophical friendship. It must therefore play an exclusive as well as an inclusive role; and this is the fundamental diaeresis of philosophical rhetoric.

In plain terms, the man who devotes himself to self-perfection by searching for true beauty is necessarily politically suspect, not to say unjust. He may make recompense for this selfishness, or defect in justice, by the gift of beauty. But the beauty of Socratic poetry is by no means accessible to the average citizen, any more than is his selfless concern for truth. Its primary political function is thus defensive, and in two senses. First, Socratic poetry must be sufficiently pious to disarm the vulgar; second, it must be medicinal or (in the literal sense) psychiatric, in order to heal the wounds inflicted by the vulgar upon the psyches of the potential philosophers. One might plausibly maintain that these two functions are mutually contradictory, as the fate of Socrates himself suggests. The claim could be strengthened by a simple consideration of the discussion of rhetoric in the final third of the *Phaedrus*. The speech of Stesichorus, in its surface bloom, exhibits a beauty of sufficient piety to repel all but the most microscopic scrutiny. But Socrates does not leave it at that. More specifically, Plato publishes the subsequent conversation between Socrates and Phaedrus in which the veiled implication of Socrates' two speeches concerning the difference between private and public poetry is extended to rhetoric. That is, the difference is stated explicitly, in and about prose, instead of being partially concealed by myth. The main thesis of the last section of the *Phaedrus* seems to be the inferiority of political to philosophical rhetoric. But this makes it unmistakable that private perfection is superior to public obligation; the beauty of patriotism, in the various senses of that term, is superseded by the beauty of truth.

In these remarks, I have referred to Socrates' mythical speeches as poetry. Despite the mask of Stesichorus, and some other briefer indications (e.g., 257a5), it is not entirely accurate to identify myth and poetry. As the general dramatic setting makes clear, the emphasis is on speech-making or rhetoric. The dialogue began with an example of Lysian rhetoric, characterized by Socrates as democratic; that is, the speech of Lysias exemplifies the contemporary decay of political virtue. For the moment we may disregard the deeper philosophical implications of this speech. The surface is clear and important in its own right. Athenian virtue has been infected by the virus of sophistry; the Athenian love of speech, and of free speech, has deteriorated into a slavish appetite for sophistical rhetoric. This appetite may be described as an erotic perversion, not simply in the sense of pederasty, but more fundamentally as a separation of gratification from spiritual principles; noble Eros has succumbed to democratic physiology. In order to prepare his refutation of the vulgar rhetoric, Socrates, like a skilled debater, first shows his technical qualifications at the level admired by his opponents. This is the surface significance of his first speech. Socrates gives a better defense of the non-lover, i.e., of the tastes of corrupt Athens, than does the non-lover's official spokesman. In so doing, Socrates wins, if not the love, at least the desire of Phaedrus, who represents what we may perhaps call the non-beloved, that is, the "youth" being courted by the non-lover. Naturally, Phaedrus is not simply identical with the democratic or debased Athenian populace, who would be immune to Socratic psychiatry. Phaedrus is an "aristocratic" version of these democratic tastes; his specific love for rhetoric makes him accessible to Socrates. And indeed, the difference between Phaedrus and the multitude is already a sign of the trans-political intentions of the dialogue bearing his name. The most one could say is that if the many are to be influenced, it cannot be by Socrates' direct intervention, but only through the intercession of men like Phaedrus, to whom Socrates accommodates his teaching.

Having attracted Phaedrus, or won him from Lysias, Socrates then presents his accommodated teaching in the form of a myth attributed to Stesichorus. This speech represents a new form in contrast to the two preceding orations, something between poetry and rhetoric. It uses elements from both modes of discourse in order to inculcate in Phaedrus the beginnings of a dialectical transformation of his love of beauty. In slightly different terms, Socrates appeals to the anti-political selfishness of Phaedrus' debased tastes. One cannot cure the demos except by transforming its "taste-makers" or "intellectuals." And these cannot be forced to replace corrupt tastes by virtuous ones, precisely because they are already corrupt. But they may perhaps be deepened in their corruption, that is, assisted in developing a spiritually deeper comprehension of the exigencies of Eros. Their love of beauty may be raised, as part of this deepening process, from base to noble ends. After the mythical indoctrination, Phaedrus is at least accessible to improvement. As he says, he will join in Socrates' prayer to Eros "if it is better for us that these things come to pass"

(257b7-c1).[1] He is presumably now ready to move from myth to logos, or from poetic rhetoric to dialectic. Let us not overestimate Phaedrus' improvement, however, and thereby Socrates' frankness. Phaedrus is hypothetically won away from Lysias (257b7-c4), but he is not yet a new man.

Phaedrus is full of wonder at the speech he has just heard. Thus he addresses Socrates as "o wonderful one" (257c4-5), the strongest appellation employed by him since that same term's previous use at 230c6 (where it indicated Socrates' unusual failure to leave Athens). To this we may compare his very restrained response to Socrates' first speech (241d4-7). Socrates, on the other hand, for the first time explicitly demotes Phaedrus by addressing him as "youthful one" (257c8); his previous qualifications of Phaedrus' name had emphasized their friendly companionship.[2] I have already explained the sense in which Phaedrus represents the beloved, or the citizens of Athens. The present relationship between Socrates and Phaedrus is a synthesis of the relationship between the non-lover and lover on the one hand, and their respective erotic objects on the other. Socrates combines aspects of the non-lover and lover, just as Phaedrus combines aspects of the corresponding "youth." As I have already shown, they are united, not by their love for each other, but by their common love for speeches, and so, by their "selfish" desire for perfection.

Phaedrus reveals his youthfulness by uttering the laughable opinion that a politician, while recently abusing Lysias, employed the term "speech-writer" in a pejorative sense (257c4-d3). According to Phaedrus, persons of the greatest power and honor in the city are ashamed to write speeches and leave them to posterity, for fear of being called sophists (257d4-8). As Hackforth points out, it is quite likely "that most prose works hitherto had come from the pens of Sophists."[3] Certainly there can be no doubt of

1   Cf. 279c6-8.
2   227a1, 238c5 (φίλε); 227b2 (ἑταῖρε); 236d4, 241e2 (μακάριε); 242b8, 243c1 (ὦγαθέ).
3   P. 113, note 1.

the close ties between contemporary political rhetoric and sophistry. Nor does Socrates deny this tie; instead, he implies that statesmen only pretend to be ashamed of their speeches. And his examples suggest the inner connection between the epideictic rhetoric of the professional sophist and the legislative oratory of the professional politician (257d9-e6). The speeches of the Athenian assembly are motivated by the same principles as the discourse, written and oral, of the sophists. This refers, not simply to contemporary political corruption, but to a more fundamental interpretation of man as a speaking animal. The function of sophistic rhetoric is to persuade, regardless of the true or false beauty of its discourse. Those who share in the illness of sophistry are like the non-lover who seeks physiological gratification independent of nobility or true beauty. The debasement of Eros from a desire for physical beauty to a desire for physiological gratification is part of a more pervasive debasement of the conception of nature. In political terms, this debasement gives rise to the "law of nature" that it is just for the strong to have more than the weak, or that might makes right.[4]

The assimilation of all modes of speech under rhetoric, and the definition of rhetoric as persuasion, when understood as sophistry, makes persuasion equivalent to force. Socrates thus accuses contemporary political life of being based, not on justice, but on the illegitimate because unreasonable rule of the stronger. Political life is then the most forceful manifestation of human or discursive life altogether. The opposition between political and philosophical rhetoric is therefore really an opposition between the political and the philosophical way of life. It remains dubious, to say the least, whether any actual political community can avoid the deterioration into sophistry. If the truly just city depends upon the rule of those who truly perceive truth, or in terms of the *Phaedrus*, beauty, there can be no doubt of the superiority of the philosopher to the non-philosophical, politically active citizen. But unless it could be shown that the philosopher is able through

4   *Gorgias* 483c8-e4.

his own nature to assume political power, this superiority has nothing to do with force. Socrates is neither Descartes nor Bacon; he does not infer the youth of his philosophy from Machiavelli's view that fortune may be mastered by strong young men. It is Phaedrus, not Socrates, who is the youth.

With the discussion of speeches, we have moved part way between the "pederastic" and the "generating" Eros. According to the myth of Stesichorus, immortality is attained, not by generating speeches, but by looking at and remembering the hyper-Uranian beings. Now Socrates implies that statesmen, who may be taken as representative of men generally, become deathless through the generation of speeches or children of the psyche (258b10-c4). Or rather, he indicates that political men suppose themselves to achieve immortality in this way. However, the erotic situation seems to have become confused. The statesman, who is normally presented as courting the councilor demos, or taking the role of lover, is now described as the admired or beloved of the council or demos (258a1-b1). The point is in fact not difficult to grasp. Those who persuade the demos by courting its applause or catering to its appetites, thereby earn the gratitude (=gratification) of the demos, and this is the demotic form of love. This relationship between the political speaker and the demos persists after the death of the original members of the relationship. One's reputation, and hence immortality, depends upon the force with which he has persuaded his audience, which includes the unborn as well as the living, to admire or love him. Thus the statesman must himself admire the skill upon which his own admiration and immortality are based (258b2-9).

If rhetoric is equivalent to persuasion, then it may indeed be called the royal art. There are, however, different degrees of monarchy. The king who rules by force (e.g., Darius) is not as genuinely a king as those law-givers (e.g., Lycurgus, Solon) who rule by persuasion. Even titular kings, although they regard themselves as equal to a god, must obey the law-giver (258b10-c6). On the basis of this distinction, we may already anticipate a third kind of monarch, the philosopher, provided that he becomes the teacher of law-givers. We cannot, however, distinguish the three kinds of monarch simply on the basis of their political status or reputation. What people suppose, whether about themselves or others, is finally a consequence of force or knowledge, that is, of false or true rhetoric. In order to know who is by nature a king, we have to know the nature of the human psyche; and since the psyche persuades by speech, we have to know the true art of rhetoric. At this point, the investigation of immortality and of rhetoric coincide. *In both cases, it is necessary to know who is truly like a god* (258c1-2: ἀθάνατος, ἰσόθεον). The true king is he who truly persuades himself about the domain of hyper-Uranian beings. There is, then, nothing shameful as such about the writing of speeches, understood in the comprehensive sense of engaging in discursive speech (258c6-d3). It is, of course, essential to distinguish between shameful (or political) and noble (or philosophical) speech-making. We cannot speak persuasively to ourselves of our recollection of true beauty unless we know the art of beautiful (=noble) speech. If knowledge is rooted in recollection, persuasion is rooted in knowledge; that is, if it is not mere force.

Therefore Socrates raises the theoretical question: "what is the way of speaking nobly and otherwise?" (258d7). The investigation is fundamental or comprehensive, and includes the two main subdivisions of speech, political and private (258d9).[5] As a fundamental or theoretical question, it is primarily directed toward the perfection of the private investigator, whatever the practical or political consequences may happen to be. Since everyone desires his own satisfaction, whoever is capable of grasping the connection between speech and satisfaction is compelled to undertake the investigation proposed by Socrates. Phaedrus interprets satisfaction as pleasure, albeit he has been sufficiently impressed by the Stesichorean speech to insist upon pure or psychic pleasures (258e1-5). And this is also in keeping with his generally

5   The distinction between poetry and prose (258d10-11) is a secondary one, and in fact originally corresponds to the distinction between public and private.

passive Eros, to say nothing of his self-satisfied recognition of himself as an "intellectual."[6] He therefore agrees with those who call adherence to bodily pleasure by the name of slavery. If anything, Phaedrus has become excessively serious, because his seriousness arises from a deeper frivolousness. Phaedrus prefers rhetoric to conversation, and he probably assumes that an investigation of speech-making consists in the making of speeches. Since perfection is for him pleasure, and that primarily in listening to speeches, his own serious desire for perfection would be satisfied by a Socratic oration on true rhetoric.

But listening to orations is a form of laziness or forgetfulness, and so may justly be called a form of slavery, or submission to a kind of psychic corporealization (259a3-6). Socrates reminds Phaedrus that a serious investigation of rhetoric is dialectical (259a1, a7). Even the passive pursuit of perfection is a kind of activity, a sharing in discursive work. At the same time, serious conversation, the "work" of free men, is playful. One cannot distinguish between the noble and the base without a noble disdain for the base. Socratic disdain, however, never takes the form of righteous indignation. Indignation, or what Nietzsche called *Rache*, would be especially inappropriate in the pursuit of beauty, since it introduces ugliness into the psyche. If I may so put it, Phaedrus' seriousness is bourgeois or "professional," whereas Socrates' playfulness is aristocratic or "amateurish" in the literal sense of the lover. Socrates thus moderates Phaedrus' seriousness by playfully reminding him of their natural environment with its divine connotations, which he specifically associates with the cicadas (258e6 ff.). These interesting creatures, as we were informed by Aristophanes in the *Symposium*, at 191c1-2, reproduce by casting their seed into the earth rather than by heterosexual relations.

---

6   Hence Hackforth shows his failure to have grasped the fundamental significance of Phaedrus by chastising Plato for having committed a "dramatic fault" in assigning these lines to Socrates' companion (p. 115, note 1). Cf. Thompson, *loc. cit.*, who, however, goes too far in taking Phaedrus as a sort of Platonist.

Their Eros symbolizes a solution to the fundamental defect of pederasty. It is therefore appropriate that Socrates selects them to mediate between human beings and the Muses (259b1 ff.). For the generation of music proceeds by the casting of seed into the psyche, rather than into the body of another. One's own psyche takes the place of the earth in the myth of the cicadas, thereby illustrating both the purification of pederastic Eros and the transition from political obligation to private perfection.

Socrates shows the extraordinary charm of music by a story about its first appearance among humans. We are so accustomed to this charm that, even in submitting to it, we do not fully appreciate its marvelous power. But the pre-musical men had no preparation for the (unexplained) arrival of the Muses. They were so stunned by pleasure that some of them continued to sing without food and drink until they died (259b6-c2). The present existence of the human race is therefore due to the ability of some pre-musical men to triumph over the Siren-song of the Muses (cf. 259a7-8). As is evident from the example of singing, or the humming of the cicadas, this triumph may be understood as one of discursivity. It is necessary, in order to be a human being, to render music articulate. Otherwise, one is transformed into a cicada. Similarly, the mere giving of speeches is analogous to the silence of music; it must be articulated by conversation or dialectic. Just as the cicadas mediate between humans and the Muses, so music (i.e., the fine arts) mediates between the human and the pre-human. Music "civilizes," but it can also reduce us to a silence which is so pleasant that we prefer it to speech. The extreme form of musical cultivation is thus equivalent to the transformation of men into beasts—into cicadas. This is the warning resonant within Socrates' playful myth.

Those who previously died because of their inability to absorb or articulate music, have now been reincarnated as cicadas. They neither eat nor drink, but spend their existence in song, and also in observing the human race (259c3-6). Presumably, then, they must have the ability to talk to themselves, but not to each other. In any event, after their death, they are able to report to the Muses about the honor that mortals pay to the arts. Three types of musical men are mentioned among the adherents to the Muses: those who honor the dance (Terpsichore), the erotics (Erato), and the philosophers (Calliope and Urania). As Socrates emphasizes, the musical men are distinguished "in accordance with the form of their honor" (259d2-3; cf. c6-7). This expresses the civilizing or political function of music. Eros, too, is domesticated by its association with the Muses, although it retains its old function as intermediary, here between the dance and philosophy. Conversely, however, Socrates makes the Muses more articulate or philosophical than they were traditionally. The most beautiful music is about heaven and accounts of gods and men (259d5-7); that is, epic poetry is here transformed into philosophy.

I may summarize the primary functions of the myth of cicadas as follows. It serves to introduce the poetic expression of the political environment of rhetoric, by giving a slight emphasis to the priority of the private to the public. In other words, given the expression of private perfection in the myth of Stesichorus, we have been led to reflection upon the nature of speech or discourse. This reflection is primarily for the sake of clarifying the meaning of private perfection. But there is a danger in the poetic approach to speech which is symbolized by the silence of music. Even though a parallel danger exists in the mathematical approach, the proper method entails a mixture of these two dialects. In our dialogue, however, the mixture will give priority to poetry over mathematics.

II.

As we begin our study of rhetoric, let us emphasize two related points. First: we are not engaged in the analysis of a treatise on epistemology, but a very intricate dramatic conversation between Socrates and Phaedrus. As the principles of rhetoric would themselves suggest, Socrates must adapt his teaching to the understanding of Phaedrus. Second: the discussion of rhetoric is a consequence of interest in Eros, and hence in perfection or immortality. This in turn is introduced by means of Phaedrus' love of epideictic rhetoric; more specifically, perfection is introduced by means of a selfish hedonism which is directed by the love of beautiful speeches. Phaedrus is concerned with persuasion rather than truth, because he perceives the persuasiveness of beauty, but not the connection between beauty and truth. For example, Phaedrus admired both of Socrates' speeches, and especially the second one, but he never bothered to ask whether there is any truth in the Stesichorean myth. For Phaedrus, truth is contained in the province of physics, not myth (229c4 ff.). Phaedrus belongs, as an "intellectual," to the camp of demythologizers, or those who possess a boorish wisdom. He must therefore be prepared for a more adequate investigation of the truth by a heavy dose of charming ignorance. Less obliquely put, it is Phaedrus' love of beauty, as an expression of his selfishness or concern for himself, which makes him accessible to Socratic rhetoric. The dissolution of the human in process physics must be combatted by an appeal to the human, all too human. Even physicists are accessible to poetry and Eros, which serve to remind them that they are human beings.

Socrates now broaches the essential question of the dialogue: "must not he who speaks well and beautifully possess a discursive knowledge of the truth about those things concerning which he is about to speak?" (259e4-6). If the answer to this question is "yes," then presumably Socrates knows the truth about the psyche, the gods, and the hyper-Uranian beings—unless, of course, we deny that his speech was beautiful. But if we assume that it was, the question arises as to how we would go about proving its beauty to those who might deny our assumption. This is the easiest way to grasp the central importance of *keen vision* for Plato: all arguments rest upon an apprehension of beauty, which is inaccessible to the psychic dullard of however powerful a logical technique. In any case, Socrates seems to claim that his discourse is true in passages like 245c3 ff. and 247c3 ff. At 246a4 ff. and c6 ff., however, he evidently admits that at least part of his discourse is not a true logos, but a likeness or product of the imagination. The speech as a whole is a myth. In what sense is a myth "true?"[7]

For example, even if we answer "yes" to the question just posed by Socrates, it is altogether possible that one who knows the truth about certain matters may give a "good and beautiful" speech about them which is not true, or not altogether true. The fact is that Socrates' question is difficult if not impossible to answer, as our recollection of his own speech shows. Did not Socrates, who normally claims to be ignorant of all but Eros, seek to persuade Phaedrus of a salutary opinion by the judicious use of beautiful lies? If Socrates lied in his first speech, how do we know that he has not lied in his second speech as well?

Phaedrus replies somewhat evasively to Socrates' question: he has heard that it is not necessary for the orator to understand beforehand "what is really just" nor "the really good or beautiful," but rather what the many opine them to be (259e7-260a4). This answer is compatible with the position that, so far as justice, goodness, and beauty are concerned, to know the popular opinion is equivalent to knowing the truth. The truth may be that there is no truth in these matters, as there is in the case of mathematics and physics. Socrates recognizes the allusion to the sophists or "wise men," and replies with a quote from Homer, taken from Nestor's martial advice to pursue the siege of Troy.[8] That is, his reply to the suggestion by Phaedrus will be a continuation of his war against sophistry, and (as Nestor's speech suggests) an erotic triumph to avenge the detention of Helen (260a5-7). It is therefore subtly related to his Stesichorean myth; in both cases, the problem is how to speak best about the highest beauty. Socrates' eristic is, however, verbal rather than corporeal; it entails "looking at" the speech of the sophists, and so is primarily passive (260a6-10). He begins with an example that is both "polemical" and "laughable." Suppose that an orator persuades Phaedrus, who does not know

---

7   Cf. *Phaedo* 114d1 ff. where Socrates says, at the conclusion of another myth about the psyche, that we ought to believe stories like this, even if they are not definitely true: καλὸς γὰρ ὁ κίνδυνος. ["for the danger is noble" – ed.]

8   *Iliad*, II. 361.

the difference between a horse and a donkey, to make war with the latter's aid, in place of the former. Phaedrus emphasizes that the situation would be ludicrous (260b1-c2). Socrates then shifts from the horse and donkey to good and evil, now asserting that the orator is as ignorant as the city he seeks to persuade (260c6-7). In the earlier example, it seemed that the orator was aware of the difference between a horse and a donkey, and was therefore able to take advantage of Phaedrus' assumed ignorance in the matter. The sophist can tell the difference between a noble and a base animal, but not between nobility and baseness. On this score, he is as much a donkey as the multitude. Nevertheless, his moral insensitivity does not prevent him from making a scientific study of public opinion, and persuading the public that evil is in fact good (260c8-d1).

Socrates' formulation of the scene implies that there is a distinction between good and evil, and moreover, that this distinction is visible to the orator, even though he does not grasp its significance. Otherwise, the orator could persuade neither himself nor his audience that good is really evil and vice versa. To this extent, he must be a clever enemy rather than a foolish friend (260c4-5). The orator already regards good as evil and evil as foolish or laughable. Hence his perception of this distinction is, although no doubt evil to good men, neither good nor evil in his own eyes, but beyond good and evil: *technical,* or enlightened. The identification of the good with the persuasive, of course, is an instance (or consequence) of the principle that might makes right. As I have already observed, this principle may be true, and therefore compatible with the principle that the good speaker must know the truth about the subjects of his discourse. In any case, the discussion is presently concerned, not with the necessity of truth for good and beautiful rhetoric (which neither of the speakers denies here), but rather with the truth about the good and the beautiful.

Thus Socrates says that perhaps rhetoric will defend itself against his boorish attack on "the technē of speeches" by retorting that it does not require ignorance of its practitioners. On the contrary, rhetoric advises those who use it to possess the truth in advance; "I make this big claim" (rhetoric continues) "that without me, knowing what is truly so (τῷ τὰ ὄντα εἰδότι) will not advance a man in the technē of persuasion" (260d3-9). Socrates personifies rhetoric, thereby rendering more dramatic her defense against his own boorish wisdom. The defense of rhetoric turns upon a distinction between what I will call technical and substantive truth. In the previous examples, the rhetorician was assigned the power of persuasion, which was tacitly equated with technical skill, and thus with knowledge of the truth about the technē of persuasion. Technical truth is now identified as necessary to make substantive truth persuasive. This defense of rhetoric is therefore not really different from the previous attack on it; the two claims are entirely compatible, even though they seem to oppose each other. But technical truth, which is able to persuade fools of substantive falsehoods, does not change its nature in persuading fools or wise men of substantive truths. In the latter case, of course, Socrates attributes to rhetoric the advice that we learn the truth, i.e., substantive truth, before employing her. But this is optional; the defense actually emphasizes the independence of technical from substantive truth. The net result is that if rhetoric is a technē, it can persuade men of substantive truth or falsehood. Perhaps it is easier to persuade them of substantive truth; hence the aforementioned advice. However, this is a technical rather than a substantive question. No substantive connection between rhetoric and truth has been shown. At best, it would seem, technical and substantive truth are reciprocally useful. But utility is measured by persuasion or power, and this means that technical truth is the articulation of power. We see here the ancestral link between pure logic and the will to power.

Socrates wishes to establish that we cannot speak beautifully without knowing the truth about the substance of what we say. He must therefore deny the validity of distinguishing (as I have put it) between technical and substantive truth, or in effect of identifying technical truth and true beauty. His next step is accordingly to consider the possibility that rhetoric is not a technē but an "unskilled practice" (ἄτεχνος τριβή).[9] To do this, Socrates calls forth some arguments whom be personifies as "noble creatures" in order to give the lie to the persona of rhetoric (260e2-261a5). These creatures seem to be repeating a Spartan maxim that there is no true technē without a grasp of the truth. The attribution of this maxim to the Spartans carries with it an unmistakable criticism of Athenian technicism, or speech for the sake of speech. To the Athenian, talk is power; to the Spartan, talk interferes with action, and is thus impotent. Spartan military virtue is then truer because nobler than the democratic rhetoric of Athens. These Spartan arguments will presumably chastise the Athenian tastes of Phaedrus; their poetic personae are the sugar-coating which will persuade him to swallow the rebuke. At the same time, however, the need for sugar-coating is a sign that the true rhetoric can be no more Spartan than it is Athenian.

Socrates now drops the personification of his arguments, and proceeds to develop the point that rhetoric is indeed a technē (cf. however 261e1-2), but not in accordance with the usual understanding. In other words, he denies the distinction between technical and substantive truth in the case of rhetoric, which, he suggests, is the technē of psychagogy or the alluring and persuading of psyches through speeches, both in public and in private, with respect to things of much and little importance alike (261a7-b2). The word ψυχαγωγία has religious overtones; as is appropriate in the context of the Stesichorean myth, it refers to the leading of psyches into the next world, and also to conjuring up the dead, or as we may say, to the return of the discarnate psyches into this world.[10] Rhetoric is thus addressed to the entire psyche, and not simply to the mind; it covers the entire range of verbal persuasion. Such a technē is in a sense defined as the reverse of a

9 Cf. Hackforth's remarks (p. 122) about the echo of and difference from the *Gorgias*.
10 Diesendruck (p. 24) points out that the noun ψυχαγωγία appears nowhere else in Plato (although the verb-form occurs in the *Timaeus* and *Laws*). No doubt its choice here is somehow connected to the fact that Isocrates frequently uses the word to describe the function of his rhetorical school.

technē; that is, it cannot be understood as a purely mathematical, theoretical, or disinterestedly instrumental way of doing something. Phaedrus is unacquainted with this synoptic conception of rhetoric which, as he understands it, has a primarily political use (261b3-5). Socrates' suggestion is so surprising that it leads Phaedrus to swear by Zeus.[11] This passage also shows that Phaedrus regards epideictic rhetoric, of which Lysias' speech is an example, as public or political by nature. Part of Phaedrus' surprise may be due to a suspicion that, if Socrates' conception of rhetoric is sound, it can no longer be cleanly and distinctly separated from physics and cosmology. He ought to be wondering whether a demythologized physics is genuinely useful.

Socrates startles Phaedrus again by asking whether he has ever heard of the technical treatises by Nestor, Odysseus and Palamedes on speech-making (261b6-8). Once again Phaedrus swears by Zeus; he attempts to mitigate his surprise by demythologizing Socrates' references. Nestor may be a cryptic allusion to Gorgias, and Thrasymachus (or perhaps Theodorus) to Odysseus (261c1-3). Socrates does not deny the implied connection between Homeric and sophistic wisdom (261c4: ἴσως).[12] Instead, he turns

11 The last time Phaedrus used this oath was at 243d2, when Socrates pointed out to him that a well-bred man of erotic experience would reject as base the "Lysian" censure of Eros. In other words, Phaedrus is startled in both passages, by the idea that rhetoric is concerned with the ἔτυμος λόγος ["true speech" – ed.] (cf. 243a8, 260e5). At 229c4 the oath occurs again in conjunction with the status of truth in mythology.

12 Cf. *Theaetetus* 153a1 ff. Palamedes is a post-Homeric hero, ostensibly put to death for treason during the siege of Troy, on a trumped-up charge conceived by Odysseus, who was jealous of his wisdom. Palamedes was subsequently associated with the sophists, and a variety of inventions, including the discovery of the alphabet, were attributed to him. Friedländer (p. 215) cites *Republic* 522d: Palamedes is said to have discovered number, without which Agamemnon could not have been an army commander. Here is another instance of the subterranean or silent presence of mathematics in the *Phaedrus*.

to the narrower conception of rhetoric just mentioned by Phaedrus. In general, Phaedrus seems to conceive of rhetoric as divided into two main parts. The first or epideictic part consists of display pieces like Lysias' defense of the non-lover, and the second of specifically political (dikastic and dēmēgoric) speeches. The political character of the first part is indirect; its instances teach us about the character of utility, or the link between political power and private satisfaction. The second part is explicitly concerned with justice and injustice (261c4-9), or what from Phaedrus' perspective we may call legal or constitutional utility, and so with what is generally "good" for the city (261d3-4). As Phaedrus conceives of rhetoric, it distinguishes between technical and substantive truth in all its parts. Theoretically, rhetoric is akin to logic and mathematics; practically, it is the voice of the will to power. In political rhetoric, then, the possession of technical truth allows us to prove the same things to be either just or unjust, good or bad, as we will it (261c10-d5: ὅταν δὲ βουλήται). The division between technical and substantive truth is at the same time a rendering autonomous of technical argumentation or dialectic. To the technical dialectician, things have no moral or political stability because they lack ontological identity. X is either good or bad because it is neither good nor bad; that is, as defined by technical skill, it is either X or non-X, and neither in its own substance (261d6-9).[13]

Is this conclusion not itself the contradictory to the one initially put forward by Socrates in this context, namely, that rhetoric, if it is a technē, is psychagogic rather than narrowly technical or dialectical? In a sense, this is precisely the point. If rhetoric is a comprehensive verbal psychagogy, then it cannot be merely a technical skill in manipulating words, but must be concerned with substantive truth, or the ends for the sake of which we speak. It must be philosophical dialectic. The sophistic dialectic,

13 This point has been excellently elaborated in terms of contemporary "relating logic" by Henry Veatch in his *Two Logics* (Evanston, Northwestern University Press, 1969).

as for example that practiced by Zeno, is an imperfect imitation of philosophical dialectic. It retains the technical skill, but detaches it from the philosophical responsibility to the ends of psychic completeness. The ostensibly autonomous dialectic of sophistry is actually attached to the debased contemporary interpretation of political excellence as power or persuasion, an interpretation which it has helped to prepare. It would be an interesting question to ask whether sophistry arose as a consequence of the non-political character of pre-Socratic Philosophy.[14] In any case, as I have already noted, the Platonic dialogues regularly link "process physics" and sophistic. If genesis is in total flux, then words, too, must share in perpetual de- or re-formation. X is then, both as a symbol and as the substance symbolized, regularly turning into non-X. Thus the sophistic technē, as one or comprehensive, "if it is such," is at the same time not such. Everything can be made like everything else, and for everyone;[15] hence dialectical efforts to deceive must themselves be "exposed" or transformed by the same lack of substantive fixity (261d10-e5).

In response to Phaedrus' question, Socrates clarifies the last point. We are deceived about the resemblance between X and Y when the difference between them is small rather than large. Similarly, if we move from X to Y by small degrees, there is a better chance of passing undetected in the task of persuading that opposites are the same. But this passage to the identity of differences or opposites (not the same thing) demands that we ourselves perceive the exact truth about the small differences or similarities which we are dissembling (261e6-262a8). According to Socrates, then, unless we know the truth about X, that is, its identity, we cannot perceive its similarity, whether great or small, to Y, Z, or anything else (262a9-b1). However, the sophist would maintain

---

14 For a similar contemporary problem, see Collingwood's autobiography.

15 I follow Robin in translating 261e3 ("de rendre toute chose semblable à toute chose, de celle, bien entendu, qui le peuvent et à l'égard de ceux pour qui c'est possible").

that X has no identity, or is both X and non-X (whether as Y, Z, or something else). Once again we may be prevented by our symbolism from grasping the force of the substantive contention. The sophist does not claim that the symbol "X" is actually "non-X" as well, but rather that "X" stands for an insubstantial congeries of motions, at least some of which are symbolizable by "non-X." The rigidity or self-identity of the symbols "X" and the like might well lead to a mathematical or logical Platonism. But this in turn leads to a doctrine of what I previously called the "ontological subject" (Chapter Three), and about which nothing discursively systematic can be said. The sophist as I interpret him would claim that "X," "Y," and the like, as symbols designating ontological subjects, are imaginary rather than ontological entities, precisely because their rigidity or self-identity does not correspond to any substance or entity in genesis (i.e., the whole). His case rests on the contention that people are easily deceived, not where there are small differences between two entities, but where there are massive similarities between two different entities. For the sophist, there are no identities, not even of differences. And Socrates has himself shifted his ground by a small degree of motion from what we may call position X to position Y. It is one thing to say that X differs from Y by a small difference, and another to say that X and Y are similar. In the second case, there must be stable identities (the massive similarity of the sophist being actually an infinite regress of differences, which we perceive as similarities); in the first case, there need not be, because the difference between X and Y could be the difference between X and itself.

If the rate of change in the flux of genesis, e.g., between X and non-X, is slow enough, or as Socrates puts it, by small degrees, then it seems possible to say "X is X" at one moment and "X is non-X" at another, and be both intelligible and correct in both cases. Since speech is discursive or temporally sequential, one can only say "one thing at a time," and also describe temporal change as it occurs. On this basis, we might argue, sophistry is no longer deceptive, but the true speech its practitioners obviously believed it to be. Even the claim that X simultaneously manifests contradictory properties is defensible if X is "more or less" similar to itself, i.e., by small degrees of difference for correspondingly small times, while continuously but slowly (relative to the speaker and his audience) undergoing change. The identity of X would then be a function of time, or a changing pattern which is able to encompass contradictory attributes, so long as other attributes are (for the time being) stable, or changing at an imperceptible rate. Massive similarity is then massive delusion, the delusion that allows us to speak at all. The difference between the two positions asserted by Socrates, and thus the refutation of sophistry, turn upon the meaning of *similar*. Socrates always tries to reduce the logic of sophistry to the extreme view that X is simultaneously and totally non-X. But this view cannot even be asserted without assuming the identity of X in the two cases of its assertion and negation, not just as a blank symbol, but as a formal configuration for which "X" is merely a symbol. Needless to say, such analyses are not presented in the *Phaedrus* but merely alluded to.

The complete refutation of sophistry depends upon a "weaving together" of arguments like those concerning noetic monads or ontological subjects, with arguments about the nature of "similarity" and self-identity. In the immediate context, Socrates' account of sophistic rhetoric is logically defective but rhetorically adequate. In general, we err with respect to similarity, or by mistaking X for Y (262b2-4). We may also agree that the technē of persuasion depends upon knowledge of "what is each of the beings" about which we are speaking, whether to reveal or to conceal their natures (262b5-9). But the problem is whether the beings about which we speak are words, things, or something else. The tacit assumption of sophistic rhetoric is that we cannot really speak about things, but only desire them; speech is not merely through, but also about, words. No doubt the sophist recognized that speech itself refers to things, but the disjunction between technical and substantive truth implies what I shall call a difference in the rate of change between words and things. If we can say whatever we wish about things (the extreme case being to say that X is at once and in the same respect Y and non-Y), then things either have no nature at all, or their nature eludes the web of speech. Now desire convinces us that things have natures; they satisfy or frustrate us with considerable regularity, *so long as we do not speak about them*. Speech has the strange power to supervene over, or to invert, our desire. It makes X good, whereas previously we had found X to be bad. Considerations of this very simple kind lead to the conclusion that the nature of things, or their identities, do not regulate speech, and certainly not technical discourse. Therefore (the thesis holds) speech about similarity and dissimilarity is speech about speech—as we would now say, about "linguistic entities."

Sophistry may therefore be attacked from two different sides. Either we may seize upon the untenable disjunction between speech and desire, as by showing the implications of the desire to speak. Or we may attack the motion of infinite regression within the concept of purely linguistic meaning. That is, for example, we may argue that if similarity is a linguistic entity, it is a construction or postulate that may be negated or contradicted at will. One may argue that the stability of technical dialectic, as in the ability to prove both Y and non-Y of X, rests upon formal structures which are not moving, and which are impervious to motion. In terms of a previous remark attributed to sophistry, there must be a form F, corresponding to the structure of X, and containing elements Y and non-Y and F must be invariant or self-identical, in order to be identified as the form containing both Y and non-Y. Or again, in order to predicate Y and non-Y of X, all three formal structures (and not just the symbols by which they are designated) must be self-identical and thus identifiable as the specific structures of the given instance of (contradictory) predication. For otherwise there will be chaos rather than contradictory predication in a given case. This is the general strategy which Socrates is currently following. As I noted earlier, however, the present discussion needs to be related to the demonstration that formal structures underlying dialectic are not instances of genesis, whether spoken or silent (i.e., the demonstration I supplied in the previous Chapter). This is what Socrates means when he says that a technē based upon the hunting of opinions rather than the knowledge of truth is laughable and nontechnical (262c1-3).

However, the discussion is already becoming too "bare" for Phaedrus; he needs examples (262c5-9). Socrates returns immediately to "the speeches" which have already been delivered; they give us "an example of how one who knows the truth, by playing with words, can mislead his audience" (262c10-d2). Scholars have been puzzled by the exact reference of the dual τὼ λόγω.[16] One of the speeches must be Lysias' (262c5-6), but which of Socrates' two speeches is the other? Presumably the first, since the scholars cannot believe that the second Socratic speech employed deception. But then the most important speech in the dialogue is improbably omitted from consideration. I believe that the partial ambiguity of τὼ λόγω ["the pair of speeches" – ed.] is intentional, since it reminds us of the interrelatedness of the three speeches. Socrates' first speech is a preamble to his second, which employs deception in the very attribution to Stesichorus. The only real problem is the sense in which Lysias could himself be said to know the truth, and this is easily resolved by our recognition that Plato, not Lysias, is the author of the first speech.

Socrates playfully and deceptively attributes the playful deceptions of the previous speeches to "local gods" or perhaps to "the prophets of the Muses," i.e., the cicadas. For he himself, he says, has no technē for speaking (262d2-6). Phaedrus does not care to debate the point; he is eager enough to return to the orations. Accordingly, Socrates has him repeat the beginning of Lysias' speech (262d7-e4). The deception which this speech illustrates is the suppression of any definition of its main subject. Socrates first divides words into two classes, those about which everyone agrees, and those which give rise to disagreement (263a2-b2). He claims in effect that no disagreement ensues about the object of words which refer to, or name, a corporeal thing. This is, of course, not the same as to exclude error from sense-per-

---

16   Cf. Hackforth, pp. 125–26, note 1. With my own discussion, see Stefanini, pp. 50–52 and 64.

ception, or the possibility of mistaking an iron for a silver object. The agreement in question concerns the name and our mental conception of the meaning of the name. But some words, like "just" and "good," give rise to disagreement, both with others and within ourselves, as to their meaning. These words are not stabilized by sense-perception; they are not "attached" to a readily specifiable body. Instead, one may say that they are themselves attached to other words, or interpretations of corporeal existence, from which they easily become detached. They wander in our minds instead of standing still, and this makes us likely to err about them (263b3-5). Rhetoric is especially powerful with respect to these wandering words, and for an obvious reason. It is easy to assert both Y and non-Y of a word X to which we can attach no fixed meaning. In general, the power of rhetoric depends upon its ability to detach words from things, and to exaggerate the ambiguity of words whose primary reference is not to things.

The remedy for this abuse of rhetoric is to find a way to fix the meaning of what I have called wandering words. One must find the stable shape or character of these words, or the noetic counterpart to the corporeal shape which stabilizes words about whose meanings we always agree. The first step in this procedure is to classify stable and wandering words in terms of their distinguishing formal characters (263b6-c2). The very fact that we can distinguish between these two classes is evidence that words have stabilizing forms which are not simply identical with perceived corporeal shapes. It is therefore irrelevant whether our intention is to deceive or to speak the truth; in both cases, one must have an accurate perception of the formal characteristics of words (263c3-6). Even on the assumption that the sophist believes what he says to be true, the truth of his discourse is proportional to the purity or acuity of his perception of formal stability. And this connects us to the earlier myth of recollection. *Linguistic forms are reminiscences or memoranda of the hyper-Uranian beings.* The name attached to a ratio of change is intelligible as the name of that ratio by virtue of an isomorphism between name and ratio which cannot itself be changing. Still more precisely, a specific ratio is visible as this identifiable or self-identical ratio, because of a formal structure which is independent of the motions expressed or identified by the ratio as a discursive sign.

To return to Socrates' example, Eros is a word which gives rise to disagreement. Its detached or wandering nature was shown by the fact that Socrates first described it as harmful to the beloved and lover alike, and then as the greatest of goods (263c7-12). One would assume from this exchange that Socrates had failed to define Eros, or at least to define it accurately, since he was able to attribute both Y and non-Y to it. Socrates himself now claims to have forgotten whether, in his enthused condition, he began his speech with a definition of Eros (263d1-3). If Hackforth is right in taking Socrates' two speeches as one,[17] then presumably he now identifies them as having been equally inspired. If the speeches contradict each other, then they must be based on contradictory definitions of Eros, and Hackforth has thus not explained why Socrates and Lysias take them as a unity. As a matter of fact, I believe that all three speeches constitute a dialectical harmony (not the same as a unity). The irony of the present passage, as evident in the ambiguous references to the three speeches, is that it identifies them all as inspired—or as non-inspired, depending upon the equivocal or wandering word "inspired," which has not itself been accurately defined. If we do not understand the dialectical harmony of the three speeches, then Socrates, despite his definitions, has deceived us, and especially so if we take his two speeches as lumped together in the lines under discussion.

No doubt the obvious response would be that Socrates' two speeches are not internally related, or that the second speech is a thorough refutation of the first. But even Hackforth has discerned that the present conversation between Socrates and Phaedrus is not intelligible on such an "obvious" assumption. I do not propose to repeat my detailed analysis of the three speeches. Suffice it to say that my interpretation is supported by the details of this section. The wandering in the definitions of Eros can be terminated

17   P. 127, note 2.

only by an accurate understanding of all these speeches. Socrates' first speech is "inspired" in the sense that it reveals part of the truth about Eros (to say nothing of Lysias' speech). Thus Socrates contrasts his speech with that of Lysias, and not his *speeches*. Again, the Socratic discourse was inspired by the Nymphs,[18] and was therefore more technical than the discourse of Lysias (263d4-6: Phaedrus swears by Zeus for the third time in this section; the technical discussion of rhetoric seems to be exciting him more than the orations themselves, although he may not be enjoying this more). All these points may be summarized in the following observation. As we learned from the *Symposium*, it is the nature of Eros to wander and deceive. Eros cannot in fact be stabilized by a definition in the usual technical or epistemic sense. We require a *more technical*, i.e., supra-technical or synoptic mode of discourse in order to encompass Eros, and this encompassing is also a regulating or directing toward the hyper-Uranian beings. The three speeches in the *Phaedrus* serve as the discursive nets in which, like hunters tracking their prey, we seek to capture the elusive and many-sided Eros. The problem is exactly analogous to that of tracking down the wily sophist, since both contain non-being as an essential dimension of their natures.

It is therefore not a sufficient criticism of Lysias to say that he failed to begin with a definition of Eros, and to order his subsequent remarks accordingly (263d7-264b2). A good speech about Eros is not a logical deduction of theorems from a set of primitive terms or definitions. This does not mean that the speech should be haphazard and disorganized (264b3-c1). In a passage of crucial importance for understanding Platonic rhetoric,[19] Socrates himself supplies the right principle of organization:

18 Note that the Nymphs are here called daughters of Achelous *and* Pan. Cf. 230b-c: the addition of Pan prepares us for the final prayer. Also the Muses do not have a common lineage; some may not be erotic (as Pan is).

19 In a commentary that illuminates the obtuse incompetence of a whole school of contemporary Plato scholarship, Hackforth calls

but I suppose you will say this at least, that one must construct every speech as though it were alive, with its own body, lacking neither a head nor limbs, but with a middle and extremities, written in such a way as to be suitable to each other and to the whole (264c2-5)

A detailed interpretation of this principle will be initiated by Socrates at a later point in the dialogue. But the main thesis is already evident. All speeches must be alive to their subject matter *and* their audience. The assimilation of discourse generally into rhetoric makes this unmistakable. Even though the philosophical rhetorician needs to know the truth, his primary function is to persuade his audience. Apart from the fact that knowing and persuading are separate if related functions, the task of persuading an audience of the truth is not simply identical with asserting the truth in propositional or deductive form. Only a person who lacks any grasp of rhetoric, and so of human nature, would believe in such an identity. The modern insistence (not uniform, of course) upon replacing rhetoric by logic has resulted in a two-fold defect. We no longer understand the rhetoric of the past, and we do not understand that logic has itself become the rhetoric of the present. I mean by this last remark that we no longer understand the extra-logical assumptions and consequences, for ourselves as well as our subject matter, of the substitution of logic for rhetoric.

A well-written speech requires a head because it must be able to think about what it will say to different kinds of audiences. Similarly, it requires limbs in order to move toward and away from different persons, and to shape its subject matter in accord with the circumstances. Its principle of organization is thus its living intelligence. This can be understood by changing our

this section "of relatively small importance . . . these things are of course matters of τέχνη but, as we might put it, of τέχνη in its purely literary, not its philosophical aspect; though indeed from the way in which Socrates speaks at 264a4-6 it may be inferred that Plato thought of the two aspects as closely connected" (p. 130).

perspective and regarding the animal body of the speech itself. All parts have a function; every aspect of the speech signifies, or contributes its meaning to the significance of the whole. The parts of the speech are like organs, bones, or living tissue; none is superfluous to the total structure. This is what Socrates means by "logographic necessity" (264b7). It follows that merely to dissect by logical analysis a speech written in accord with this principle is equivalent to murdering it. At the best, we are engaging in anatomy or physiology, but we are not conversing with this living speech. In rhetoric, surgery must be preceded by political intercourse or friendship. The significance of the logical structure of a speech is dependent upon its psyche, and this is the easiest way in which to grasp the relation between the two main parts of the *Phaedrus*. We must know the psyche in order to know how to speak, both with respect to distinguishing between true and false speeches and with respect to persuading men of different types. And the psyche is essentially erotic, or desire striving for the perfection of self-consciousness, which leads finally to the transcendence of the self. Need I add that all of this applies directly to the interpretation of a Platonic dialogue, the outstanding example of a living speech?

The parts of Lysias' speech may be shuffled about in any arrangement (264c6-e2). This is not to say that the speech is meaningless; we have already found it to possess a rather complex teaching. The point, I believe, is rather that the principle for the interpretation or meaning of the speech is external to it. In himself, the non-lover is continuously turning into the lover. For all his significance, the non-lover is not intelligible in himself as a complete interpretation of the human psyche. The epitaph quoted by Socrates from the tomb of Midas is in fact rather misleading in the present context. Even though its lines may be arranged in any order, it retains a single identifiable meaning. But it is as dead as the corpse it commemorates; it cannot walk away from unsatisfactory readers, or adjust its message in accord with the nature of its audience. I do not believe it is fair to say that Lysias' speech is simply a corpse. On the other hand, it is not a self-organized whole, not quite alive if not quite dead. Like Eros, it is constantly changing into the opposite of its present condition. Perhaps it would be best to describe the speech as an aspect of the human psyche, dependent for its identity upon its place within the psyche as a whole. The interchangeability of the lines in Midas' epitaph thus does not stand for the interchangeability of the sentences in Lysias' speech; that is obviously impossible. It does no doubt refer to the looseness of the order in which the points of the speech are introduced; taken simply as an oration, Lysias' speech lacks logical organization. But it is therefore a splendid example of how much can be said or taught without such organization. The "interchangeability" lies in the significance of that teaching; the non-lover is a wanderer, and he can be stabilized only through harmony with the lover.

III.

Phaedrus seems to grasp that Socrates is now exaggerating the formal defects of Lysias' speech, and accuses him of ridiculing it (264e3). Socrates does not quite deny this charge, but suggests that the matter be dropped, so as not to vex Phaedrus. In passing, he observes that Lysias' speech contains a host of what I shall call negative examples (264e4-6). One should not imitate Lysias' oratorical technique, and in that sense, it has much to teach us. But negativity is the engine of Lysian dialectic in a more profound sense. Let me summarize the whole issue for the last time. There is a "good" and a "bad" negativity in the speech of Lysias. The good negativity expresses the need to render Eros determinate, and consequently to limit it. The bad negativity is the nothingness within which the sophist hides, or rather continuously transforms his identity, just as in the sophistic rhetoric one may predicate Y and non-Y of X. In more concrete terms, the bad advice of the non-lover is a perversion of the reasonable thesis that philosophy and friendship both include a strong element of detachment or passivity, and hence demand a certain absence of erotic desire. Socrates' first speech was designed to restate this thesis in a fuller and more complex fashion. But in so doing, it sharpened rather than resolved the conflict between the good and the bad negativity. We may understand his second speech in these terms as the effort to achieve such a resolution. As we recall, the non-lover reasonably identifies Eros as a form of madness. Socrates' procedure in his second speech is to show that sobriety, or the ostensibly good negativity of the Lysian teaching, is in itself, or when allowed to dominate the psyche, a kind of madness which deteriorates into the very corporeal Eros it strove to contain. The "sophistic" character of Lysias' speech is exemplified in the fact that the good negativity transforms itself, by the very act of self-positing, into the bad negativity. Sobriety is thus revealed as a self-deceived form of human madness; the good negativity is then incorporated into divine madness, or the procedure whereby Eros is regulated and limited by the vision of the hyper-Uranian beings. In the second speech, the self-positing of Eros initiates the dialectical completion, and in that sense termination, of Eros. As a result, divine madness is seen to be more sober than the merely human sobriety. Sobriety and madness are reconciled in the divine negation of Eros.

Socrates passes from the speech of Lysias to his own two speeches, which he characterizes as "opposites" (264e7-265a3). I have just explained the sense in which this is to be understood. Socrates alludes to the dialectical connection between his two speeches by a joke; when Phaedrus calls them both "manly" (ἀνδρικῶς) Socrates replies: "I thought you were going to say the truth, that they [proceeded] madly (μανικῶς)" (265a4-5). The joke is in fact serious, for the truth is that the two speeches, taken generally, stand for human and divine madness—or if you prefer, for human and divine mixtures of sobriety and madness. Thus Socrates takes his two speeches together, although he proceeds to introduce the theme of division and collection by what is apparently a specific reminder of his second speech (265a5 ff.). Socrates reminds Phaedrus that madness was previously divided into two kinds (εἴδη), one caused by human sickness, and the other by a divine alteration in our usual customs (265a9-10). Again, this refers indirectly to the difference between the two speeches, although the content of the reference is taken from the second speech. This in turn illustrates my earlier remark that the speeches about the non-lover do not contain their own principle of interpretation.[20] Just as one must know the monad of madness before it can be divided into species, so madness cannot be distinguished from sobriety without a higher perception of a more comprehensive genus. The same might be said about every pair of opposites Y and non-Y; one must first perceive the monadic X of which they are possible predicates. Every act of division is an articulation of an internally differentiated formal monad. One cannot speak of limbs except with respect to a body, nor of species except with respect to a genus. But the apprehension of the monad as both a unity and a *relevant* object for this specific division cannot itself be a consequence of division. In this sense, collection, i.e., the synthetic unification of a manifold, whether in active projection or passive reception, is always prior to division (and to the "collection" of divided parts).

To divide is to see two elements as separate from each other which were previously joined together. One cannot know that one has performed a division unless by way of a prior synopsis of the junction. This prior synopsis is not accurately expressed by the words for "collection" or συναγωγή, which mean literally a "gathering together" or "assembling" of disparate individuals, whose community thus becomes visible only *after* they have been brought together. It is of course true that, after perceiving a horse, a man, and a lion, we may "collect" them together under the genus "animal." But the perception of a horse, a man, or a lion is of a monadic structure which serves as a whole to another set of attributes. The division of these attributes depends upon the perception of the monadic structure, and the classification or collecting of that structure under a genus (e.g., "lion" under "animal") depends in turn upon the division of the monad into attributes which subsequently identify the generic home of the given

---

20   With this modification, cf. Stefanini, p. 52.

monad. By chance, the Socratic teaching on this point is expressible more clearly in English than in Greek. Collection, or the gathering together of the formal elements of a perceived monad, is
dependent upon recollection, or the anticipation of the pattern to
be formed by an apprehension of the relevant noetic monad. Since
perception is more visible by difference than by sameness, we
tend to overlook the unity which is already present in any conscious sensation, and to concentrate our attention on the hetero-
geneous details of the unity, thereby contrasting it with other
unities, but with reference to the differences. The sameness is then
noticed afterwards, when we are in the process of sorting out the
details, or collecting the differences. Since the sameness is seen
by virtue of its differences, we are led to believe that the sameness
is somehow a consequence, not merely of the differences, but of
the perception of the differences. The sameness is then conceived
as a creation, construction, or perspectival projection, whether of
sensation alone, or of the subsequent acts of linguistic classification. It is seen as an individual, or as itself a difference. At this
point, the Socratic critique against sophistic rhetoric becomes applicable. If X is itself a difference, then it must be different from
itself, or not simply both Y and non-Y, but non-X as well as X. For
to preserve its self-identity, it must exhibit a formal structure
whose unity is not reducible to a series of discrete properties.
Such a reduction makes the series itself a discrete property: $p(p_1,
p_2, \ldots, p_n)$ is itself the kth P of an infinite series of properties $P_1,
P_2, \ldots, P_n, P_{n+1} \ldots$ each of which is unique with respect to all oth-
ers, and infinitely diverse with respect to itself, since, as pure difference, its structural significance is determined by the
perspective of the speaker. In short, there is an infinite regress of
properties and of perspectives of speeches.

Collection (συναγωγή), then, is grounded in recollection
(ἀνάμνησις). This means that we must noetically apprehend a
formal unity before discursive division is possible. In the present
discussion, our primary example of this issue has been the psyche, whose elusiveness makes it an excellent reminder of the discursive silence that characterizes noetic apprehension. In addition

to this, the psyche, even within the myth of the palinode, is tacitly divided from the hyper-Uranian beings on the one side, and from the body on the other. In other words, the apprehension of noetic monads is not the same as the perception of absolute genera. The classification of kinds by species and genera is dependent upon, but not the same as, the apprehension of noetic monads, because within diaeresis, what counts as a genus in one context may count as a species in another. The psyche is a genus with respect to madness and sobriety, but it is a species with respect to what Socrates frequently calls "the whole," which we may tentatively and mythically identify as the monadic structure whose elements are the Ideas, psyche, and body. This in turn means that there is an at least partial disjunction between our knowledge of the whole— more accurately, of the parts within the whole—and our noetic apprehension of the whole. Still more specifically, we could not know anything except because of a prior noetic apprehension of that thing. But the noetic apprehension is not knowledge, if to know is to classify discursively by division and collection, as for example in sorting out genera and species.

The *Phaedrus*, of course, is concerned primarily with neither ontology nor epistemology, but with mythology, which, to avoid misunderstanding, I had better identify at once as philosophical myth.[21] Science is always concerned with the determinate particular, and can never perceive, let alone provide us with a logos of, the whole. Ontology intends to give us such a logos, but for "technical" reasons it cannot succeed. Apart from the various logical paradoxes and restrictions on completeness, an ontological speech, even if it were complete and coherent, would by virtue of its mathematical nature say nothing about the phenomenological world of human experience. The function of philosophical

---

21 Stefanini (p. 32) exaggerates somewhat, but points at an essential truth, when he asks us to regard the *Phaedrus* "come il *dialogo dell'irrazionale*." Similarly with his statement that none but perhaps the *Symposium* (up to the *Phaedrus*) is "meno eleatico del *Fedro*." Its Eleaticism is represented as *silence* (the consequence of monism).

myth is to provide a horizon for ontology and descriptive phe-
nomenology by rendering common sense self-reflexive. And the
function of the *Phaedrus* is to exemplify this bonding function of
philosophical myth. It can therefore not be understood on the
basis of views like Hackforth's, who sees the *Phaedrus* as an an-
nouncement that "the ontological and epistemological flights of
the *Republic* have been superseded by something less magnificent,
but perhaps more practicable"; that is, "the whole of the dialogue
is centered upon the present section" about collection and division. "What is now contemplated is a piecemeal approach to
knowledge, consisting in a mapping out of one field after another
by a classification *per genera et species*." This view, however, raises
the immediate question: what is the relation between this ostensibly central passage and the long myth of Stesichorus? Hackforth
replies that the myth is indeed "too magnificent and too long"
relative to the formal structure of the whole dialogue. It is, however, totally relevant to the "main purpose of the dialogue, the
vindication of the pursuit of philosophy as the true culture of the
soul . . . It is because the structure of the dialogue is accommodated to a less important purpose, namely the enunciation of a
new *method* of philosophy, that the formal defect has come
about."[22]

According to Hackforth, then, the dialogue is centered upon a
section which not only does not express its main purpose, but which
leads us to feel that the main formulation of the main purpose is too
long and too magnificent. And furthermore, the excessive magnificence of Socrates' second speech thus serves to introduce his new
and less magnificent stage of epistemological development. It is
very instructive to ask how Hackforth came to so absurd a conclusion. The answer, I believe, is unquestionably his conviction that the
key to the dialogue is its role in conveying the state of Plato's historical development during his middle years, and hence as a transition from youthful excess to the sobriety of old age (which is
suspiciously like English nominalist epistemology). It is easy to see

22 Hackforth, pp. 136–37.

here the positivist and historicist presuppositions of such a conviction. But let us simply argue from the text. The fact is that the present passage *cannot* be central, and the manifest proof of this is precisely the magnificence and length of Socrates' second speech. Hackforth's interpretation is sheer speculation, and based upon hypotheses for which there is no evidence in antiquity, let alone in Plato. It leads to the judgment, however swathed in compliments to "the poet, the enthusiast, and the mystic," that the speech about perfect speeches is itself imperfect, and grossly so. By Hackforth's judgment, the poet Plato was an incompetent poet, who obscured the epistemological purpose of the *Phaedrus* by an excessive outburst of enthusiasm.

The simplest and most obvious approach to the unity of these two aspects of the dialogue emerges as soon as we jettison extraneous hypotheses about historical development and study the text itself. The main purpose of the dialogue is to provide the mythical speech about psychic perfection or wholeness which serves as the living environment for the method of division and collection. Without that environment, the method is a kind of surgery or butchery. And even within it, the method remains subordinate to the synoptic or regulative function of mythical speech. If philosophy, as Hackforth wisely says, "is the true culture of the soul," then there can be no philosophical supercession of speech about the psyche by speech about genera and species. Plato's later dialogues are not lacking in myths about the psyche; and one of the latest, the *Philebus*, presents us with Socrates, again engaged in his usual ironic (and erotic) dialectic about the nature of the best life. The only proper method for understanding Plato is to follow his own instructions and evidence. We must take the longer way, and study each dialogue as a living or self-contained whole, before we can hope to see the teaching of the Platonic corpus.[23]

23 If the thesis of historical development is correct, then no dialogues prior to the *Phaedrus* could illuminate it, since (by hypothesis) Plato has now advanced to a new stage. But no dialogues *after* the *Phae-*

With all due attention to epistemology, let us not forget that it is madness which we are collecting and dividing. Collection (συναγωγή) depends upon a manifold of separate but relatable individuals; but the individual is initially perceived by an act of synopsis or recollection. We are now equipped to return to the text. Socrates "sanctifies" his division of the divine madness by assigning each species to a god (or gods) in order to emphasize the divine supervision of his secular dissection, whereas in the earlier classification (244a8 ff.), he was less precise. Prophetic inspiration is associated with Apollo, telestic with Dionysus, poetry with the Muses, and Eros with Aphrodite (265b2-5). These, then, are the four most important divinities (taking the Muses collectively) to be associated with the teaching about Eros in the *Phaedrus*. The only one of these to be unambiguously identified with madness in traditional thought is Dionysus. Aphrodite does not represent madness so much as attraction, to use Walter Otto's distinction.[24] Apollo, the god of light, proportion, form, and clarity, serves to emphasize that even divine madness contains a strong element of sobriety (and we recall that Dionysus was not mentioned among the gods leading the psychic procession in the myth of Stesichorus). This note of sobriety is even visible in the species of divine love, which is now attributed jointly to Aphrodite and Eros. In addition to these celestial resonances of sobriety, Socrates reduces the intensity of his palinodic revelation by reminding us that, although "not altogether untrustworthy," it may well have gone astray occasionally while reaching for the truth. It was "a kind of mythic hymn," and the verb used for "singing" in this sentence also means "to joke" (265b6-c3: προσεπαίσαμεν). Lest there be

---

drus are relevant to it, since they embody stages not yet achieved by the author of the *Phaedrus*. The net result of the historicist thesis is to cancel itself out.

24 "Von [Aphrodite] kommt nicht so sehr der Rausch der Verlangens, als der Liebreiz, der es erregt und hinreisst." in *Die Götter Griechenlands* (Verlag G. Schulte-Bulmke, Frankfurt, 1961), p. 161; cf. pp. 102 f.

any mistake about this, Socrates repeats the verb in its root form seven lines later: the myth "seemed to me on the whole to be really playing" (265c8-9: παιδιᾷ πεπαῖσθαι).

We have here another of those extremely interesting, and normally neglected, passages in which Socrates (or the main speaker in the dialogue) characterizes a very important and extensive discussion or speech as a game or playing.[25] The general significance of this habit can only be determined by a study of its exercise within the particular dialogues. But certain points are obvious enough. If a man repeatedly characterizes what seem to be intensely serious speeches as jokes or games, we must necessarily assume that he is warning us against taking those speeches too seriously. This does not mean that they are to be simply disregarded. Serious games are always worthy of the closest scrutiny. Differently put, if men can only be playful with respect to the highest or deepest things, that in itself is enlightening. If Zeus is a playing youth (παῖς παίζων), the highest human activity must be to devise an ontology of play. It remains a question whether such an ontology is itself playful. The only way to decide is by studying the speeches in question. And our study of Socrates' palinode has demonstrated that Socratic playfulness is compatible with the most serious and detailed teaching. The simplest way to appreciate the playful character of the palinode is by remembering Socrates' characterization of a perfect or living speech. A perfect speech adjusts its teaching to the audience, or says less than it knows to all but the most careful auditor. In order to do this, it must be sufficiently intricate to present a surface appropriate to the different types of men. Consequently the surface must be like a game or puzzle in that it serves as an entrance to widely different levels of comprehension. In order to win the game, we must penetrate the surface and attain to the deepest level of understanding. As in any game, this requires extreme skill and meticulous attention to detail. Socratic games are not merely edifying. They cannot

---

25   Cf. *Republic* 536c1, *Laws* 769a1, *Philebus* 30e6-7, *Parmenides* 137b2 for examples.

be played, and indeed, they cannot even be noticed, by those who lack an appreciation for aristocratic irony.

Socrates now proceeds to divide off a part of his earlier game which brought considerable pleasure to Phaedrus. According to Socrates, the division itself, or getting hold in a technical way of the kinds (εἰδοῖν) of collection and division, will not be unpleasant (265c4-d1).[26] The first occurs when, "looking at both together, we lead a scattered multitude into one kind (ἰδέαν), in order to define each [unity] and thus make clear what in each case we desire to teach" (265d3-5). This is essentially the translation of Robin and Hackforth, and it is certainly the easiest way to understand the sentence in its context. One might, however, translate εἰς μίαν τε ἰδέαν συνορῶντα as "looking synoptically at one Idea."[27] In this case, recollection would precede, and regulate, collection. In my opinion, we are meant to hear this resonance within the sentence; but even those who are deaf to resonance will admit that we must first see a form, and its relation to scattered individuals, before we can gather together the right individuals under the form.[28] As an example of collection, Socrates cites the recent definition of Eros, which, whether right or wrong, provided a clear and self-consistent basis for the speech (265d5-7). To which definition is Socrates alluding? His use of the singular, as well as the explicit statement in his next remark, make it evident that he is taking his two speeches together to provide one definition, and so, one collection and division, of Eros.

Before considering this further, let us look at the description of the second kind or form (265d8: εἶδος). "Going backwards, we are able to divide in accordance with kinds,[29] by

26 Cf. 265b8, c4 and d1.
27 Von Arnim (p. 199) draws the comparison between (συνορῶν) as used here, and *Republic* 537c.
28 Cf. Robin (*Phèdre*), p. clviii, on the limitation of the dividing intelligence with respect to the indivisible species.
29 Cf. Robin's note on the sense of κατ' εἴδη.

the natural joints; we are not to try merely to break off any part, acting in the manner of an incompetent butcher" (265e1-3). The eidos is here tacitly contrasted to the living speech. It possesses a structural articulation which guides the activity of division, but it is not alive; not even skillful butchers dissect living animals. The joints of the eidos are fixed; they not merely guide, but compel. The eidos, as self-consistent and self-identical, always says the same thing to everyone, regardless of whether the addressee hears (or sees) it properly. It provides the fixed, reliable point by which the living speech can guide its own rhetorical motions. In a word, as Socrates' example shows, what we are dividing is "like a body," *but not like a psyche*.

Socrates draws his example of division from his two speeches taken together, which, he says, grasped or assumed jointly "the one common eidos of senselessness [=madness] of discursive intelligence (τὸ μὲν ἄφρον τῆς διανίας: 265e3-4)," or *paranoia* (derangement of intelligence: 266a2). On the basis of our detailed interpretation of the first two speeches, we see here an accurate and illuminating summary by Socrates. Both of his own speeches *did* concern themselves with madness. In referring to the eidos, Socrates uses the phrase "senselessness of discursive intelligence" to cover both the human madness of excessive sobriety and the divine madness in its various forms. In his first speech, Socrates called the human madness "hybris." The excessively sober man speaks of Eros as hybris, but he is himself hybristic in attempting to separate his desire from love. His discursive intelligence suffers from the madness or hybris of opposing the gods. In his second speech, Socrates means by "discursive senselessness" the submission of discursivity to myth, recollection, or the silent hyper-Uranian beings. This submission to a "divine fate" is not explained discursively, and to a demythologizer less susceptible than Phaedrus to beauty, it makes no sense. In accordance with Socrates' remarks (266a1-b1), let us sketch the pattern of the indicated diaeresis:

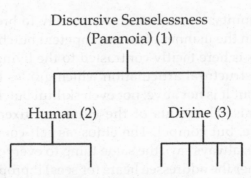

Discursive Senselessness
(Paranoia) (1)

Human (2)   Divine (3)

It is, however, true that Socrates did not use a consistent schema of division in his initial classification, as can be seen from the above simplified diagram. Our present passage is faithful to Socrates' speeches in that everywhere the problems of dividing like Eros, psyche, or madness are poeticized and concealed, rather than explicitly stated.

Let us briefly recall the difficulties involved here. The major difficulty turns upon the impossibility of uttering a determinate logos about the hyper-Uranian beings, or noetic monads considered as ontological subjects. Secondly, the diaeretic method "wanders" in its determination of the genus to be divided; this choice varies with the intentions of the dialectician. The forms may be given by nature, but not the classifications of the logician. Finally, in the particular case, there is no form of Eros, and one may well wonder whether there can be a form of psyche. For all three reasons, but especially the last, it would be a total misconception of the *Phaedrus* to attempt to reduce it to a consistent diaeresis or schema of classification. The psyche is a mathematician, but cannot itself be mathematicized. Thus Socrates is a lover of divisions and collections, which make it possible for him to speak and think (266b3-5). But it would be true only in a poetical sense to say that he divides and collects himself. The speaking and thinking psyche is itself neither a speech nor a thought. This explains the qualifications with which Socrates calls those who are able to divide and collect by the name of "dialectician" (266b5-c1). The *Phaedrus* makes evident, perhaps better than any other dialogue, that philosophical speech cannot be restricted to the "dead" or lifeless technique of diaeretic classification. Dialectic includes, beside myth and diaeresis, the detailed testing and educating of the living psyche through conversation. In short, the Platonic dialogue itself is dialectical in a more comprehensive sense than the technique of division and collection.[30]

The specific, contextual purpose for the introduction and praise of diaeretic dialectic in the *Phaedrus* is to criticize the epideictic dialectic of sophistic rhetoric. In that context, and with Phaedrus as an audience, Socrates is very brief in his description of diaeresis. What Phaedrus needs to hear is this: the man who divides and collects in accordance with kinds is the man who can give stable definitions of his terms. He thereby knows what he is talking about, and indeed, knows how to talk. How he knows the kinds in accordance with which he divides and collects, is another question. The philosophical dialectician in the full sense of the title knows both how to talk and what to say to a given person. He is therefore not simply a technician, like the mechanic who tunes the engine of our automobile, but does not tell us where to drive it. The philosopher is the true king, since his knowledge enables him to rule by persuasion. On the other hand, sophists like Thrasymachus rule by force rather than by knowledge; Phaedrus is right to deny that they are "epistemonic" kings (266c1-7). Having grasped this point thanks to Socratic persuasion, he himself makes a correct division between the eidos of dialectic and that of rhetoric. But the interesting thing is this: the division is correct even though no definition has yet been offered of rhetoric (266c7-9). The rhetorician is correctly distinguished from the dialectician

---

30 Cf. Robin (*Phèdre*), p. liii: "Dire d'autre part que la dialectique en est la méthode, c'est dire qu'elle est un entretien, car il n'y a pas de dialectique sans dialogue." This excellent observation does not quite square with Robin's earlier remark (p. v) that "Enfin il ne me parait pas douteux que le 'lieu supra-céleste' du *Phédre* ne soit rien d'autre qu'un doublet mythique du 'lieu intelligible' de la *Republique* (VI 508bc, 509d; VII 517b)." The presentation of dialectic in the cited passages of the *Republic* needs to be corrected or supplemented by the argument of the *Phaedrus* as a whole.

by his indefiniteness. Whereas both can assume many forms, the knowledge of the dialectician gives a stability and order to his transformations that is lacking in the rhetorician. The dialectician's powers are regulated by the actuality of the fixed forms of things, whereas the rhetorician's actualities are only momentary illuminations on the grey battlefield of power. The indefiniteness of the rhetorician (like the non-being of the sophist) comes from his subordination of actuality to possibility.[31]

Socrates insists that some determinateness be given to the unphilosophical rhetorician; if he has a technē at all, we must be able to say "what it actually is" (266d1-4), or be able to discover the eidos of the rhetorician, which cannot be epistemically defined merely by negation. A correct division is thus by no means equivalent to formal knowledge. Similarly, knowledge of the particular techniques of rhetoric is not equivalent to knowledge of the rhetorical technē. One has not written a beautiful speech merely by exemplifying the skills or devices of the art. These must be collected together under the recollected form, or unified within a living example of the non-living eidos (266d7 ff.). It is curious that, when the devices of rhetoric are collected together in such a way as to exhibit the structure of the eidos, the individual speech itself comes to life, or achieves a mobility and consciousness which are alien to the eidos. The difference between the speech and the eidos is reminiscent of the difference between a Platonic dialogue and a diaeretic classification of the logical structure of a dialogue. In order to mediate between the eidos and the psyche, the speech must participate in both domains. What this amounts to, of course, is the denial that non-philosophical rhetoric is a technē at all, and this is the main point in the ensuing inspection of contemporary rhetoricians.

In order to "compose a whole" (269c3) or living speech, one must possess the knowledge of the dialectician. Since only the dialectician knows the kinds of forms, we should not be surprised to find that the non-philosophical rhetorician cannot define his

31 Cf. *Sophist* 254a4.

own eidos. Granted that the end of rhetoric is persuasion, we cannot explain persuasion except by a knowledge of forms and psyche; we cannot explain power except by reference to actuality. Thus Phaedrus' division between dialectic and rhetoric was in fact a division between philosophical and non-philosophical speech. As soon as we discover the eidos of rhetoric, we find ourselves once more within the eidos of philosophy. The indeterminateness of non-philosophical speech makes it impossible for us to achieve epistemic knowledge of it. We can "know" it only in the paradoxical sense that Socrates claims to know his own ignorance. Non-philosophical speech is infinite, and hence self-negating. The non-philosopher can say, not merely that X is both Y and non-Y, but that it is non-X as well. The indefiniteness of X and non-X in "ordinary discourse" makes it impossible for us to *count on* them, or to choose between them.

Something of this indefiniteness is reflected in Socrates' review of rhetorical devices and their particular contemporary champions (266d7-267d5). It is worth noticing that, of the nine sophists mentioned, three have given their names to Platonic dialogues (Gorgias, Hippias, Protagoras), one plays an important role in the *Republic* (Thrasymachus) and one in the *Gorgias* (Polus); one, Prodicus, is mentioned often in the Platonic corpus (e.g., *Euthydemus, Protagoras, Theaetetus*), and one, Evenus, is mentioned in the *Apology* and *Phaedo*. Nor does this in any way exhaust the role of the sophists in the dialogues. The present passage serves to underline the dramatic function of sophistry for Plato; it gives a kind of definiteness and animation to the central problem of non-philosophical speech, thereby rendering visible and accessible to dialectical investigation what has in itself neither an eidos nor a genuine technē.[32] Without entering

32 In *Sophist* 258d6 ff., the Eleatic stranger identifies the form of non-being as "otherness." But the inadequacy of "otherness" to serve as the form of sophistry is obvious from the fact that it is interwoven with speech altogether, and so it is no surprise that the sophist is constantly appearing in every division. One has only to look at the

into historical hypotheses, the following suggestion about the internal order of the dialogues may serve to illustrate this point. The *Phaedrus* and *Republic* serve as a transition between dialogues like the *Protagoras, Gorgias* and *Symposium*, and the *Theaetetus, Sophist* and *Statesman*. Without a synoptic comprehension of the psyche and its modes of speech, it would be dangerous to enter into a technical analysis of philosophical speech; and this is one way to express the defect of so much contemporary Platonic scholarship. Technē becomes meaningful and responsible only with respect to an appropriate *telos*.

I have called attention on several occasions to the similarity between Eros and sophistry as subjects of diaeretic analysis. One way to express what this means is to say that Eros in itself cannot supply us with a portrait of the philosopher. Two comments must be made in this connection. First, Socrates offers only one example, in his brief discussion of division and collection, of an appropriate subject for diaeresis: Eros (265d5). But in the myth of Stesichorus, it is Eros which leads us up to the hyper-Uranian beings. Socrates never suggests that Eros is included among them, nor would this be intelligible in view of what the *Symposium* teaches us about its nature. This supports my contention that the forms of diaeresis are not the same as the hyper-Uranian beings. They are forms of discursivity, and hence are subject to the domain of genesis. They contain Eros, and are not fixed but wander, unless they are made stable by the arts of the dialectician. Second, Eros would seem to instantiate the great genus of "otherness," introduced in the *Sophist* to account for non-being. It has an eidos in the same sense that "otherness" is called an eidos there (*Sophist* 258d6). The selection of Eros as *the* example of division and collection is another sign of the comic nature of the *Phaedrus*. The refutation of sophistry is being carried out by means of a diaeresis

final summary of the diaeretic pursuit of the sophist to see that his "definition" is intelligible only on the basis of a knowledge of the eidos of philosophical speech. This is why, in looking for the sophist, the interlocutors happen first to discover the philosopher (253c6-9).

on a surrogate for sophistry. The serious meaning of this comic procedure is the insubstantial (but not worthless) nature of diaeresis as an independent technē. The *Phaedrus* invites us to achieve the reflexive awareness of the link between its myth and its analysis of rhetoric. Like every good teacher, it does not simply state that link for us to memorize. Instead, we must *recollect* it.

IV.

Having made visible the pseudo-technē of rhetoric by a series of examples, Socrates now tries to gather them together, in order to see "what kind of power" it possesses (268a1-2). There is a play here upon the sophistic identification of persuasion and force, as well as upon the Socratic or Platonic thesis that "to be," and therefore to have an eidos, is to possess a power to act or to suffer.[33] Phaedrus, of course, takes the term in its prior sense; rhetoric has great strength in the assemblies of the multitude (268a3-4). But Socrates illustrates with a series of further examples his contention that the (non-philosophical) rhetorician cannot define his profession because he is ignorant of dialectic (269b6-7). He cannot do so because there is no determinate eidos for rhetoric apart from philosophy. The formal elements of speech-making are not woven together into a seamless pattern (268a5-6), are not hyper-Uranian beings. Socrates' illustrations are in dramatic form, like miniature dialogues within the dialogue. The immediate reason for this is that Phaedrus has not understood the discussion of division and collection; he has not been convinced by the previous informal survey of oratorical devices that rhetoric lacks real power. This is why Socrates ironically addresses him as "o daimonic one" immediately after Phaedrus asserts the power of rhetoric in assemblies (268a5). Socrates must now try to charm him into conviction with animated examples.

---

33 Cf. 270d2 ff. and *Sophist* 247d8-e4. To say that "beings" are "powers" is of course not the same as to say that eidos is potential rather than actual.

The first example involves medicine and Eryximachus, both very important for Phaedrus. There is nothing new in the substance of the example; a knowledge of particular medical skills is not in itself equivalent to knowledge of the medical technē. Phaedrus, as valetudinarian and beloved of a physician, understands the problem here. The practitioner must also know "to whom, when, and for how long," or the relation between specific power over the body and the health of the individual patient (268a8-c4). Otherwise, he is to be rejected as a madman in the pejorative sense of the term. It is easier to see this in the case of medicine than it was in that of rhetoric, because now the question is one of strict utility, and not of an individual's taste concerning beauty. The technē of medicine has a kind of fixed visibility that is not present in the case of speech-making, because the end of corporeal health is more accessible than the end of psychic health. This makes medicine useful for illustrating how an end is the principle of unity within the manifold of diverse technical procedures. It does not, however, make medicine adequate to the task of serving as the paradigm of human completeness; here the perception of beauty, although harder to define than the desire for health, is radically superior. Having focused Phaedrus' attention on the need for formal unity within a technē, Socrates therefore moves from medicine to tragedy. Here the point of the illustration is the relation of whole to parts (268c5-d5) rather than (as in the case of medicine) of means to end. A tragedy exhibits this relation of a living speech better than does an oration. In a tragedy, speech and deed are unified by the plot, and again in a way independent of one's personal apprehension of beauty. We know that a tragedy is complete if its parts contribute to the working out of events in accordance with traditional myths that we *recollect*, having heard them prior to the dramatic performance. These myths constitute the horizon of our human experience, and even the air we breathe. And of course, the speeches are given life by the immediate presence of the *dramatis personae*, who enact highly formalized paradigms of fundamental human situations.

In the case of tragedy, its special complexity is dramatically represented by the fact that Socrates constructs an example within an example. Sophocles and Euripides are portrayed as responding to the incompetent tragedian just as a musician would reply to an incompetent pretender to the art of harmony (268d6-e7). The tragedians speak "musically" or not boorishly (268e1-2),[34] whereas this is not true of the doctor, who called his incompetent imitator a madman (268c2). The musical man accommodates his speech to the person, even when assigning blame, whereas the doctor, who measures speech by a standard of scientific accuracy, takes no such rhetorical steps. Hence the medical speech, although its end is the preservation of life, is not itself alive in the way that musical (=poetic) speech is. There is another interesting difference between the two examples. Music or harmonics is in itself a more "abstract" technē than medicine, inseparable from, even in part identical with, a branch of pure mathematics.[35] Thus the musician emphasizes necessity and uses the word μαθήματα in his dialogue (268e3, 6); neither feature occurs in the far briefer speech of the doctor. The musical man, who is not simply equivalent to the tragedian, has his own kind at mathematics, which includes both the numbers of harmony and those of "measuring" speeches to fit particular psyches. And in the summary of these examples, the musical man serves as the paradigm of both the tragedian and the doctor. He is wider than both, or illuminates what is proper in the differing examples of each (269a1-4).[36]

Medicine tends the body; music, and more specifically, tragic poetry, tends the psyche. The exemplification of unity or wholeness

---

34 The same point follows whether we accept the mss. reading of ἀγρίως or change it to ἀγροίκως as do Osann and Hackforth. The latter reading, of course, would be especially suggestive in light of 229e3. ["Both ἀγρίως, "savagely", and ἀγροίκως, "boorishly", mean at root "living in the fields" – ed.].

35 Phaedrus' reply, ὀρθότατα γε ["That's most *correct*, at least" – ed.], is more "mathematical" than others he might have used.

36 Sophocles is now made the spokesman for Euripides and Acumenus for Eryximachus. Are we to assume that Socrates regards the first in each pair as the more articulate of the two?

in discourse has become steadily more concrete and alive, beginning with the altogether abstract and dead rhetorical techniques. Having thus constituted the living individual, Socrates turns logically to the example of political rhetoric (269a5 ff.). The city is the completion of the individual—except, of course, for the crucial case of the philosopher. It is therefore a beautiful feature of this dramatic example that Adrastus[37] and Pericles, a king and a democratic leader, chastise Socrates and Phaedrus, a philosopher and an intellectual. Political rhetoric chastises private rhetoric. The statesmen, who are said to be "wiser than we" (probably quite true as far as Phaedrus is concerned), rebuke Socrates and his companion for their boorish (ὑπ' ἀγροικίας) and uneducated language toward the rhetoricians (269b1-3). As we know from the *Gorgias*, Socrates regarded Pericles to be himself a practitioner of corrupt rhetoric. The ironical character of this speech is obvious from Pericles' assertion that we must excuse those who are ignorant of dialectic and cannot define the "what is it" (τί ποτ' ἔστιν) of rhetoric (269b5-7). Despite his studies with Anaxagoras, Pericles can scarcely be thought to possess the requisite knowledge of dialectic. I believe it is clear that this passage continues the criticism of Pericles expressed in the *Gorgias*, and does not modify it, as some have claimed.[38]

The political example completes the previous examples of medicine and music, but it also ironically exhibits its own insufficiency. The entire thrust of the *Phaedrus*, from its dramatic setting to the details of its content, is designed to show the superiority of private or philosophical to political or sophistic rhetoric. And this is inseparable from the crucial theme of "immortality" or the perfection of the individual psyche. The speeches of Adrastus and Pericles share the essential defect of sophistic rhetoric, indicated here as ignorance of dialectic. Nevertheless, we must not forget that Plato could scarcely have preferred the private rhetoric enjoyed by Phaedrus to political rhetoric at its best. In addition, the necessity of politics provides some justification for defending

37 Cf. Robin's note, *loc. cit.*
38 Cf. Hackforth, p. 149 (on 269e1 ff.).

public against private wisdom. It is only from a philosophical viewpoint that political knowledge must be regarded as a necessary preliminary to higher understanding (269b7-c1). From the political viewpoint, to which the voice of tragedy corresponds more closely than that of the philosopher, there is indeed something boorish and uneducated about the abstract articulations of dialectic.

The preceding examples, then, have taught us something about the necessary preliminaries to the true art of rhetoric: means are subordinate to the end, parts to the whole, particular to general perfection. But Phaedrus still does not know the definition of the true rhetorical technē (269c6-d1). After all this discussion, he has still not grasped what Adrastus and Pericles explicitly said a moment ago: the true art of rhetoric is a consequence of the true art of dialectic. It is the technē possessed by the philosopher. Although this can scarcely be taken as a testimonial to Phaedrus' intelligence, we should not be too severe with him. For the claim that the philosopher alone possesses the true art of rhetoric is sufficiently unusual to puzzle a brighter man than Phaedrus. Socrates himself, as he appears in the writings of his contemporaries, does not emerge as a specially persuasive man, and certainly not toward the multitude in assembly. All the more reason for Socrates to persuade Phaedrus. Instead of rebuking him for his ignorance, Socrates begins again, this time with a commonplace formula; a natural gift, together with knowledge and practice, will make one a famous speaker (269d2-6). And once again, he distinguishes his "method" from that of Lysias and Thrasymachus, both, incidentally, noted for their ability to persuade the multitude (269d6-8).

Socrates begins to illustrate his method with a strange, not to say comical, expression. All the great arts have need of garrulity and "high-flown speculation" (as Hackforth well translates μετεωρολογίας) about nature (269e4-270a1). This sounds very much like Aristophanes satirizing Socrates. In fact, it is Socrates satirizing Pericles and Anaxagoras. Pre-Socratic physics does not provide a stable basis for political wisdom because it distinguishes sharply between the divine and the human. The conception of nature is reserved as a theoretical term for the cosmos of number, bodies, and motion, or for ontological processes and structures; human experience is relegated to the domain of *nomos*. Throughout the dialogues, pre-Socratic "process physics" is associated with the political and rhetorical teaching of the sophists; and we have already discussed the connection as it is treated in the *Phaedrus*. In the present instance, Anaxagoras is one of those men of boorish wisdom who teaches that the sun is in fact a stone rather than the god Apollo. His scientific demythologizing results in a disjunction between political man and the natural world, which could only be bridged by a rhetoric of concealment and noble lies. It certainly presents no interpretation of the nature of the psyche that could serve as a foundation for dialectical rhetoric. As a student of Anaxagoras, Pericles is filled up with "meteorological" speculations; the "nature of mind" in this teaching has cosmological or ontological significance, and of a kind that turns our attention away from the specific differences among men.[39] If Pericles' political rhetoric is Anaxagorean, then it must be seriously defective, to say the least (270a1-8). What we need is precisely a conception of nature whereby human experience acquires a stable basis in the cosmos or whole.

The Anaxagorean mind must be reinterpreted as the medium within which the individual psyche achieves stability by encountering, as the term of its motions, the hyper-Uranian beings. In slightly different terms, memory unifies the dianoetic kinēsis of mind and thereby allows the unity (noēsis) to apprehend the perpetual or unmoving paradigms of genesis. Political philosophy becomes possible when the rhetoric of Pericles is stabilized, and therefore redirected, by the mnemonic intentionality of mind. Hence the reconstitution of rhetoric as a technical adjunct of dialectic retains the superiority of the philosopher to the citizen, or his transcendence of the city. But it also enables the philosopher to provide a stable or discursive interpretation of traditional

39   Cf. Anaxagoras, Fr. B12 in Diels and *Phaedo* 96a6 ff., esp. 98b7 ff.

notions of political virtue and utility. Even though the purpose of the *Phaedrus* is extra-political, it nevertheless pays its debt to the city. Socrates' ironical criticism of contemporary political rhetoric is thus by no means purely negative. Political health is as dependent upon correct discourse as is philosophy. And correct discourse, as the myth of Stesichorus showed, depends upon a synopsis of the whole which precedes and regulates the articulation of its parts. Our own understanding of Socrates' attempt to persuade or educate Phaedrus, for the sake of the city, is thus dependent upon our synoptic vision, just as political rhetoric is dependent upon cosmic synopsis.

Socrates turns once again to medicine in his effort to revise Phaedrus' understanding of nature. The example is appropriate for more than one reason. The most important is that medicine makes visible, with all the tangibility of the body, that a technē is not the same as a series of techniques, but is defined by an end. Since the end, in this case health, cannot be simply identified with the healthy body, but is visible within that body, it also serves as a preliminary example of the forms or joints of nature, which mark off the collections and divisions of the dialectician. The end of health serves to unify the techniques of the art, because it also expresses the perfection of the object of that art. The end defines the unity or completeness of the nature of the object. A genuine understanding of the art, whether medicine or rhetoric (bearing in mind the double sense of "healthy"), therefore depends upon knowledge of "the nature of the whole" object to which the art is applicable (270b1-c2). By the same token, the philosopher cannot be said to have understood the art of dialectic unless he has understood "nature as a whole." Since dialectic includes the art of psychic persuasion (as follows from its absorption of rhetoric), it may more modestly be said to depend upon knowledge of "psyche as a whole."[40]

40 My interpretation is intended to show that 270c2: τῆς τοῦ ὅλου φύσεως must be taken to refer to both psyche and nature. It makes no difference which of these is the primary signification in the text;

Phaedrus shows his interest in the example of medicine by introducing Hippocrates as an expert on the method for understanding the body (270c3-5). This is the point at which he shows the clearest grasp of Socrates' argument, and his companion is quick to take advantage of this fact by associating "the true account" of speech about nature with the medical speech of Hippocrates (270c6-10). Medicine is a bond between Phaedrus and Socrates; it makes them "comrades" (270c6). There is then no reason to assume that Socrates is citing a genuine Hippocratic writing; his language indicates that Hippocrates' words must first be compared with the truth, in order to see whether there is a harmony between the two. As Hackforth observes (p. 151), Socrates is about to "interpret" Hippocrates in order to bring him into agreement with the truth. The truth is that, in order to obtain discursive understanding (διανοεῖσθαι) about any nature at all, we must follow a determinate procedure. First, we must decide whether the nature about which we desire technical competence is simple or multiform (270d1-2: ἁπλοῦν ἢ πολυειδές). If it is simple, there will correspond to it a specific technique; if not, it requires further division. In either case, diaeresis precedes the task of determining the "power" of the given nature to act or to suffer. That is, the collections and divisions of diaeresis are not the same as the task of determining the *being* of the thing (270d3-7). And the dividing up of the multiform nature into its formal atoms is a kind of counting (ἀριθμησάμενον) which is reminiscent of the "divine gift," described in the *Philebus* (16c10 ff.), of sorting out the number of forms in everything composed of the one and the many.

In the present passage, the process of collection and division is described as though it were analogous to anatomy. In anatomy, we first trace out the "joints" of the body, or determine its parts, by a process of visual inspection which is not the same as a study

cf. Friedlander, p. 218, n. 29. For a more extensive discussion of the relation between medicine and philosophy, cf. Rosen (*Symposium*), Ch. IV.

of the natural functions of those parts. Similarly, Socrates describes the enumeration of diaeretic forms as though it were a visual process independent of the study of the power of the forms. Socrates thereby silently assimilates diaeresis to the "visual" character of noetic apprehension of hyper-Uranian beings. In both cases, theory is understood in the literal sense of seeing what presents itself to the mind's eye. In the *Phaedrus*, the "phenomenological" character of noetic and dianoetic thinking harmonizes with the visible character of beauty, the most splendid or manifest aspect of the hyper-Uranian beings (250b5 ff.) and also of sensuous reality. We cannot determine the "power" of a nature until we have seen its form "in act" or "at work." Through the perception of beauty, we see genesis "at work" (to use again the Aristotelian phrase), and our psyche is erotically stimulated to participate in that work. Vision therefore mediates between the corporeal desire for generation and the psychic work of classifying and understanding forms. It is the road along which we move toward immortality, and in this sense it is a *methodos*. Those who do not follow it are indeed blind, in the deepest sense of the word (270d9-e2).

V.

At the beginning of the discussion of rhetoric, Socrates asked whether he who speaks well and beautifully must not possess a discursive knowledge of the truth about the objects of his discourse (259e4-6). He now summarizes the results of the investigation engendered by his earlier question as follows: "but it is clear that if someone is to give a technical account, he will precisely exhibit the being (οὐσίαν) of the nature of that about which he offers the accounts" (270e2-4). Nothing is said here about the dependence of fortunate or beautiful speech upon possession of truth. The entire discussion has shifted subtly from the question of beautiful to that of true speech, through the mediate question of whether rhetoric is a technē. This is of course not to deny that for Socrates technically true speeches may be beautiful, but the present issue is whether speeches may be beautiful even if they are not technically true, and, despite Socrates' silence, there can be no doubt that the answer is "yes." The shift from beautiful to true speech is itself an icon of the inexpressible visibility of beauty as the unity of form. Similarly, the silence of beauty represents the (discursively) unspeakable nature of the conditions (ontological subjects) of speech. We have moved from beautiful to true speech because our Eros for the beautiful cannot be satisfied without reflexive or technical discourse. But we must remember both beauty and truth, or the noetic as well as the dianoetic formal monads. In sum, the vision of form, incited and focused by beauty, enables us to repair the divisions of discursive experience by a recollective function of discourse itself.

In the particular case, we need a technical account of the psyche (270e4-5); namely, as precise an account as we can obtain. Socrates next gives a resume of the method of such an account, using Thrasymachus as the representative of sophistic rhetoric, perhaps in order to emphasize the difference between persuasion by force and by truth (271a1-4). The first step corresponds to a verbal imitation or model of the formal structure of the psyche, with all (if any) of its eidetic parts specified or classified by diaeresis (and need I repeat by now that the diaeretic form of the psyche cannot be the hyper-Uranian form—if such a one exists). This, Socrates adds, we call "pointing out [its] nature" (271a5-8). The pointing or showing (δεικνύναι) is a kind of discursive poetry (γράψει τε καὶ ποιήσει), akin to contemporary "phenomenological description" in which precision replaces beauty, and which makes the form determinately visible: the perception is translated into language.

Showing the nature is not yet explaining its "being" or power. The second step in constructing the technical logos of being is thus the explanation of the action or passion of the nature whose form we have determinately described (271a10-11). These two steps were previously associated with Hippocrates in formulating the procedure for speaking truly about nature (270c9 ff.). But now Socrates adds a third step, which joins his remarks about living discourse to the nature of technical logos. We must also classify the kinds (γένη) of speeches and psyches, and examine all the causes by which psyches are affected, in order to harmonize speech and psyche for the purpose of persuasion and dissuasion (271b1-5). This third step is not Hippocratic or technical in quite the same way as the first two. The classification is not of the eidetic parts of psyche simply or "abstractly," but rather of the typical incarnations, the existential variety of human beings, and the diverse kinds of speeches to which they respond. This step requires what might almost be called prudential rather than theoretical intelligence. It requires a sensitivity to the nuances of political and spiritual life, or knowledge of the particular; and so, it is again similar to sense-perception. The unity apprehended by the master of this third step cannot be generalized in scientific logos precisely because of its particularity. We have to *see* the individual man in order to make a proper adaptation of the scientific logos to his particular circumstances. This is something like the empirical judgment involved in medicine, except that the doctor does not need to see the specific psychic unity of his patient in order to choose the particular remedy. Despite the variety of corporeal circumstances in medicine, the unity in question is always the same: health. The specific personality of the patient being healed is either irrelevant or is itself reduced to the level of a particular factor to be considered in pursuing the same health for every individual.

Socrates proceeds to elaborate upon this third step in the technē of rhetoric, which is the most important for the main purpose of the dialogue. Although Phaedrus greeted the previous account of this step with high praise (271b6), he is obviously not clear about its nature (271c5). In a way the first two steps must be superficially more familiar to him, since they have something to do with natural science, and are linked by Socrates with medicine. Phaedrus' love of rhetoric, on the other hand, is directed toward epideictic or set speeches, which say the same thing to everyone. Socrates once more rejects this kind of rhetoric as not technical, since it "conceals," i.e., is ignorant of, the psyche (271b7-c4). His restatement of "how" one must speak in order to be "as technical as possible" (271c6-8) concentrates upon the method of setting speeches into motion, or rendering them animate. Phaedrus knows the medical importance of setting the body into motion (222a2-b1). The speeches and conversation of Socrates are intended to teach him about the motions of the psyche.

The "power" of logos, that is, its "being," expressed as work, is psychagogy: the leading, persuading, or charming of psyches. In order to adjust speech effectively to the individual, the rhetorician must know the kinds of psyche. Again, this entails knowledge of the particular, in the case of speeches as well as of psyches. The technē of fitting together speech and psyche requires not merely theoretical comprehension, but also practical experience, a "sharp perception" of how the individual man is affected by individual speeches (271c10-e2). This is the heart of the matter, and Socrates, as is his way in conversing with Phaedrus, repeats the point, animating it by telling us what the genuine rhetorician must be able to say to himself upon perceiving an individual man (271e2-4). "This is the one, and this is the nature, now actually present before me, about which the [pedagogic] accounts were previously given; in order to persuade [this nature] of so-and-so, I must apply these speeches to it in these ways" (271a1-3). As a consequence of this theoretico-practical mastery of the particular case, the genuine rhetorician knows when as well as how to speak, and when to remain silent (272a4). And finally, he must know when to use the various kinds of rhetorical techniques (272a5-7). In this tripartite division of step three, Socrates stresses that knowledge of the particular includes a perception of the ripe or propitious occasion. The right speech for a particular psyche at one time may be altogether inappropriate at another. The beautiful and complete mastery of the rhetorical technē is therefore equivalent to a complete understanding of human nature, as both formally articulated and as being-at-work in the specific circumstances of everyday existence (272a7-b2; cf. 270c1-2).

This is an extraordinarily arduous task for a Socrates, to say nothing of a Phaedrus. As though to buttress his pupil, Socrates associates himself with Phaedrus as addressee of the hypothetical teacher of true rhetoric (272b2-4). Phaedrus is forced to agree with the personified argument, although he complains of the difficulty it imposes (272b5-6). To this complaint, Socrates replies for the only time in the dialogue, "you speak the truth" (272b7).[41] And so, necessary as it is with Phaedrus as a pupil, Socrates repeats his main criticism of non-philosophical rhetoric. These repetitions are an essential part of Socrates' pedagogic technique; he is tacitly attempting to mold or activate Phaedrus' memory. As Socrates puts it, they must turn over the previous arguments, inspecting them closely to see whether they necessitate taking "the longer way," or whether there may be a shorter and smoother road (272b7-c2). And then, amusingly enough, instead of reviewing all the previous arguments, he himself takes a shorter way by asking Phaedrus for help. Does Phaedrus recollect anything he has heard from Lysias or someone else that would assist the investigation? In other words, it would be pointless to review all the arguments, just as it is pointless to suppose that Phaedrus could take the longer way. Phaedrus will be trained, not by dialectic, but by the repetition of discourses, myths, and conversation lightened by animation or personification of the issues discussed. Phaedrus will be forced to remember generally or superficially a teaching which we must remember specifically and internally, if we hope to be more than a semi-conscious intermediary between philosophy and the multitude.

Phaedrus fails the test here, not so much because of his own defects, but because, as we have already seen, there is nothing to recollect that would enable us to become rhetoricians by the shorter way (272c5-6). Socrates hopes to impress this fact onto Phaedrus' memory by giving him this last, direct opportunity to

41 At 228c9, Socrates says that Phaedrus has truly inferred his intention not to leave until the speech of Lysias is delivered. In the discussion of Eros and dialectical rhetoric, Socrates very seldom praises the responses of Phaedrus. Instances thus far: 263d1, 266d7, and indirectly, at 270c6.

defend the sophistic rhetoric he so much loves. But Socrates reinforces this negative lesson by himself presenting a last formulation in defense of non-philosophical rhetoric. He thereby
illustrates this pedagogic principle: one should always state the
popular or opposed teaching as justly as possible (272c7-11). The
opponents (literally, wolves, as opposed to the philosophical dog)
say that the upper and longer way is unnecessary. In order to be
a satisfactory speaker, we need not "participate in the truth" concerning just or good things, in themselves or concerning men who
are so by nature or upbringing (272d2-7). The examples cited remind us that sophistic rhetoric is essentially political; its goal is
not knowledge, and not really education, but rather power. The
sophist does not deny that there is truth, but rather he maintains
it to be true that there is no truth about human or political things.
But now Socrates modifies his earlier statement of the sophistic
teaching, and at first glance, makes it seem more reasonable than
before. What counts in the law courts is not truth but what persuades, "and this is the likely" (272d7-e1: τὸ εἰκός). Socrates emphasizes this contention by repeating "likely" four times in four
lines: the technician of likenesses or images can say farewell to
the truth (272e1-273a1).

We should not blur this very interesting point by translating
τὸ εἰκός as "the probable." At the beginning of the discussion of
rhetoric, Phaedrus introduced a view which he had heard, to the
effect that a good speaker must understand, not what is really
just, good, or beautiful, but what the many opine them to be
(259e7-260a4). Phaedrus did not recollect having heard this view
when Socrates asked him for a defense of the vulpine rhetoric.
Socrates politely reminds him, without explicitly mentioning that
he is doing so (cf. 273d2 ff.). Up to a point, then, the view he has
heard (272c7-8) is the one originally introduced by Phaedrus.
However, Socrates makes two modifications. First, he suppresses
"the beautiful things" from the account of what one need not
truly understand. And second, he replaces "opinion" (δόξα) by
"the likely" (τὸ εἰκός). The first change improves upon the version of Phaedrus. An expert on persuasion must certainly know

the truth, or some part of the truth, about beauty, precisely because it is beautiful speech, in the form of images or opinions, that
persuades the majority of men. Even if beauty is altogether "subjective" or relative to the perceiving individual, the competent
sophist must know which kinds of men are persuaded by which
kinds of beauty. If however the sophist maintains that even the
individual's tastes are in continuous flux, so that X may appear
to be both beautiful and ugly to the same man under the same
circumstances, then Socrates can reply that persuasive speech, or
at the very least a technē of persuasive speech, is impossible.

The sophist can deny a stability to the just and the good, but
not to the beautiful. However, in granting (as he must) the stability of beauty, he also necessarily admits that man has a nature,
namely, as the lover of beautiful speeches, and more specifically,
that men of natural types $T_1, T_2, \ldots, T_n$ love beautiful speeches
of the type $S_1, S_2, \ldots, S_n$. Therefore the sophist admits that there
is a stable truth about the nature of man and speech. This brings
us to "opinion" and "the likely." We might be inclined to suggest
that Socrates substitutes one for the other because they are inter-
changeable, or that opinion is the mode of cognition appropriate
to images. However, opinions are not themselves necessarily images of the truth; if there is no truth about X, then opinions O_1,
$O_2, \ldots, O_n$ are equally inaccurate, false, or distinct from X, and
can scarcely be said to provide icons of X or "reflect" the truth in
varying degrees. The differences between O_k and O_{k+1} will then
necessarily be due to contingent and subjective factors. On the
other hand, to say that O_k is a likeness, is to admit that it reflects,
whether well or badly, the truth about X. If the persuasive is the
likely, then there must be a truth by which the likely is distinguished from the unlikely; and this truth must be accessible to
the audience with sufficient clarity for them to discern the likely
as likely. Thus sophistry itself depends upon stability (X=X) and
truth; it cannot depend upon the subjective persuasiveness of
beauty alone. Even the improved version of the sophistic teaching
leads to its self-refutation.

In view of the changes between the present and the earlier

formulation, it is amusing to find Phaedrus now recollecting the original discussion (273a2-5). His tardy memory is in fact inaccurate, but very few auditors could be expected to recall details which are accessible to careful students of the printed text. This in no way alters the pedagogic value of repetition, but serves to underline the difference between Socrates' external and internal teaching. Socrates now connects the two formulations with a further reference to Tisias who, he says, teaches that "the likely is nothing other than what the many opine" (213a6-b1). As we have just seen, this implies the Socratic thesis that doxa is an icon of truth. More precisely, if the likely is distinguishable from the unlikely, it must be by access, even though only in doxa, to a rational order of events, or causes of events. In this sense, opinions may be classified into "right" and "wrong" on the basis of the study of likelihood or probability. However, icons do not in themselves provide us with an adequate foundation for an epistemology. Socrates illustrates this inadequacy by means of an icon (ὡς ἔοικε) which is again animated (273b3-c5). The example is political and involves the familiar story of the weak but brave man who has stolen the cloak of a strong coward. Such a theft is unlikely if we turn away from the psychic quality of the individuals involved, and look only at their bodies. The many are swayed more by the corporeal than by the psychic in arriving at their opinions. One may add to this, as Socrates does not quite do (273c2-4), that the thief in our example will probably escape punishment if he is sufficiently clever at sophistic rhetoric. What is ostensibly an absurd consequence of Tisian doctrine actually tends to support the efficacy of that doctrine. There is, then, a difference between success in politics and in epistemology; lies are perfectly adequate to the law courts. Nor can one appeal to a higher conception of success except on the basis of the distinction between the psyche (truth) and the body (force).

In sum: the sophists cannot be refuted merely by appeals to justice or conventional opinion, but solely by logical or dialectical analyses. This entails a dialectical analysis of icons, as for example by division into the psychic and corporeal, which is not itself iconic. Hence the absolute indispensability of the recollective intuition of form (i.e., the recollection within or as accessible to discourse of hyper-Uranian being) prior to discursive division and collection, which, like any linguistic or semantic activity, is already permeated by icons. If the forms are themselves linguistic constructions, there is no stable basis for distinguishing between the likenesses of language and that of which they are likenesses. There is a second implication of the example from Tisias that needs to be mentioned here. The sophists are inaccessible to "orthodoxy" or arguments from justice, because their psyches are corrupt. But the consequent necessity to meet them on their own ground of dialectical disputation raises the great danger that the cure is politically as dangerous as the disease. From this perspective, the private thesis of the love of beauty has a political virtue: the ambiguity of the connection between the love of beauty and the love of justice can be concealed by philosophical rhetoric. This is exactly what Socrates proceeds to do in his apostrophe to Tisias. Socrates states explicitly that the likely is generated by similarity to the truth, and is therefore "most beautifully" discovered by the man who knows the truth (273d2-6). The implication is that, if the jury knows the truth about likenesses, it will detect the guilt of the weak but clever liar. But there is obviously no stable basis for such an implication. In the first place, by Socrates' own teaching, knowledge of the truth is inaccessible to the many, and therefore to all but the most extraordinary of jurors.

Secondly, knowledge of the truth is not the same as knowledge of empirical fact; the liar might be sufficiently clever to conceal the truth from even a philosophical juror. But third and most important of all, it is by no means self-evident, on the basis of the central thesis of the *Phaedrus*, that philosophers are always politically just. The philosopher seeks his private perfection in the vision of beauty, which guides him, not simply above the city, but beyond the heavens as well. Of course, we are told that the fallen psyche may improve its lot in subsequent incarnations by living justly (248e4), but the philosophical psyche is already in the highest level of incarnation, "philosophy plus pederasty," which is equivalent to passive vision and the activity of dialectical collection. I do not mean to assert that the philosopher is unjust, but simply to remind the reader that there is something unjust about philosophy. The man who devotes his life to the interior vision of beautiful memories is not *likely* to be a sharp-sighted witness of external or political justice.[42] We shall return to this subject below; here, the reminder may suffice that, if justice is "minding one's own business," and the business of the philosopher is perfection, it would be unwise to attribute demotic justice to him without the closest consideration. As we are about to see, not even the art of philosophical rhetoric is directed primarily toward a political end, although it may certainly be employed by philosopher-kings for secondary political purposes.

Meanwhile, Socrates revises another earlier contention by asserting that the acquisition of technical rhetoric depends upon mastery of an enumeration of the natures of prospective auditors, the diaeresis of beings in accordance with forms, and the classification of each thing under one Idea (μιᾷ ἰδέᾳ: perhaps the literal translation should be "kind"). This is the third description of philosophical dialectic in five pages (273d6-e4). At 270c10 ff., the steps in the dianoetic study of nature were said to be:

1. determine whether the thing is simple or polyform;
2. if simple, find its natural power to act or suffer;
3. if polyform, enumerate its forms and find the corresponding power of each.

At 271a5 ff. the steps were presented with respect to the psyche:

1. determine whether the psyche is simple or (like the body) polyform;

42 The supra-celestial identification of justice as co-present with knowledge and moderation has no necessary connection with political or demotic justice. Everything turns upon the nature of *philosophical* justice.

2. describe its natural power to act or suffer;
3. order the kinds of psyche and of speech, showing which of the latter are appropriately addressed to which of the former.

This account seems to assume that the psyche is a formal monad, albeit internally articulated; at least it leaves out the second step of the first account, and adds the third step about matching speeches to psychic differences. In the present or third set of steps, step 3 of set two is here first, although in attenuated form; we are told to classify natures, of presumably psyches but not speeches. The present step 2 corresponds approximately to step 1 in each of the two previous descriptions. But the present step 3 (classification of each thing under one Idea or form) is at best implied by step 2 of list one; it does not appear at all on list two.

I believe that we can make a reasonable conjecture about the difference between the second and third lists. List three describes the technē of rhetoric *without any reference to speech*, and so is more like the first list, which adapts dialectic to the study of nature, than the second list, which adapts it to the study of the psyche. The lists, when we collect them together, remind us that the psyche speaks, whereas nature and technē do not. We should also observe that the three lists emphasize division far more than collection, which is scarcely mentioned. It appears most clearly in list three, where the term ἰδέα is used without comment. In other words, the *Phaedrus* is silent about silence, or exhibits it but does not offer a reflexive articulation of this most elusive and most necessary monad. The living speeches of the genuine rhetorician are like soldiers guarding the interior solitude of the philosopher. It is precisely in this sense that Socrates continues: the effort required for becoming a technical speaker is not invested for the sake of talking and acting with human beings, but rather "to be able to say what is gratifying to the gods, and to do all things in as gratifying a way as possible" (273e4-8). In terms of Socrates' second speech, this refers finally to participation in the heavenly processions for the sake of "blessed visions" (247a4), and ultimately, visions of hyper-Uranian being. Nothing is said anywhere about conversation with or by the gods; for all we are told to the contrary, speech begins with incarnation, and is altogether absent from heaven.

In the *Phaedrus*, blessedness would seem to be equivalent to a species of silence. Speech that gratifies the gods can only take place while man dwells on earth; it marks his love or desire for, but not his achievement of, wisdom or perfection. Recollection, the sole earthly link with heaven, is also silent, albeit the necessary condition for speech. The study of rhetoric, then, is a *long detour* undertaken to gratify, not our fellow slaves, but our good masters, whose origin is good (273e8-274a2). The great things for the sake of which we take the roundabout way are thus the things of the Stesichorean myth. And the same may be said of the first two speeches on the non- or concealed lover. The speech on manic silence is the center of pre-and post-manic speech: there can scarcely be any question about the structural unity of the Phaedrus, once we have analyzed it in detail.

VI.

So much, then, for the marvelous wisdom hidden in the technē of Tisias (273c7-10).[43] Phaedrus is now convinced, after so many repetitions and so much discourse of varying kinds, that what Socrates advocates is "altogether beautiful" (274a6-7). Socrates turns now from the discussion of skilled and unskilled speeches to the propriety and impropriety (=comeliness or beauty and ugliness) of writing (274b3-8). As in the case of speech, Socrates will divide writing into two kinds, external (=books) and internal (=recordings in the psyche). His conclusion will be that internal writing, or in other words, silent monologue, is the only serious kind. More precisely, it is better to speak than to compose books, but the best speeches are planted like seeds in a suitable psyche, which gives them animation and intelligence. Psychic writing thus permits defensive speech by the man who

43 Cf. Hackforth, p. 153, n. 4.

knows (276a5-7), but its primary function is obviously to assist in the achievement of self-perfection. The planting of verbal seeds in another man's psyche is also an act of education or philanthropy, but again, the purpose is the perfection of the other, and not conversation. As Socrates says, external writing is a playful extension of the memory; we may assume that internal writing is the serious effort to recollect the original silence of noetic synopsis.

Socrates has already defined the task of the noetic speaker (τὸν νοῦν ἔχοντα) as gratification of the gods (273e5-274a2). He returns to this point, or repeats for Phaedrus' education how most to gratify god in the matter of writing or speaking. This is necessary, because Phaedrus has forgotten, or not yet absorbed, the import of the previous discussion (274b9-11). We should ourselves not forget that the extensiveness and variety of discourse in this dialogue are due primarily to Phaedrus' bad memory (cf. 227d6 ff.). Socrates now repeats a story he has heard, handed down from the ancients or forefathers, of which they alone know the truth. It seems to be a doxa, and perhaps an *orthē doxa* (correct opinion), but however instructive, only a preliminary version of the truth we desire (274c1-3). It is therefore playful or laughable (274c4), despite or because of its serious content. The playful account of the playful art of writing, which is also intended as part of Phaedrus' instruction on how to gratify a god, concerns the discovery of writing by the Egyptian god Theuth.[44]

The Egyptians are famous for their antiquity, their memories, and their piety. In this sense, it is appropriate for Socrates to use an Egyptian tale in returning to the origins. It would have been inappropriate for him to employ a Greek god, in view of his criticism of writing. Nor is it an accident that the only conversation in the *Phaedrus* between god and man, the only instance of a speaking god, takes place among the Egyptians. Unlike the Greek gods as described in the myth of Stesichorus, Theuth lives among men in their earthly abode. Socrates calls him a

---

44 Cf. *Philebus* 18b6 ff.

"daimon," thereby suggesting that he is not a god in the same sense as the Olympians, but despite his antiquity, intermediate between men and the genuine or unqualified divinities (274c5-7). No doubt it is this daimonic nature which permits Theuth to speak, and to present mortals with such techniques as number, calculation, geometry, and astronomy, such pleasant games as draughts and dice, and such an ambiguous gift as writing (274c8-d2). When Theuth presents these gifts to Thamus, the king asks in each case what benefit they possess (274d2-7). In the case of the other or mathematical arts, Thamus judges them to be noble or base, and so accords them an appropriate mixture of praise and blame (274d7-e3). In the case of writing, however, where Socrates brings his character to life, the king has nothing but criticism.

Theuth associates wisdom with memory, and claims that writing is a drug that will affect both advantageously (274e4-7). Whereas Theuth refers to writing as "knowledge" (τὸ μάθημα), Ammon demotes it, together with the other gifts, to the status of "things of art" (τὰ τέχνης) and even addresses the daimon as "greatest technician Theuth." One person is able to generate such things; but another must judge concerning their portion of harm and utility for those who are about to use them (274e7-9). The utility of a technē is dependent upon its end, and decisions about the hierarchy of ends do not belong to the technical man, but to the king or statesman. The king is concerned with wholeness or perfection; he is the practical imitation of the philosopher. But political wholeness is almost as conspicuous by its absence from the *Phaedrus* as reflexive discussions of silence. Socrates needs the example of Theuth and Thamus in order to criticize writing vividly or animatedly. At the same time, he "depoliticizes" it as much as possible by making the dialogue between a daimon and a king, instead of between a king and one of his human subjects. This is why, a few lines later, Socrates refers to Ammon's speech as a "prophecy" (275c8: μαντείαν). Nevertheless, the legend of Theuth and Ammon, together with certain aspects of the discussion of rhetoric, are enough to remind us that the philosopher cannot simply transcend the city in his quest for solitary perfection. Speech is necessary for perfection, and speech is necessarily political.[45]

The father of writing is too fond of his offspring to tell the truth about its disadvantageous nature for men.[46] If implanted into the psyche, it will engender forgetfulness; thanks to confidence in external marks, men will cease to exercise their memories, and thereby to recollect things from within themselves. Writing is then a medicine for reminding,[47] not for remembering (274e9-275a6). It "externalizes" man, or takes him away from self-reflexivity, and so from the pre-discursive apprehension of synoptic unity. If a thought is an icon of a noetic form, then the written word is an icon of an icon, or three steps from the king. Hence Thamus calls writing a doxa or "semblance" of wisdom. The many will suppose themselves to be wise or to know many things, whereas in fact they will be ignorant for the most part, doxosophers instead of wise men (275a6-b2). In these lines, Thamus links "manyness" (πολυήκοοι, πολυγνώμονες, τὸ πλῆθος) and "semblance" (δόξαν, δόξουσιν, δοξόσοφοι); as Socrates previously established, what the many opine is a consequence of iconic heterogeneity of the absence (=forgetting) of synthesis. This is not to be taken as a total repudiation of doxa, but rather of the opinions of the many. Right is distinguished from wrong opinion by gathering together or unifying the excessive division of externality. The principles of this unification are accessible only through internal self-reflexivity, and thereby through recollection.

Phaedrus' initial response to this Socratic memory is to regard it as a poem (275b3-4). But this does not mean that it was pedagogically inappropriate; even demythologizers can be charmed

---

45 Cf. Hiram Caton, "Speech and Writing as Artifacts" in *Philosophy and Rhetoric*, Vol. II, No.1, Winter, 1969, pp. 21 ff.

46 Cf. Pieper, p. 101.

47 For a more favorable interpretation of ὑπομνήματα, cf. 249c6-8. See also 266d7, 277b4: "reminding" is here associated with Phaedrus.

by poetry.[48] Socrates thus provides Phaedrus with what only can be called a poetic demythologizing of the Theuth legend. According to the priests of Zeus' temple at Dodona, the first prophecies came from an oak tree. The ancients, who were not "wise" like contemporary young people, "were satisfied in their simplicity to listen to oaks and rocks, if only they spoke the truth" (275b5-c1). These allusions to Zeus, trees, and rocks echo the opening scene of the dialogue.[49] Socrates thus illustrates the correct way to indicate the sober content of a myth without lapsing into boorish wisdom, as Phaedrus was about to do in the case of Boreas. Phaedrus takes the point; he accepts Socrates' rebuke and agrees with Ammon's account of writing (275c3-4).[50] Treatises are neither clear nor steady, because they are dead rather than alive; their apparent stability is in fact a complete lack of defensive or polemical ability (275c5-d3).

The immobility of writing makes it comparable to painting; taken together, the two may be said to provide icons of the psyche and body.[51] Both are "silent" in the sense that neither can respond to questions (275d4-7). As I have just indicated, this form of rhetorical or political silence is bad because it interferes with the

48 Socrates began the dialogue by referring to Phaedrus as his friend (227a1). This term of address appears twice more in the early section of the dialogue (228d6 and 238c5), and then disappears until 271b7, after which it is used at 275b5 and 276e4. The least one could say is that Socrates and Phaedrus appear to be friends at the beginning and end of the dialogue; in the middle, they are companions.

49 Zeus: 227b4-5; trees: 229a8, 230a7 ff.; rocks: 229c6 ff.

50 Phaedrus very rarely says that Socrates speaks the truth. The two occasions: 266b2, after a summary of the three discourses which illustrates diaeresis; 238d4, in response to Socrates' claim that he is speaking dithyrambs (242d8 is hypothetical: *if* you speak the truth). He usually says something like "you are right" or "you speak beautifully." And these are his regular responses for the balance of the dialogue, on occasions when he might have said "you speak truly": 275d3, e6, 276e1, 277a5.

51 As Hackforth points out, γραφή and ζωγραφία are etymologically closely related.

psyche's internal march toward recollective or noetic silence. Just as in the case of madness, there are two kinds of silence, the divine and the human. Divine perfection is dependent upon human discourse, which permits the potential philosopher to be educated safely in the presence of the non-philosophers, and which also preserves the city from the vicious rhetoric of sophistry.[52] As dead speeches, books have only external motion; they cannot control the nature of their readers. Most important, they do not know when to speak and when to keep silent (275d7-e3). Their speech, as continuously self-identical or monotonic, is equivalent to silence in the pejorative or human sense. Very far, then, from being able to defend their fathers, books require the authors to come to their defense (275e3-6). Rhetorically and polemically, they are worse than useless. But let us not overlook their epistemic defect, either. The entire discussion of writing is designed to convey the harmony in human existence between knowledge and intelligence. One does not know men, and consequently, what it means to be a real or true man, unless one knows the effects, noble and base, of epistemic speeches upon the variety of human psyches. Without this understanding, one cannot know oneself, and thus the way to perception is blocked at the outset. The telos of knowledge is blessedness, not erudition. The psyche that is filled up with disconnected facts and arguments is the human equivalent to a dead book.

The legitimate son of a genuinely procreative psyche is thus the writing inscribed with knowledge in the psyche of the man who understands. Socrates calls this the "defensive" writing, because it knows when to speak and when to remain silent (276a1-7). At long last, Phaedrus seems to have remembered something: "you refer to the living and ensouled speech of the knower, of

---

52 One could well question Socrates' analogy between books and paintings on a variety of grounds, none of them relevant to the present example. I will note merely that the problem of rendering books and paintings defensively articulate is soluble in essentially the same way.

which one could justly call writing an icon" (276a8-9). But
Socrates, although he is pleased with this answer (276b1:
παντάπασιν μὲν οὖν), knows Phaedrus too well to leave it at
that. He therefore plants one more seed in Phaedrus' psyche, by
comparing writing to the art of farming. The noetic farmer (ὁ
νοῦν ἔχων γεωργός) is able to distinguish between the serious
and playful planting of seeds (276b1-c2). The distinction turns
upon the occasion or purpose of the planting, as well as the character of the soil and the time allotted for ripening. One might
playfully suggest that to these will correspond the justice (purpose), beauty (depending on the richness of the soil), and goodness (maturity) of the crop. In any case, these are the qualities
cited by Socrates as he shifts from the farmer to the writer (276c3-
6). The epistemic or noetic man, who grasps the just, beautiful,
and good things, will not write seriously with pen and ink, because the result is "watery" language that cannot defend itself or
teach the truth adequately (276c6-10). The act of writing or verbal
communication is the philosophical locus of the harmony between theory and practice. The discussion of speech throughout
the last third of the *Phaedrus* is itself pedagogic or defensive, and
may be called an essential element of philosophical politics. Its
function is not to provide an interpretation of the myth of Stesichorus, but rather to plant in the reader's psyche the seeds of the
technē by which he may himself acquire that interpretation.

Let me illustrate this point with a further observation on the
present reference to just, beautiful, and good things. The passage
is reminiscent of the description of the divine nature in the myth
of Stesichorus, which is said to be "beautiful, wise, good, and
everything of that sort" (246e1). Granting the ambiguity of the
supplementary phrase, it is nevertheless interesting that justice is
not explicitly attributed to the divine, but is, so to speak, replaced
by wisdom. This observation is in itself, of course, altogether in-
conclusive and perhaps arbitrary. But it can be given a "poetic"
reinforcement by a study of all the passages in Socrates' second
speech where the term "justice" is used. I have already had occasion to mention that "justice" is altogether absent from the first

two speeches on the non-lover, and that this is a mark of their baseness as synoptic interpretations of man, however valuable they may be in illustrating particular facets of human nature. Since the third speech is designed to raise the first two speeches by completing or transforming their teaching, we may expect it to use the term "justice" as an essential aspect of its noble interpretation of man. And indeed, the most important mention of justice places it among the hyper-Uranian beings, together with moderation and knowledge (247d5-6). On the other hand, this edifying reference is considerably tempered by Socrates' assertion at 250b1 ff. that justice, moderation, and the other honored qualities lack the innate splendor possessed by beauty in their earthly likenesses. It is the perception of beauty, and not of justice, moderation, and the rest, which stimulates man's Eros and leads him up toward noetic recollection. It is therefore comprehensible that justice is not predicated of the divine nature, nor for that matter of the discarnate psyche (e.g., at 253c7 ff., where it might appropriately have been mentioned). In fact, it is not even mentioned in connection with the achievement of blessedness by the philosophical lovers on earth, but seems to have been replaced here by moderation (256a7-b7; cf. 256e3 ff.).

The real function of justice in the third speech is to characterize the behavior of fallen or incarnated, and non-philosophical psyches, as well as their reward or punishment for behavior while incarnated for the first time (248e4-5, 249a5-b1, 250a4, 252c6). The only occurrence of justice in conjunction with philosophy is at 249c4, where Socrates says that "justly, then, the philosophical dianoia is alone winged," a passage of considerable ambiguity which I have previously analyzed at length. And not even this passage says that the philosophical dianoia is just. The precise examination of the role of justice in the third speech, then, supports the thesis that its primary function there is edifying rather than philosophical. Perhaps more justly, one could say that justice functions as the political virtue, as distinct from beauty, which represents the theoretical or noetic virtue. But the role of politics in the *Phaedrus* is "philosophical," or altogether subordinate to the main theme of the private, extra-political desire for immortality or perfection.

Thus, the edifying character of justice in the speech about silence is replaced by the defensive character of rhetoric in the speech about speech. The noetic or epistemic rhetorician exercises justice in generating speeches which are appropriate, not for his own ascent to perfection, but for the psyches of non-philosophers, among whom the potential philosophers must here be included.

A failure to grasp the difference between philosophy as living speech, expressive of the pursuit of unity or perfection, and pedagogical writing, underlies much of the confusion which the present passage has elicited among scholars. Equally responsible for this confusion is the failure to distinguish between Socrates, to whom the complaint against writing is assigned, and Plato, the author of the dialogue. The dialogue-form is itself a pedagogic or defensive form of rhetoric, the living speech which says different things to the readers of varying natures, and nothing at all when silence is appropriate. It should be evident from the fact of the dialogues themselves that Plato subscribed to the principle of Socrates' criticism of external writing, but that he believed himself to have devised a way of writing immune from the Socratic objections. This evidence is obscured by a combination of defective sensibility and ideological prejudices, which make dramatic form invisible, and give birth to "arguments," extracted from the dialogues like skeletons plucked from living animals. This procedure is equivalent to physiological dissection as practiced by a mad butcher, who discards the flesh and retains the bones for his bemused clientele. On the other hand, one can learn from academic perplexities that Plato's solution is by no means perfect. In times like our own, it is no solution at all to write dialogues. We require instead commentators, at least so far as the study of Plato is concerned.

The agricultural icon is used by Socrates to make a final comparison between the writer of books and the playful farmer (276d1-8). Books are treasuries of seeds sown παιδιᾶς χάριν which I would interpret to mean "for the sake of playful pedagogy or παιδεία." The playfulness of books must be understood in two senses. First, the education of the young, or the non-philosopher (276d4-5), is playful in comparison with the mature or serious activity of philosophizing. But second, there is a playfulness about philosophy itself, corresponding to the relative lack of seriousness in human life, when contrasted with the heavenly or even with the hyper-Uranian. Let me restate this last observation. Philosophy is play rather than work, because work is for the sake of leisure, whereas philosophy is what the best men do at their leisure. And the best of the best are always at leisure; they are σχολῇ, or "scholars" in the only serious because most profoundly playful sense. Books, then, are memoranda (ὑπομνήματα) for the forgetfulness of old age; when one understands them properly, or is no longer "young" (=uneducated), and has allowed their seeds to reach maturity in his psyche, then they serve "to initiate him into the final mysteries, and he alone becomes perfect" (249c6-8). And this initiation indeed remedies forgetfulness by serving to raise recollection to its highest and most comprehensive stage. In sum, philosophy prevents us from lapsing into human forgetfulness, for which old age, instead of expressing the perfect fulfillment of man's existence, becomes a second childhood, neither playful nor serious, but "a tale told by an idiot, signifying nothing." While other men, then, pass their leisure time in such youthful ways as symposia, perhaps listening to and themselves delivering speeches on Eros, the philosopher will amuse himself by writing books, in which perhaps men will be depicted as discoursing on Eros, whether at symposia or elsewhere (276d1-8).

This little speech rightly strikes Phaedrus as "altogether noble" or "beautiful" (παγκάλην). It even moves him to praise the game of discoursing "on justice and the other things you mention" (276e1-3). I take this as a playful indication by Plato that Socrates has taught Phaedrus justice, so far as that is possible, through the discussion of rhetoric. And Socrates rewards Phaedrus' improved condition by addressing him as "my friend Phaedrus" (276e4). However, he takes no chances with Phaedrus' bad memory, but summarizes the main points of serious, dialectical, or psychic writing: planting and sowing epistemic words in a suitable psyche, which, upon maturing, can defend themselves and the planter, and generate new words, or thinking, by which they achieve immortality for themselves and blessedness (εὐδαι-μονεῖν) for the man in whose psyches they dwell (276e4-277a4). This summary, as is Plato's way, contains a new point; the seeds or words are themselves for the first time said to gain immortality. I believe that this can easily be understood in conjunction with the previous speech about writing; if a man is able to write books which possess the attributes of living dialectic, then his words will continuously reproduce themselves, but also achieve "immortality" (i.e., live beyond their author) in and as themselves. Again Phaedrus affirms the greater beauty of dialectical to external writing (277a5). But once again we are shown how limited is Phaedrus' memory. Socrates suggests that the task of criticizing Lysias' speech on the basis of technical rhetoric has been adequately completed (277a6-b3). "So it seemed," says Phaedrus, "but give me another reminder" (277b4). Phaedrus had characterized the first two discussions of dialectic as "beautiful" (271b6, 274a6). This was also his response to the speeches about playful (276e1) and serious (277a5) writing. On the whole, Phaedrus perceives the beauty of what Socrates is saying, but not its truth. His failure to remember reminds us that there is no necessary transition from beauty, despite its splendor, to truth.

We have, then, still another summary of dialectic (277b5-c6). First: one must know the truth about the subject concerning which one speaks or writes. This entails being able to isolate or define it in itself (κατ' αὐτό), and then to divide it in accordance with its formal joints (κατ' εἴδη) until one reaches the uncuttable or eidetic monad (277b5-8). Second: one must have the same insight into the nature of the psyche; that is, one must know which form of speech harmonizes with each psychic nature, how to construct and adorn the relevant speech by speaking intricately to an intricate psyche and simply to a simple one (277b8-c3). Otherwise, one will fail to acquire the technē of rhetoric, whether for purposes of teaching or persuading; "thus our previous discussion altogether revealed the matter to us" (277c3-6). If we compare this summary with the earlier ones, there are several points of difference. First, Socrates omits all mention of determining the power, whether active or passive, of a given nature. Second, although he emphasizes diaeresis, nothing is said about enumerating the resultant kinds. Third, Socrates adds a new point, or at least a new way of expressing an implication of two old points: one must speak intricately or simply, depending upon whether one's auditor is intricate or simple. Perhaps the two omissions may be taken as a kind of simplification for the sake of Phaedrus. But I believe it is more important to observe that there is now a greater emphasis on speaking, and especially on ornate and intricate speech, than in the previous accounts. The earlier accounts tend toward silence, a silence of which Phaedrus is incapable, but which does not explain either the capacity or the need for the intricate rhetoric of Socrates and Plato, as embodied in the *Phaedrus*. The last word on dialectic, and no doubt the word which Phaedrus will recall, turns upon defensive rhetoric.

VII.

Now that we have had the discussion of serious and playful writing, we can define dialectic as a synthesis of diaeresis, definition, the determination of powers, knowledge of the psyche, and an ability to speak, i.e., to plant seeds or stimulants for the memory in the appropriate psyches, while at the same time defending oneself and one's speeches from forgetfulness or unintelligent attack. But there is a very serious problem which the *Phaedrus* in no way solves. Recollection, as well as division and collection, are essentially silent and visual. *How is it possible to pass from vision to speech?* My analysis of the meaning of the hyper-Uranian beings showed that it is not possible to give a discursive logos about the formal monads which I called the ontological subjects of discourse. But it did not show how discursive logos follows upon the noetic apprehension of those formal monads. Recollection is

not συναγωγή or "bringing together what was previously separate." The formal monads were never previously separate. The
point can be stated, however, independently of the difference between the hyper-Uranian beings (=ontological subjects) and the
forms or kinds of diaeresis. One must first see the form of the
unity which directs us how to collect particulars correctly, before
we can actually perform that collection. If "collection" is understood as the gathering together of separate individuals under a
common form, the apprehension of that common form cannot be
the result of the collection, but must precede it. And then, having
performed correct collections and divisions, or isolated the formal
monads on the basis of anticipations of their unity, we must next
"weave together" these monads in such a way as to render speech
possible. One can of course reply that diaeresis itself assumes the
power to speak, or that we perform it only after a high level of
verbal sophistication is reached, and so that it is retrospective or
recollective in this simple, empirical sense. But such a reply
scarcely explains how, without diaeretic and dialectical knowledge, we were able to begin speaking in the first place, which is
a matter from the beginning of predication, and so of collection
and division. One may predicate Y of X without knowing how
(or even precisely what) one is doing. But once one achieves self-
consciousness, an explanation of this initial power is mandatory.
According to Plato, speech depends upon noetic apprehension,
whereas we do not know that we are noetically apprehending
until afterwards, by means of a *recollection*, and hence through
speech. So far as its accessibility goes, then, noetic apprehension
depends upon speech.

   In sum, there are two problems connected with speech that
the *Phaedrus* does not answer. The first is the logical or syntactic
problem of the interweaving of noetically accessible, stable, de-
numerable, monadic and yet internally articulable forms. The second is the psychological problem of the discursivity of thinking
as dianoetic vision. To rephrase this: we have the problem of how
to speak about forms, and the problem of how to speak *when there
are no forms*, or none that can be readily identified. The second

problem is best posed in terms of the difference between myth and logos. Virtually the entire discussion of the psyche in the *Phaedrus* is mythical rather than epistemic or logical (cf. especially 246a3-6 and c6-d2). It is no accident that, whereas Socrates gives several determinate or logical accounts, however brief, of dialectical diaeresis, he never gives an equivalent determinate account of the nature and varieties of psyche. The closest we come to a discussion of the varieties of psyche is in the Stesichorean myth at 248c2 ff., where the order of psychic incarnation is introduced by a reference to the decree of necessity. This passage, with all its intricacy, could scarcely be called a logos in the technical or epistemic sense.

Discursive or dianoetic speech is conducted by means of recollections of noetic form. Again disregarding the difference between the two, we must say that dianoetic speech is speech *of* or *by means of,* formal apprehension. This is apparently the whole point of the elaborate discussion of diaeresis and weaving in the *Sophist.* We cannot here begin a detailed analysis of that dialogue. But it is not necessary, so far as the problem in question is concerned. The great paradox or mystery of the *Phaedrus* is that it provides us with an extraordinarily intricate speech about the psyche which, although obviously amenable to discursive interpretation, cannot itself be the consequence of noetic or dianoetic vision. Whether or not we are prepared to go so far as to deny that there can be an Idea (noetic monad) of the psyche, it is evident that the assertions in the myth of Stesichorus could not be reduced by analysis to a series of weavings together of noetic (or dianoetic) forms. I would insist that ordinary discourse, entirely apart from myth, cannot be so reduced, and on this point, if I have understood the dispute, I agree with the "ordinary language" philosophers in their quarrel with the "ideal language analysts." Unfortunately, the former discard noetic forms altogether, thereby making discourse altogether unintelligible. The real difficulty lies in the fact that some speech is "formal" and some is not; differently put, the logical form of a statement is by no means equivalent to its ontological form. Or still more accurately, there are some statements whose ontological significance does not seem to be equivalent to formal structures of any sort, methodological or ontological.

At the center of the *Phaedrus*, there is a core of silence. Socrates never explains how he knows what he relates about the psyche. This "knowledge" is precisely *divine madness*. Little wonder that it has been ignored by a generation of epistemologists who equate knowledge with discursive or dianoetic speech. Socrates gives us no reason to assume that the core of silence will be replaced by speech through the progressive transformation of myth into logos. The historical development of the sciences of psychology, linguistics, and semantics would seem, incidentally, to have had the net effect of hacking the psyche to pieces, or of transforming it into the body. So far as the history of science goes, it would seem to testify to the conclusion that an excess of discursivity leads to the destruction of the psyche. Certainly this has been the case as a consequence of an interpretation of discursive reasoning as cutting, classifying, and enumerating in accordance with kinds (*ordo et mensura*), together with the determination of active and passive powers (empirical science). I do not mean to suggest for a moment that such speech is undesirable. I do, however, insist upon the undesirability of interpreting *all of rational speech* in this way. Most speech, not merely about the psyche, but about speech itself, is not diaeretic in the sense just described. And this means that it is a mistake to define all speech as visual, or in terms of the model of vision. The Platonic myths are not visions of noetically accessible formal structures, although this is partially disguised by the fact that, as in the *Phaedrus*, they are often called "prophecies." To take the two crucial cases, no one has ever *seen* the psyche, or what Socrates calls "the whole." One is tempted to suggest that speech about the visible owes its possibility to man's capacity for speech about the invisible. For regardless of the chronological moment at which one "sees" a form or Idea, the process of speech as a whole or unity functions by means of words and conceptions which do not correspond to Ideas. There is no Idea of speech: as discursive or kinetic, speech is a mode of Eros. And this is why it is amenable to an unending variety of analyses. Discursive speech, in a literal sense, is *the language of love*.

Socrates has not taught Phaedrus how to speak about silence, but rather instructed him to do so by a variety of myths and icons which appeal to his love of beautiful discourse. One set of these myths concerns the philosophical technē of dialectic, but we have ample evidence to doubt whether these speeches will remain for long in Phaedrus' memory. Nor, given their brevity and inconsistency of expression, is there any reason why they should, unless perhaps as an odd variant on technical procedures employed by the sophists and some scientific investigators like Hippocrates. Phaedrus is not a classical scholar of the 19th or 20th century, searching for the historical development of Plato's conception of dialectic. He is an aesthete, a dilettante, and an intellectual; therefore, he will exercise great influence over his fellow Athenians. Socrates devotes considerable effort to the edification of Phaedrus. But the choice of Phaedrus as protagonist is not simply a political act. In both the *Symposium* and *Phaedrus*, Plato shows the trans-political nature of Eros, and hence of philosophy, by deriving it from the fundamentally nonpolitical, selfish, and passive nature of Phaedrus. Philosophy is the solitary pursuit of self-perfection by an essentially passive vision of ungenerated beings. But, if for no reason than that the philosopher is not a disembodied psyche, it is also something more. The limitations imposed by Plato on the *Symposium* and *Phaedrus* thus correspond very generally to the defects of Phaedrus' nature. The goal of Eros as its own negation is itself negated by man's residence in genesis, which differentiates his unity, and so threatens it with dissolution. Hence the need for speech (and political existence), by which man seeks to recollect his original or "heavenly" unity. In sum: Phaedrus loves both beautiful speeches and process physics; his Eros encompasses both myth and logos, but without the capacity to humanize them. In the two dialogues in which he is the father of the logos, Socrates appeals to his love of beauty, because the theme of these dialogues is wholeness or unity, and the perception of beauty is the most splendid, visible, or accessible manifestation of unity, whether in the perception of form or the desire of Eros.

However, the terminus of the love of beauty is silence. Even for philosophy as a private activity, the love of beauty must be supplemented by a re-interpretation of the love of physics, or more generally, of the mathematical study of nature. But this study, too, must lead inevitably to silence, as is already evident from the *Phaedrus*. The silence of mathematics about human existence leads us to suspect that the love of mathematics is a special case of the love of beauty. Therefore, both these "private" forms of Eros must be completed by a third: the political Eros. It is necessary for humans to do as well as to speak: to make love as well as speeches about love. In the *Symposium* and *Phaedrus*, there is a regular abstraction from desire or the body. The correct synthesis of the lover and the non-lover involves a proper recognition of the psyche's dependence on, as well as its rule over, the body. As human beings, we need to descend as well as to ascend. The major concern of the *Phaedrus* is ascent, and therefore it contains a long defense, explicit and implicit, of prophetic speech at the expense of external writing. Living speech must prophesy about the nature of the psyche, with respect both to its unity and its diversity. It must relate the awareness of unity to the particular aspects of diversity—that is, to the particular in its particularity. Its nobility or beauty depends upon direct contact with the individual, and so upon conversation. External writing, whether for private or public ends, is base or ugly if regarded as "secure and clear" (277d1-10). Clarity and distinctness are obtained by a loss of consciousness, both of the self and the other. The unconscious speaker is thus unable to distinguish between dreaming and waking discourse about justice and injustice, or about the specifically human. He might be able to distinguish between mathematical truth and falsehood, which is the same whether we be awake or asleep (277d10-e1). The crowd praises dreams about justice and good things, but philosophical politics requires constant wakefulness, even at night (277e1-3).

The wakeful man who understands the necessarily playful

character of external writing, or its inability to engage in inter-
rogatory examination and pedagogy, may indulge in it blame-
lessly (277e5-9). For he recognizes that the purpose of external
writing is either to persuade or, in the best case, to remind those
who really know (277e9-278a1). Persuasion and reminiscence, we
may add, are the two recollective functions of external writing,
corresponding to the difference between the many and the few.
Books (or set speeches) are thus at best icons of speeches implanted within the psyche concerning just, beautiful, and good
things (278a2-4). I take the absence of truth in this phrase to be
part of the exaggerated condemnation of books to an essentially
political role. In any case, clarity, completeness, and seriousness
are exclusively properties of psychic writings, which may be
called a man's genuine sons, first in themselves, and secondly in
the form of their sons and brothers who have been properly engendered in the psyches of the speaker's audience. As the absence
of any reference to women underlines, genuine pederasty, become
capable of reproduction, is philosophical education (278a4-b2).

Socrates prays that he and Phaedrus will become writers and
speakers in the noble or wakeful sense, and Phaedrus wishes as
well as prays for the same result (278b2-6). The dialectical game
has therefore achieved a measured, moderate, or sufficient fulfil-
ment (278b7). Socrates now directs Phaedrus to deliver a message
to Lysias which summarizes the results of the dialogue under
three main headings, all of them attributed to musical words
overheard at the stream of the nymphs. Speechmakers like Lysias,
poets like Homer, and law-givers like Solon, are all charged to
designate themselves by a name other than "author," provided
they conform to the standards of serious writing. That is, they
must have written with knowledge of the truth, be able to defend
their speeches, and also to point out their paltriness (278b9-d1).
Rhetor, poet, and law-giver require the sanctification of the Muses
because they constitute the three fundamental aspects of political
discourse. The messages directed to these three types are in a way
equivalent to the teaching of the three main parts of the dialogue:
the two rhetorical exercises, the myth of Stesichorus, and the

conversation on rhetoric. This, I believe, is what Socrates "prays'" that Phaedrus will remember of the long exchange of speeches. Philosophy is accessible to Phaedrus only as a purified version of public discourse, which will rule or regulate the technical speeches of physics and medicine that also command his attention. The distinction between wisdom and philosophy, however, can be taken in a comprehensive sense: only a god may be wise, because (in the *Phaedrus*) the gods are silent, or purely noetic beings. Speech is a mark of the absence and the pursuit of wisdom, of the desire to recollect what has been divided by genesis (278d2-7). And external writing is but an icon of living speech or, as I said above, three steps from the king (278d8-e3).

Now that the technical discussion has been concluded, Phaedrus regains some of the spiritedness he demonstrated at the beginning of the dialogue. Just as Socrates has teased Phaedrus for his association with Lysias, Phaedrus now teases Socrates by asking what message he will deliver to "the beautiful Isocrates" (278e4-9). Of the many conjectures which have been made concerning this reference, one thing is reasonably clear. Socrates, and presumably Plato, have a high regard for Isocrates' nature and writings. The least that can be said for Isocrates is that he exemplifies thus far (278e10: νέος ἔτι) in his orations something of the animated discourse which Socrates regards as necessary for defensive psychagogy.[53] This pre-eminence of Isocrates stems from the fact that his discursive intelligence has something of philosophy within its nature. Hence the prophecy that Isocrates will one day be led by a more divine impulse (278e10-279b1). This prophecy is both very favorable toward Isocrates, and at the same time expressed with some caution. Socrates does not call Isocrates a philosopher, nor predict that he will become one in the future. Neither does he guarantee that Isocrates will achieve a more

---

53 See the excellent doctoral dissertation on *The Political Philosophy of Isocrates* (University of Chicago, 1955) by Allan D. Bloom, for a discussion of the Socratic content of Isocrates' rhetorical teaching, esp. pp. 43, 116, 167 and 221–29.

divine status than he presently enjoys. We may respond with the same caution to Socrates' obviously ironical remark that Isocrates is his sweetheart, just as Lysias is the sweetheart of Phaedrus (279b1-3). Both Socrates and Phaedrus have been adequately revealed as lovers of speeches, not of bodies.

Socrates began the dialogue with a prophecy about Phaedrus (228d7). After completing his first speech, he identified himself as a playful prophet (242c3-4), in connection with a reference to his daimonion, and the sin of his defense of the non-lover. The daimonion is there absorbed into the prophetic nature of the psyche generally (242c7), but Phaedrus seems to lack this gift, which may be related to the memory. In his discussion of madness, Socrates cited two kinds of prophecy, the telestic and purificatory (244a8 ff.). Apparently this division was incomplete, for as the prophecies about Phaedrus and Isocrates indicate, there is also a kind of divination about human nature. (The daimonion may perhaps be classified under the species of purificatory prophecy.) This reinforces our earlier observation concerning the mythical nature of speech about the psyche, or more generally, in all cases of non-eidetic discourse. Whatever may be true of other dialogues, the *Phaedrus* teaches that there is no logos of the psyche. It is therefore appropriate that Socrates close the dialogue with a prayer (279b4-7). At 237a7, Socrates introduced his first speech with a prayer to the Muses; one may therefore say that his major discourses in the *Phaedrus*, including the discussion of rhetoric and dialectic, and which contain in their center the eschatology of the psyche, are surrounded by piety. In the *Phaedrus*, Socrates appears as the prophet of the Muses and of Pan, the legendary rival of Apollo—a god of music, the countryside, and lust.[54] His piety is therefore playful, as is fitting in the task of educating Phaedrus. The final prayer is

---

54 Cf. 263d4, where Pan is identified as one of the fathers of the Muses. In his note to the present passage, Robin (*Phèdre*) says that "la prière à Pan rappelle la prière au Soleil du *Banquet* 220d"; but he forgets the rivalry between Pan and Apollo. Friedländer (p. 221) cites *Cratylus* 408d, where Pan is said to be "der Alles zeigende."

dedicated to "friend Pan and the other gods of this place," and distinguishes between internal beauty and external wealth, thereby echoing the two kinds of writing. Wisdom is a characteristic of internal beauty and moderation, or, as we may now say, of the prophetic dialectician (and not simply of the master of diaeresis: 279b8-c3). Nothing more is needed here; the sun has begun its descent (279b4-5), and Socrates caps the measured playfulness (278b7) of the dialogue with a suitably measured prayer (279c4-5). "Pray for me, too," Phaedrus graciously adds (and moderately: he himself does not pray); "for friends have common possessions" (279c6-8). Phaedrus thus accepts some of Socrates' possessions, thanks to the Muses, or his love of beauty.

CHAPTER FIVE:
Conclusion

I.

It is now time for us to exercise our capacity of recollection, or to perform a synopsis of the complex divisions we have sorted out in our analysis of the *Phaedrus*. We may take our bearings by the general question of the relation between the *Phaedrus* and the *Symposium*. The most striking theme of the *Phaedrus* is that of the divine madness. This theme is altogether absent from the *Symposium*, where madness is mentioned only by Alcibiades, the only intoxicated speaker at the banquet. But the madness and the intoxication of Alcibiades are all too human; with the exception of his love for Socrates, the erotic excesses of Alcibiades are sober instruments in the service of a political rather than a divine hybris. One may say that the essential sobriety of Alcibiades' ambition makes it impossible for him to understand his love for Socrates. In suppressing his yearning for divine beauty, Alcibiades loses his immortality, and the *Symposium* is, among other things, the dramatic enactment of his psychic shipwreck. Apart from the speech of Socrates, then, the erotic peak of the *Symposium* is a portrait of failure. As is perhaps clearest in the speech of Aristophanes, Socrates' companions are restricted in their comprehension of Eros by a fundamental sobriety. But this sobriety is defective because it is sundered from philosophy; differently stated, it is rooted in the body rather than the psyche. And therefore, it is subject to all the contradictions of corporeal appetite. These contradictions lead inevitably to a deterioration of the corporeal sobriety into merely human madness.

Let us put the teaching of Diotima to one side for a moment. It is clear that none of the other interpretations of Eros is sufficiently comprehensive. The interpretations are all too sober because they try to give a comprehensive account of genesis *from within the horizon of genesis.* The specific or dominating appetite of each man is taken as the basis for an interpretation of genesis, whereas, in fact, it is only a perspectival view of genesis. Eros, or the human experience of genesis, considered in itself, has no stable form, and therefore, no "horizon." It is always ceasing to be what it was, and beginning to be what it is not. Thus the speeches about genesis prior to (and after) that of Socrates actually reduce to silence, as is most evident in the speech of Aristophanes. But the teaching of Diotima also fails to give a comprehensive account of the whole. Let us first see how this is so with respect to genesis. Diotima's interpretation of Eros is not altogether consistent. For the most part, she explains Eros as love of the beautiful. But much if not most of genesis is ugly, as it is experienced by man. One might claim that the ugly aspects of human experience become beautiful when transformed by the understanding of philosophy. However, this transformation cannot take place except by an initial attention to the ugly as ugly. The Eros for understanding is either comprehensive or perspectival; if the latter, it reduces to one or another of the positions represented by the other speakers at the banquet. The same difficulty is evident in the passage in which Diotima identifies love of the beautiful as a kind or part of love of the good. Love of the good is itself identified as a repudiation of the bad, in the way that a man desires to have a sick limb amputated, even though it belongs to his own body. Hence the cosmos is once more cut in half. Besides this, the definition of Eros as love of the good is explained by corporeal imagery which alludes to the speech of Aristophanes, and is shortly replaced by the definition of Eros as the desire to generate in the beautiful. If the beautiful and good are defined in terms of genesis and the body, then we return to the multitude of interpretations of genesis: what is beautiful and good becomes relative to the body, or what seems to be beautiful and good to each individual. And the result, of course, is not philosophy but sophistry.

According to the traditional understanding of the *Symposium*, Diotima escapes the paradox of an account of genesis solely in terms of genesis. But the "final mystery" or ascent to the vision of the beautiful itself is once more incomplete. First of all, the ascent to the beautiful is a consequence of generating in beautiful instances of genesis. It is therefore compromised from the beginning by its origins: it would seem itself to be a generated thing, i.e., a *poem* (and I mention parenthetically that, at 205b, Diotima identifies *poiēsis* as a species of genesis). This raises all the difficulties involved in the effort to choose between alternative or contradictory poems. Second, the ascent takes place through the intermediary of a guide (210a) who is never identified, but who is usually assumed to be an experienced lover or philosopher. However, if the account of the ascent of the neophyte is defective, it cannot be used as an explanation of how the guide ascended before him. In this account, the neophyte ascends from generated bodies to generated deeds, and thence to generated speeches; in sum, to what Diotima calls the vast ocean of beauty (210d): again, the language of genesis. By viewing this ocean, and generating many beautiful philosophical speeches, the neophyte will ostensibly gain in strength until he perceives the science of beauty itself. But Diotima offers no explanation as to how this erotic induction takes place. It cannot be explained by identifying the guide or motivating principle as Eros, because Eros is "polymorphous perverse" and himself stands in need of guidance. As I expressed this difficulty in a previous study:

> We need to make the final ascent from beautiful particulars of the highest kind to beauty simply or in itself as the unity of those particulars. Unfortunately, such an ascent takes us from speech to silence. Every speech is a particular and generated individual, a wave of the sea rather than the sea itself; it is itself a unified manifold, but one which cannot speak its own unity. The visibility of the beautiful particular rests upon the prior intuition of beauty in itself; but every attempt to speak

of beauty in itself merely generates another particular. Silently present within the interstices of Diotima's account of the ascent is an unspoken and unspeakable descent, the "guide" who directs Eros in the right way at each stage of transcendence. Eros is the physiological or physical striving of genesis; not he but the guide has already seen that toward which the neophyte is being directed.

Prior to the ascent of any mortal to beauty itself, there must be a *descent* or revelation to the erotic psyche, which opens the horizon for a comprehensive and stable account of genesis. This is the premise for the transition from the *Symposium* to the *Phaedrus*. In a fundamental sense, the problem faced by both dialogues is the same. The attempt to give an account of genesis in terms of genesis is equivalent to the attempt to give an account of discursive speech discursively. Diotima's negative description of beauty itself is as much a confession of the impossibility of this attempt as a prophecy of a higher revelation. The *Phaedrus* supplies us with this higher revelation, although not without ambiguity; but revelations are not exercises in logic, and the expurgation of ambiguity is equivalent to the suppression of human existence. The key to the difference between the *Symposium* and the *Phaedrus* is the recognition that the way up is not the same as, and in fact is posterior to, the way down. This is dramatically represented by the promotion of Eros from the status of daimon to that of god. Man's comprehension of genesis is rooted in his transcendence of genesis. In more prosaic terms, an adequate language of love is not accessible on the basis of an infinite regress of meta-languages. Those who insist upon an initial linguistic sobriety always terminate in one form or another of arbitrary madness. We need a reinterpretation of the excessively sober Eros of the *Symposium*, and this is the function of the first two speeches of the *Phaedrus*. The reinterpretation is complicated by the fact that it is necessary first to criticize in part the apparent identification in the *Symposium* of philosophy and Eros. The mixture of madness and sobriety in the daimonic Eros is inadequate to support such an identification; in this sense, the speeches of the non- and concealed lover amount in part to a rehabilitation of sobriety or temperance. But they also present a critique of sobriety understood as corporeal or for the sake of the body. They prepare us for the prophecy that genuine sobriety depends upon a divine (and not a daimonic) madness understood as psychic or for the sake of the psyche.

The first speech (of the non-lover) is a parody of a utilitarian calculus in the service of corporeal hedonism. This speech has two different levels. One contains a reasonable criticism of erotic passion as an obstacle to friendship and the pursuit of the useful, the just, and the true. At the second level, there is a base reduction of intelligence to logistics and of love to physiological desire. The second speech (of the concealed lover) starts from the same premise as that of the non-lover: the prudential calculation of or sober deliberation on desire. This speech also has two different levels. First, it criticizes the inconsistencies of the non-lover's effort to place intelligence at the service of corporeal hedonism or physiological gratification. Second, however, we must remember that the concealed lover actually has the same goal as the non-lover, namely, physical enjoyment. But his criticism of Eros leads finally to a praise of moderation and philosophy, rather than to the achievement of his (partially concealed) goal. He can avoid surrendering this goal only by himself turning into the non-lover, that is, by enacting the contradiction implicit in the subordination of intelligence to corporeal desire. Nevertheless, the initial sobriety of his assumed stance makes it impossible for his praise of philosophy to be transformed into philosophy itself. Despite or because of the sobriety of his critique of Eros, the concealed lover is still circumscribed by the domain of genesis.

The relation between the first two speeches makes it difficult to summarize either apart from the other. But we can present the main thesis of the first speech. An initially moderate desire is persuaded by an appropriately restricted or sober intelligence to disregard all factors in the human situation but that of the gratifying of physical desire. Intelligence, because of its low erotic strength, cannot in this context aim higher than at efficient gratification. But if "intelligence" means "efficiency" and efficiency in turn is defined by bodily pleasure, then the distinction between intelligence and desire disappears. Intelligence is not merely an instrument of desire, but the finally unintelligible projection of desire. The autonomy of corporeal desire leads to a deterioration or debasement of the technical conception of "efficiency" or to the self-negation of desire by the debasement of the beloved, and hence of the non-lover, who is in fact a concealed lover. And that in turn takes us to the second speech.

II.

In the transition from the first to the second speech, an agreement is struck between Socrates and Phaedrus. Socrates accepts the task of defending the non-lover, but reveals him to be in fact a concealed lover. In other words, Socrates begins Phaedrus' education by revising and assimilating Lysias' teaching into a higher, more comprehensive interpretation of Eros. This can occur because Phaedrus' love of base speeches transcends the love of the baseness of what is said. We see here an important clue to the fundamental nature of human Eros as the desire for (comprehensive) speech about desire. Selfishness may thus be converted into a disinterested perception of beauty. This was already prefigured in the sobriety of the non-lover; in the proper psychic mix, this sobriety plays its role in the transition from the body to the psyche. The concealed lover takes an important step forward on the basis of the same premise as that of the non-lover: prudential calculation. But he "rationalizes" this premise by making explicit the dependence of desire on knowledge of the object desired. He does this by what amounts to a distinction between appetite and deliberation. This distinction is implicit in the simplest instance of desire, which is thus seen to consist of two contradictory elements. In the given case, the erotic appetite, in order to be satisfied, gives rise to a deliberation which is itself non-erotic. In more general terms, man's fundamental or comprehensive desire is to deliberate, and thus to speak, about his desires, and so finally about his nature. In order to do this, he must regain possession of himself from the initiating appetite, literally *recollect* himself, yet without losing the impetus toward activity that only appetite provides. He must conceal his Eros from himself as well as from the object of that Eros; this is the difference between the non-lover and the concealed lover.

The concealed lover presents this difference publicly as one between the lover and the non-lover. In the *Symposium*, the distinction turned upon the desire of the lover for the beautiful; but this is inadequate, because the non-lover also desires the beautiful. Instead, the concealed lover distinguishes between (1) a natural desire for pleasure, and (2) an acquired opinion aiming at the best. This distinction is reminiscent of the distinction between appetite and deliberation, except that it isolates deliberation from human nature, which is identified with appetite. The concealed lover teaches implicitly that it is necessary for man to improve on nature; desire is in itself called "hybris," whereas the acquired opinion is identified as "temperance." The examples given of hybris are the excessive forms of eating, drinking, and Eros: all necessary for human existence, in their temperate forms. But temperance is not furnished by nature; the concealed lover does not identify the source of the humanizing deliberations by which man is preserved from bestiality. We shall have to wait for the third speech in order to learn that the humanity of man is a divine gift. The teaching of the concealed lover, on the contrary, amounts to a version of linguistic conventionalism. Man presumably masters his erotic appetite by talking about it. In terms taken from my analysis of the first speech, the position of the non-lover leads to a reification of desire, or to a split between humaneness and desire. Man is *alienated* from his desire, and subsequently enslaved by it. The equation of intelligence with efficiency leads finally to a deterioration of efficiency, to the debasement of the beloved, and thereby, to self-debasement, or to pain rather than pleasure. The implication of the concealed lover's analysis is that the non-lover is in fact a concealed lover, whereas he himself is the non-lover. As the ostensibly genuine non-lover, the concealed lover must commit himself to the criticism of Eros or nature. Therefore he must distinguish between deliberation and nature, or identify his greater intelligence and articulateness with an opinion about the best that is not natural (or corrupted by Eros) in its origin.

Since the source of the opinion about the best cannot be Eros, the concealed lover, who is in possession of this opinion, is forced to undertake the role of non-lover. Indeed, we may say that he was foredoomed to this role by his initial acceptance of the identification of intelligence as prudential calculation. If, then, the concealed lover succeeds in seducing the beloved with his discourse, he will at once fail, since there will be no reason for the beloved to gratify him. The handsome youth has been turned, not quite toward philosophy, but toward the masters of prudential calculation, or the sophists. That is, if he obeys the instructions of the concealed lover, the youth will associate sexual gratification with skill in deliberative rhetoric. At the same time, the principle of such skill must be opinion or convention rather than nature. But opinions differ, not merely with each other but with themselves. For example, men praise temperance publicly while denying its excellence in private. Obedience to opinion is thus obedience to a master divided against himself, and this contradiction can be resolved only by what we may somewhat playfully call a "theory of types." The contradiction between public and private discourse on temperance or human excellence can be resolved for the time being by separating the two, and rendering each autonomous in its own domain. This separation is already prefigured in the difference between the psyche and the body. But a house divided against itself cannot stand; the question soon arises as to which opinion, the psychic or the corporeal, is of the higher or ruling type. On the one hand, this would seem to be a matter of opinion, in accordance with the initial separation of intelligence from nature. On the other hand, however, differences of opinion are usually settled by persuasion or force, and in the given case, the private surrender to intemperance is equivalent to a triumph for the opinion of the body. The difference of opinion is in fact a concession to the "law of nature" that might makes right, and that the body is mightier than the psyche. For otherwise we should be forced to admit that the superior strength of the body is a mere matter of opinion, which is clearly absurd. Opinion will triumph only with the triumph of temperance in deed as well as in speech. But so long as victory is merely a matter of words, the body insists upon its status as natural standard. The sophistic position thus returns us to the reification of desire which was a consequence of the non-lover's teaching. In sum: the non-lover and the concealed lover are continuously transformed into each other; each ceases to be what he was, and becomes what he is not. Eros has not yet been tamed or guided on its upward ascent.

III.

The non-lover and the concealed lover are personifications of Eros. The speech of each persona contains an inadequate interpretation of the human experience of genesis, although each has its contribution to make to a genuinely comprehensive discourse on man. This brings us to the third speech in our dialogue, or the myth of Stesichorus. The first two speeches attributed evil effects to Eros, or in effect admitted their own incompleteness. This is also shown by the fact that Socrates is willing to criticize the lover, but refuses to praise the non-lover. In other words, the non-erotic component of philosophy must be furnished by a trans-human source, if it is to avoid the contradictions we have just summarized. Contradictions among opinions must be settled by recourse to nature in a sense other than that furnished by corporeal desire in its emancipated form. Eros must be purged of its evil effects. Socrates employs a medicinal rhetoric to accomplish this purge, similar to the medicine by which Stesichorus regained his sight. That is, just as Stesichorus recanted about Helen, so Socrates will now give a poetic restatement about beauty as the object of Eros.

The defense of Eros begins with a distinction between good and evil madness. Socrates implies that Eros, as an instance of good madness, and a divine gift to humans, is itself free from evil. To this we may add that its divine status raises it above the human division between good and evil, or beauty and ugliness, which plagued earlier efforts to derive a comprehensive interpretation of experience from a principle immanent to experience itself. Whereas in the *Symposium* (and the first two speeches of the *Phaedrus*), Eros was equivalent to the human experience of genesis, this is no longer true. As we shall see, there is a principle of experience higher than Eros: noetic apprehension of hyper-Uranian being. If, however, Eros is divine or good, then there must be a principle *lower* than Eros, which is responsible for evil and ugliness in the world of genesis. This principle is never explicitly described in the myth of Stesichorus; it must be inferred from reflection on the first two speeches of the dialogue. One cannot simply identify it with the base horse in the image of the psyche, since both horses are moved by erotic appetite. Neither can it be identified with the body (or more abstractly, with the "receptacle" of the *Timaeus*), since the human conflict between good and evil is described as occurring within the psyche, and in terms of the two horses: there is no reference in the myth to the *chariot*, or to the body as a principle of activity. As we shall see, the solution (to the extent that it is a solution) lies in distinguishing between the attractive and separative functions of Eros incarnate. One could say that evil and ugliness arise from the union of psyche and body, provided we add to this that the principle of activity is within the psyche. *But this means that Eros continues to have evil effects.* The human experience of good and evil is evidently rooted in a divine necessity, which is at the same time the condition of human perfection.

We see from this reflection the continuity between the *Symposium* and the *Phaedrus*. If left to its own devices, Eros bifurcates in its embodied form, and the ensuing contradictions between its two divisions make coherence and comprehensiveness impossible in human experience. By calling Eros a god, Socrates indicates that it is subject to a higher principle, which it transmits to man, and which is capable of bringing unity to its internal divisions.

In the first two speeches of the *Phaedrus*, Eros was obtained by a division of human desire. In the third speech, Socrates divides madness rather than desire, and Eros is a species of the divine form of madness; to exaggerate very slightly for the sake of clarity, Eros is subordinate to madness. Somewhat more precisely, human desire may be divided into two elements, the manic and the erotic, which correspond to what I call the separative and the attractive components of corporealized desire. Although both play their part in the conversion to philosophy, it is evident that the manic or separative component must predominate. The difference between the *Symposium* and the *Phaedrus* is the manic component of desire, with all that it implies. Without divine madness, Eros is forced to supply mankind with good and evil, but it is too unstable to preserve them as separate and self-identical. Lacking the divine madness, the Eros of the *Symposium* is too sober, and its sobriety is too unstable: hence it deteriorates into human madness.

Socrates separates out four kinds of divine madness. The first is prophecy, of which he gives exclusively feminine examples. The function of prophecy is to perceive, silently or passively, a vision of beauty, by which we may be inspired to perform noble deeds. It is like the noetic apprehension of a formal monad; and hence, although we must speak about and somehow "divide" prophecy, the activity itself is pre-discursive. This silence affects the clarity of the diaeresis in which Socrates is now engaging. The prophetic division of madness leads to ambiguities in the joints of the division; for example, the second kind of madness, or "purification," is also a kind of prophecy. We are thus prepared poetically for the mathematical paradoxes which ensue from every attempt to state discursively the ontological or logical structure of noetic monads (=hyper-Uranian beings). The first kind of prophecy looks to the future, whereas the second kind is guided by the desire to be freed from the past. The difficulty in distinguishing the two arises from the interrelatedness of the temporal dimensions, or the impossibility of defining desire in terms of the priority of past or future events. If there is a standard for the establishment of such a priority, it cannot itself be an instance of desire, or a temporal event. The third and fourth kinds of divine madness, poetry and Eros (somewhat misleadingly) understood as philosophy, are the decisive rivals for sovereignty in what one may call man's prophetic attempt to encompass, organize, and hierarchically order the instances of temporality. They offer alternative ways in which to seek unity within the manifold of existence, and consequently blessedness or perfection.

In Socrates' treatment of it, poetry is closely associated with temporality, and is therefore as difficult to distinguish from the two kinds of prophecy as they are from each other. Poetry is making or generating. It is an expression of individual desire and imagination; it subordinates the discursive element of speech to the silence of illumination or manifestation. That is, poetry is presented as terminating, like prophecy, in beautiful deeds, or as a praxis rather than a *theōria*. The non-discursive character of making or doing requires a verbal interpretation to establish its significance, or to stabilize the "poems" and deeds from the discontinuity of time. For this reason, a poetic interpretation of philosophy must be supplemented by a reflexive appropriation or discursive analysis of the prophetic horizon of human experience. This peculiar combination of speech and silence pertains to the fourth kind of divine madness, which originates in, and is measured by, noetic and dianoetic perception of the hyper-Uranian beings and their discursive or logical icons. In order for this perception to occur, there must be some relation between the psyche and the hyper-Uranian beings. Socrates tries to establish this relation by attributing perpetuity to the motions of the psyche. However, even assuming that this can be done, it is in itself insufficient to establish the truth of personal, self-conscious immortality. The personality of the individual psyche is a function of its temporal, and hence corporeal, experiences. If all persons share perpetual motion, they must do so as instances of a common form, and the form which they instantiate is not the same as their personality. Perpetual motion is formally the same in every instance; after death, and the loss of private or corporeal identity, there would be no way to distinguish between one perpetually moving psyche and another.

Socrates' discussion of immortality actually results in a doctrine of two motions or *psychic dualism*. One motion is cosmic or circular, and leads the psyche through the perpetually recurring motions of genesis; the other motion is vertical, and leads the psyche upward, directing its vision out beyond the heavens even as the circular cosmic motion is being described. It is the second motion that is characteristic of the individual or personal psyche, and it need not recur in the particular case. There is no necessary connection between immortality and personal blessedness or perfection. In other words, speech about psyche as the principle of motion is not the same as speech about psyche as the principle of speech. The problem of discursivity, and so of self-consciousness, is only implicitly present in Socrates' second speech, not merely because of the poetic silence of myth, but because the psyche is never shown to be speaking within the myth itself. Socrates reserves the discussion of discursivity for the post-mythic or reflexive section of the dialogue. Unfortunately, it is not clear from that discussion how discursivity is connected to the passionate striving or noetic apprehending attributed to the psyche in the myth itself. Instead of dealing with speech, Socrates introduces the image of the charioteer and winged steeds. The wing, which is the key motif in this image, is a poetic vector of vision and desire; the psyche's upward journey is apparently as silent as its circular or cosmological motion. The personality or self-consciousness of the individual psyche is then exhibited in its pre-verbal origin as the dual attraction toward an equally silent beauty.

IV.

The function of the wing is to translate the initial equine motion into the journey upward toward the roof of the cosmos. The vision which awaits the successful psyche, says Socrates, has never been celebrated by any previous poet. Nor is his own revelation of the hyper-Uranian beings an adequate account of their nature.

Indeed, the reference to poetry, and the details of the present myth, indicate the obstacles which face any effort to provide a determinate or systematic logos of what have traditionally been called the "separate Ideas" (a phrase not used by Socrates). They are separate from the motions of genesis, and consequently lack all sensuous properties; yet they may be apprehended by a special kind of psychic or mental vision, and understood as the "true beings" and objects of true knowledge. Since *discursive* speech, as the etymology of the term implies, is a moving resident of genesis, and thereby inseparable from sensuous being and perceiving, it is not clear how one can speak about the hyper-Uranian beings. This difficulty is underlined by the fact that, in the myth, the psyche apprehends them silently, and that Socrates describes them directly in almost exclusively negative terms. One is led to suggest that nothing determinate can be said about their formal structure, but only about their ontological function. This function may be illustrated by an example from contemporary linguistic theory, which is also helpful in understanding the discussions of sounds, words, and letters that appear in the later dialogues in a similar connection.

Theoretical linguists distinguish between the "formal units" or "expression-elements" of a language, and their "substantial realization" as sounds and letters.[1] These formal units of semantic structure "are quite abstract elements, independent of the substance in which they are realized."[2] That is, if we consider them apart from their manifestation as sounds or letters, they have only two properties in themselves: a *combinatorial* capacity to join with one another in complex structures by which we identify and distinguish words and sentences; and a *contrastive* function—their difference from one another. According to John Lyons, "the

---

1   I follow the presentation of John Lyons, *Introduction to Theoretical Linguistics* (Cambridge, Cambridge University Press, 1968), pp. 58 ff.

2   Lyons, p. 61. For purposes of simplicity, we may ignore other ways to realize expression-elements, such as by light, gesture, etc.

principle of *contrast* (or opposition) is fundamental in modern linguistic theory."[3] In making this point, Lyons refers to the assertion of de Saussure that expression-elements are essentially negative in nature. This example from linguistics may help us to interpret the relation between hyper-Uranian beings and their representation in genesis, whether as words or things. The formal unit or expression-element corresponds in my interpretation to the hyper-Uranian being understood as a *noetic monad*, whereas their realization in sounds or letters corresponds to the words or things of genesis. Let us restrict our attention to the correspondence between noetic monads and speech. It is obvious that neither the sound nor letter which we use to exhibit the expression-element is that element, nor for that matter a copy or imitation of it. The particular sound or letter is in each case arbitrary or conventional; the "true being" which underlies the conventional symbol is the expression-element, which, in keeping with its essentially negative character, can never be manifested *in itself*. And yet it is equally obvious that there must be expression-elements, or that they differ absolutely from their symbolic realization, as well as from each other. For, although the symbols are arbitrary, the difference between words composed of these symbols is not. The words "bet" and "pet," although conventional linguistic constructions, manifest absolute and unchanging semantic structures, which would be unaffected even were we to change every element of their symbolic representation. Similarly, although the words are changing in speech, or distinguishable from each other by a matter of continuous variation, "there is no word of English which is in some sense half-way between the two with respect to its grammatical function or meaning."[4]

Just as expression-elements correspond to noetic monads or hyper-Uranian beings, so sounds and letters may be taken to represent the discursive symbolism by which we attempt to manifest these noetic monads. The noetic monad is in my terminology the

3   Lyons, p. 67.
4   Lyons, p. 68.

ontological subject of discourse, including formal or logical discourse. Differently put, the logical analysis of the formal structure of discourse is not the same as an analysis of the formal structure of the ontological subjects of discourse. The continuous variation of the sounds by which we try to designate the different letters *b* and *p* does not affect the absolute difference between their expression-elements. Still more perspicuously, we can literally see the formal difference between *b* and *p*, even though differences in pronunciation might make it impossible for us ever to state that difference in an absolute or unvarying sense. (And the fact that we might decide to represent *b* and *p* by two different symbols, say *l* and *r*, would in no way alter the "ontological" difference between the two symbolized expression-elements, nor the visually apprehensible formal difference between *b* and *p*.) In general: every attempt to describe the formal structure of an ontological subject is actually a description of a logical or discursive representation of the ontological subject. A failure to distinguish between these two domains leads to hopeless paradox in every effort to demonstrate the so-called "Platonic theory of Ideas." We cannot, therefore, identify the forms which are sorted out by the method of division and collection with the noetic monads or hyper-Uranian beings. Perhaps this will suffice as a summary of the complex analysis which I devoted to the problem in the text above.

The *Phaedrus* is a self-reflexive or persuasive account of speech as persuasion. As the subsequent philosophical revision of rhetoric shows, "persuasion" is not to be taken in a trivial or merely sophistic sense. The serious function of discourse is to instruct or persuade oneself and others of the truth, and by extension, of the beautiful and the good. The difference between philosophical and non-philosophical speech turns ultimately on the capacity of the speakers to be persuaded by the *evidence* of truth, beauty, and goodness. According to Socrates, this evidence is not empirical but "hyper-Uranian." The visibility of these principles of speech can be illuminated by a reflexive analysis of speech itself. But the mode of discourse appropriate to the principles of speech is not the same as speech about the consequences of those principles. In non-poetic language, we see here the origin of axiomatics. However, the poetic portrait also indicates that Socrates' conception of axiomatics is not simply reducible to meta-mathematics. A vision of the principles of speech that is compatible with the richness of human experience includes the "numbers" of music or poetry as well as those of arithmetic and the forms of geometry.

The hyper-Uranian beings are "axioms" in the literal sense of beings worthy of honor and respect. For those who can see them, they are altogether persuasive. Socrates describes the capacity to apprehend these noetic beings as a function of Eros guided by a divine fate or gift. Sexual appetite is the most powerful of all human desires. Its goal is reproduction, and therefore self-preservation in a double sense, turning upon the difference between the carnal and the psychic apprehension of beauty. When the latter predominates over the former, the psyche is, or may become, detached from the carnal expression of need, or absorbed in and satisfied by the psychic awareness of beauty. Should the appetite for beauty be joined to a sufficiently powerful (=winged) intellect, satisfaction is dissolved by reflexivity, or the desire for perfect beauty, and subsequently, for perfection. The non-verbal fact of desire is thus an icon of the silent perception of the principles of speech. And poetry is the mode of speech most appropriate to the task of portraying the silent perception of beauty.

V.

Every psyche yearns for the ascent to the roof of the cosmos, but its capacity to accomplish this journey is determined by the dialectical encounter between the noble and base horses. Here again, we see the distinction between cosmological and personal immortality. Socrates restates this distinction in terms of degrees of forgetfulness, and thereby assumes (contradicting the earlier classification of psyches) that all human psyches have seen something of the hyper-Uranian domain. He then proceeds to classify kinds of embodied existence in terms of the degree of recollection of discarnate vision. As it now seems, every human psyche is personally as well as generically immortal, albeit at different levels of dignity or intensity. The most striking characteristic of the classification of lives is the absence of any explicit reference to the mathematician, or to the mathematical study of nature. The lives may be organized into these groupings: those primarily dedicated to the care of the psyche, the city, or the body, respectively. The analysis of these lives repeats the emphasis upon care in the previous account of the gods who tend to the motions of the cosmos. The suppression of mathematics is undoubtedly related to this emphasis upon care, self-concern, or self-consciousness, which are necessary attributes of the yearning for, and (possible) achievement of, personal immortality.

A second striking characteristic of the classification of lives is the low status given to prophecy and poetry. There is a disharmony between the myth as a whole, which stresses and exemplifies the importance of these two forms of madness, and the discussion within the myth of the order of psychic descent. I have suggested that the effect of this disharmony is to raise the status of philosophy among the forms of divine madness, or more sharply put, to force us to reconsider the connection between philosophy and the two related activities of poetry and prophecy. On the other hand, the absence of any reference to mathematics and epistēmē, and the very low rank given to the *technai*, shows the radically incomplete nature of the portrait of philosophy in this section at least of the *Phaedrus*. "Incomplete," however, does not mean "worthless" or "dispensable." The primary function of the myth of Stesichorus is to exhibit the connection between care and persuasion, or the pre-philosophical, "everyday" significance of desire and speech, and of philosophy understood as the perfection of desire and speech. The function of the *Phaedrus* as a whole is to mediate between the reflexive or self-caring rhetoric of genesis or historical existence, and the mathematico-technical aspects of philosophy, in which a reflexive self-caring is minimally present or altogether absent. Those who forget themselves in their absorption with division and collection cease to be philosophers in the Socratic sense of the term, regardless of the sophistication of their logical techniques. But the same is true of those who forget to divide and collect, thanks to an excessive self-absorption. The result is in the one case sophistry, and in the other, tyranny.

Since the philosopher alone genuinely remembers his discarnate apprehension of truth, he alone may be genuinely said to choose his form of life, and hence to be free. The other choices correspond to varying degrees of forgetfulness, and so are correspondingly determined by necessity. Nevertheless, according to the myth, the possibility of living a just life is available at each stage of the psychic descent. But there is obviously a difference between philosophical and non-philosophical (or demotic) justice. Thus, the non-philosophical psyches are given the opportunity to choose a superior life for their second (or later) incarnation, but they are never said to be able to choose a philosophical life. As Socrates puts it, only the philosopher's intelligence is winged. Every human psyche has seen or remembers something of the truth, but only the philosopher has seen or remembers enough to achieve freedom, and therefore responsibility. Philosophical justice is derived from the reflexive desire for truth, and so from the essentially private desire for perfection. But the peculiarly selfless or self-transcending character of self-perfection frees the philosopher from the selfishness or erotic restriction which necessarily marks the non-philosophical lives in decreasing intensity as we descend toward the tyrant. This selfless self-concern constitutes the philosophical madness: the wings of the philosopher raise him above the city (beyond political justice), and so above the ordinary desires of political man. Whereas the human psyche is erotic, or implicitly directed upward, only the philosophical psyche is reflexively erotic, or perceives that the true end of its appetite is not the immediate object of desire.

Philosophical Eros enacts the dialectic of attraction and separation implicit in visual perception, the mode in which beauty most directly presents itself to man. (One might well complain that the Platonic analysis of beauty neglects music, or the sense of sound. But visual beauty is silent, like the noetic apprehension of hyper-Uranian beings; in addition, it is connected immediately with Eros or corporeal sexuality, as music is not.) We are attracted to the beautiful body, yet vision, the primary medium of attraction, requires a separation from the body. This distance permits the beautiful form to stand forth as distinct from the particular body desired. And thus the form is perceived as more desirable than the body itself; the world of genesis, thanks to its sensuous beauty, manifests the path by which the philosopher is enabled to transcend genesis. This philosophical transcendence is prefigured by sexual reproduction; these are the two forms of immortality accessible to man: through the children of his body or those of his psyche. Discourses are the children of the psyche, and this reinforces the previous reference to the link between philosophical madness (or the vision of hyper-Uranian beings) and persuasion or rhetoric. The psyche achieves immortality by recapturing or recollecting in discourse, poetic as well as mathematical, the silent apprehension of eternity. In the *Phaedrus*, eternity is represented by beauty, which, thanks to its dual nature of attractive separation, mediates between, and therefore unifies, the noetic and sensuous cosmos. Eternity is thus accessible in the visible form of genesis. We are now able to restate the connection between the non-lover and the lover as the personification of the separative and attractive dimensions of Eros. In order to transform physiological desire into noetic admiration, the philosopher must be a non-lover as well as a lover.

Thus far, Socrates' interpretation of the human psyche has drawn a sharp distinction between the philosopher and the non-philosopher. This distinction, although essential to the conception of philosophy as recollection or reflexive desire, is nevertheless unjust to the higher forms of non-philosophical Eros, which make indispensable contributions to the richness of human existence. Socrates now makes amends for this previous neglect by giving four examples of divine madness, corresponding to Zeus, Ares, Hera, and Apollo, which we may tentatively identify as the philosophical, martial, political, and geometrico-musical. There can be no doubt, however, that Zeus or philosophy is the genuine or trans-political king. The end of Eros, as inflected by divine madness, is perfection, and therefore unity or self-identity. The philosopher must overcome the divisions implicit in the polymorphous nature of Eros by achieving a synoptic vision, capable of being discursively recollected, of the ends of all desires. These ends are achieved, as we have in effect already seen, by the separation from the initial attraction of desire. We may summarize the stages of this process of separation by saying that philosophy raises the individual above the divisive appetites of political life, although these appetites must first be excited in order for the ascent to take place.

We are now able to understand the struggle between the good and the bad horse as the equally necessary attractive and separative functions of Eros. These functions may obviously be interpreted in a heterosexual as well as a pederastic sense. To give only the decisive example, philosophy is impossible without existence, and more specifically, without the political perfection of existence. In personal terms, one must first desire a beautiful body in order to desire the beauty as distinct from the body. The degree of perfection which the individual attains is dependent upon how he resolves this internal "difference" (in the Hegelian sense) within desire. The erotic psyche achieves divinity only by overcoming the divisions within itself that arise from the necessarily diversified expression of its desire for unity. Human beings may be corrupted or even destroyed by their very desire for perfection. Since the philosopher remains a human being rather than a sage or a god, his "immortality" is intermittent, or dependent upon the strength of his memory. And so he, too, as a resident of genesis, is also engaged in the struggle against dissolution. He, too, must generate, or engage in both poetry and mathematics. The philosopher must remind himself that he is a human being, lest he divide himself away by his divisions and collections. He must preserve the integrity or unity of his "ordinary language" by the discovery of modes of analysis which are faithful to its extraordinary diversity.

VI.

The persuasive character of speech is rooted in what one might call the overcoming of the division between subjectivity and objectivity. Although Plato does not employ these terms, it is not difficult to see the sense in which they apply to his enterprise. Persuasion is a condition of the psyche, and not simply a power of speech considered as a detached formal structure. If, for example, we are concerned exclusively with the deductive properties of a speech, it is necessary, by whatever process, to *see* or mentally apprehend the form of the speech. However mechanical may be the procedures by which the form is certified, its persuasiveness depends upon the "appropriation" of that certification by one or more self-conscious persons. The persuasiveness, as distinct from the logical validity, of the form, stems from the recognition of the relevance of the concept and techniques of determining validity to the excellence or *goodness* of deductive arguments. The question with which we are concerned is not one of the techniques employed to certify validity, but how one sees the point or persuasiveness of validity. One must see the form, but also the relevance of the internal structure of the form to the subjective or psychic goal of persuasion.

The problem becomes still more complex when we turn to the content of speeches, whether formally valid or not. A sophist might easily employ valid argument-forms to establish conclusions which by some other standard are irrelevant, unpersuasive, or bad. Similarly, a philosopher might easily employ invalid arguments in order to persuade his audience of conclusions which, by other standards, are relevant and good. What counts as a persuasive speech, then, depends upon three factors: the visibility of the form, the relevance of the form to an end, and the conviction in the audience that the speech is compelling or relevant to the subjective desires and intentions of the members of that audience. This last factor is not simply reducible to the first two. One may wish to be persuaded while denying the general relevance of formal validity to persuasion, or one may admit the general relevance of validity but deny its persuasiveness in this particular case. The speech in question may be rejected as formally sound but materially inappropriate to the end in view. The audience may perceive the form but not the end, or vice versa, or they may perceive neither, while still being persuaded in any of these three cases, for a variety of other reasons.

In sum, the persuasiveness of a speech turns upon two different kinds of visibility, formal validity and relevance to an end. As Plato might express the point, one must not merely see a form, but one must also love it. The function of rhetoric is not to make us see forms, but rather to love forms which we have already seen. Even if the rhetorician seeks to persuade us of a form we do not presently see, he must do so by arousing our love for other, presently visible forms, which, because of their relation to the invisible form, will prepare us to love it as well. This explains the connection between Eros and rhetoric, but it also bears upon the silence of the psyche in its ascent to the roof of the cosmos, and it sheds some light on the initially mysterious doctrine of recollection. Recollection may be defined as the silent procedure by which we see the point of a speech. It may therefore refer to what I previously called the ontological subjects of discourse, but it may also refer to the formal or logical subjects. In either case, we may say that the speech exhibits its own formal structure, but points toward its significance for the auditor, who may fail to see it even while grasping the formal structure. The significance is thus separate from but related to the form of discourse. In this sense, recollection is the act by which we see the significance of the form; it is a re-arranging or re-assessing of what we already know or see without knowing. When we see the significance of a speech, it ceases to be an external, objective form (in the logical sense of form), but has been subjectively or reflexively appropriated. In Platonic language, we love it: it is now our own, or participates in the satisfaction of our desire to know (for whatever reason). (This argument applies by extension to ontological form which is indirectly accessible via a combination of poetic and mathematical discourse.)

At the same time, the form, as what we see (τί ποτ' ἔστιν) is not ours but itself (καθ' αὐτό). Thus we may study the method of recollection independently of its erotic function, or extend the domain of philosophical rhetoric to the analysis of the logical form of what we see. Plato calls this analysis by the names of dialectic or diaeresis. Diaeresis, the division and collection of forms, depends upon the prior vision of a complex formal structure (and the reader will remember that I am not speaking of the noetic monads or hyper-Uranian beings). For example, in order to arrive at a logos of the sophist, we must first possess an apprehension of what a sophist is. At each stage of the division, we refer to, and in that sense recollect, our apprehension of the sophist, in order to see how to divide, and which half of the division to pursue. The correct division and collection of the formal elements of the sophist is not self-generating. As in the application of any technē, we have to see what we are doing. We have to see the significance of each step in the division to the desired end of acquiring a definition of the sophist. And so we have to be persuaded that we are on the right track. This self-persuasion is one version of recollection: *we see the point*. (The other version, to repeat, is the capacity to apprehend the discursively "invisible" ontological subject from reflection on the form anterior to diaeresis.) The point, however, is visible, not as a part, but as a whole, as the (discursive) formal monad that illuminates our logical dissection of what is in itself indivisible. In short, the monad "sophist" does not become visible point by point, beginning as it were with the *tabulae rasae* of the dialecticians; it must be visible, as a unit, at each point of our dialectic. The points (or cuts) of dialectical diaeresis do not generate but discover or recollect formal monads by providing us with a discursive portrait or icon of their internal structure. As discursive animals, we cannot bespeak the monad except point by point; but we could not speak correctly if we had no apprehension of what, at each point, we were saying.

According to Socrates, one cannot divide or sort out the properties of a formal structure unless that structure possesses an internal coherence, stability, and self-identity. The "motion" of discriminating properties $p_1, p_2, \ldots, p_n$ both from each other and from their contradictories, *rests upon* a stability intrinsic in those properties themselves, and not merely in the formal structure as a whole. In the act of analysis, we see $p_1, p_2, \ldots, p_n$ seriatim, and therefore tend to overlook the fact that they could not have been discriminated except by virtue of an implicit or explicit "recollection" of the series as a monadic formal structure, in terms of which the analysis of properties is continuously checked for relevancy and accuracy. Similarly, we see as analysts the "motion" from p_1 to p_2 and therefore overlook the fact that the visibility of this motion rests upon the stability of p_1 and p_2. This tendency to be confused by the motions of analysis produces the blurring of vision which is a characteristic of sophistry. The sophist takes the motion of words to be identical with the motion of things, or more precisely, of the formal properties of things. He therefore "forgets" (fails to recollect) that the name of a ratio of motion is intelligible because of an isomorphism between name and ratio which cannot itself be changing. The structure of the ratio cannot itself be a ratio of motions whose structure would then itself be a ratio of motions, *ad infinitum*.

One may therefore compare the structure of a speech to the form of a living being, which is to say that its motions are held together by its "psyche." Since the psyche is itself moving, one cannot understand the speech (without even mentioning its ontological pre-structure) except by grasping the ends that define this motion. These ends are of two kinds. First, they include the forms of the discourse itself, and second, the purpose of the discourse, or the nature of the psyches which it is intended to persuade. An argument is a proposal or effort to persuade; and so the "logic of the argument" is neutral with respect to the significance or relevance of the argument: it is not equivalent to, but only a part of, the logos of the argument. It is therefore no accident that Plato introduces the technē of diaeresis within the context of a discussion of rhetoric, and more specifically, of living speech. The logic of a logos is self-identical and determinate; it always says the same thing to everyone. But the psyche of the logos is a unity containing difference within its core; it says different things to different kinds of people. The psyche inflects the logic of a logos in way differing with the changing content of its environment. The simplest example of this is the variety of interpretations given to the significance of speeches, even when there is no difference about the logic of these speeches. And this interpretational difference may be about the logic itself, rather than the content. Even a determinate or self-identical form has a rhetorical horizon, whether with respect to the perspicuity of its symbolic notation or its meta- (=onto-) logical significance.

We can now state the difference between philosophy and sophistry. Both are synoptic or syllogistic, in the sense that both desire and talk about everything. Therefore, they cannot be distinguished as rhetorical enterprises, except in terms of the units, content, or constituents of speech. The sophist is undefinable because he does not know, or cannot define, what he is talking about. No unit of sophistic speech is really distinguishable from any other; X is not merely both Y and non-Y, but it is also, and at the same time, non-X. Philosophical rhetoric, on the contrary, is defined by diaeresis in the sense of the technē by which we are able to give an account of "what it is" that we are talking about. It must immediately be added, however, that this definition of philosophy is manifestly partial, because diaeresis is itself possible only thanks to noēsis in its two senses of the recollective apprehension of ontological and logical form as unities or monads. One might be tempted to say that, although the philosopher can be distinguished from the sophist, he cannot himself be defined. There is no discursive account of the formal structure of philosophy. Hence the need for myths to supplement the various modes of logos employed by the philosopher in distinguishing himself from the sophist. The point of the dialogue-form, then, is that it exhibits the unity of myth and logos in the living philosopher. Those who disregard the dialogue-form in their study of Plato are disregarding the Platonic conception of philosophy. Their dissection of "arguments" abstracted from the text is thus murder rather than dialectic.

Socrates personifies his arguments, criticisms, and examples concerning rhetoric, or allows them to become characters within the dialogue, in order to emphasize the connection between diaeresis and living speech. For the same reason, the choice of medicine to illustrate the diaeretic method is an especially appropriate one. Phaedrus is both a valetudinarian and the beloved of a physician. Philosophical rhetoric is the medicine of the psyche, and medicine is the life-oriented technē par excellence. The transition from the discussion of beautiful to the discussion of true speech is effectively mediated by the example of medicine, which reminds us of the need to supervise Eros by discursive knowledge, and also that the end of knowledge is the perfection of life. The beauty of the speech about Eros depends for its truth on the medicinal interpretation of discursive logos, which divides and collects in order to give an account of what is in itself visible but silent. A complete diaeresis of the psyche would then be equivalent to a verbal icon of noetic intuition. But an imitation of life is not alive; the diaeresis must not be radically sundered from the reflexive unity of self-consciousness.

The subsequent discussion of rhetoric, it must be remembered, itself conforms to the *ad hominem* character of every Platonic dialogue. Socrates is attempting to educate Phaedrus, and indirectly, his readers. Part of the reader's education is to grasp the connection between dialectic and the psyche, or the existential, and therefore particular, unity of speech and deed. Hence the many repetitions within this section of the dialogue; Socrates is stimulating Phaedrus' memory. At the same time, the reader is expected to remember each of the repeated formulations, and to observe their differences as well as their similarities. If one does not perceive Socrates' own rhetorical practice, one cannot fully understand his rhetorical theory. If, as Socrates insists, it is necessary to speak differently to different kinds of men, then we need to perceive with precision and in detail how he actually speaks to Phaedrus, and what kind of man Phaedrus is. Not only is this a living exemplification of Socratic rhetoric, but the example, as speech directed *ad hominem*, needs to be corrected by inferences drawn from its particular features. To give only the decisive instance, the refutation of sophistic rhetoric turns finally upon the possibility of distinguishing the likely from the unlikely. A persuasive likeness implies a stable formal structure as the measure of the difference between the likely and the unlikely. Socrates' conversation with Phaedrus is an imperfectly persuasive likeness of what we may call a "perfect" conversation between two equally competent interlocutors; that is, between two philosophers. The defects of the conversation with Phaedrus are visible as such only because and to the extent that we are able to "recollect" the paradigm which it imperfectly reflects. The psychagogic function of the dialogue-form may also be expressed as a stimulus to the reader's memory.

The discussion of rhetoric may be said to terminate in the problem of silence, which was poetically exhibited in the myth of the psyche. The discussion of rhetoric is silent about the role of noetic apprehension as the necessary precondition for diaeresis, to say nothing of its function in the rhetorician's perception of the particular case. The *Phaedrus* tells us nothing about what is called in the *Sophist* the "weaving together of forms," and therefore it does not tell us how anything can be said (predicated) of anything. There is a missing link between the silent apprehension of hyper-Uranian beings and the subsequent divisions and collections of kinds of lives, deeds, and speeches. In order to complete the teaching of the *Phaedrus*, we would have to understand the mediation between speech and silence. One may assume that this problem will be treated more exhaustively in dialogues like the *Sophist, Parmenides* and *Philebus*. We have not, therefore, completely answered the question raised by the *Symposium*: which comprehensive speech about genesis is best? We know, to repeat, that the answer requires a supervision, limitation, or definition of Eros by speech about formal structure in the two senses of noetic apprehension and dianoetic diaeresis. If, however, the erotic perception of beauty initiates the flight of the psyche to recollect its vision of the hyper-Uranian beings, and if such recollection constitutes immortality or perfection, what is the role played by speech in this apparently silent process? Is not the absence of a detailed explanation of the connection between the hyper-Uranian beings and the forms of division and collection a mark of the comic nature of the *Phaedrus*? More generally and more fundamentally, if there is no speakable connection between the two kinds of form, then does not all speech, and even more so, all writings about the nature of speech, take on the nature of comedy?